The West Country

The principal sights

< Lift flap for map

D0967598

St Ives, by Alfred Wallis

Peter Sager

The West Country

WILTSHIRE, DORSET, SOMERSET, DEVON AND CORNWALL

Translated by
David Henry Wilson

PALLAS GUIDES

Front cover: Granite rocks over Zennor
Inside front cover: Patrick Heron near Zennor, and his window at the Tate Gallery, St. Ives
Back cover: Royal Crescent, Bath
Inside back cover: Façade, Kingston Lacy
Frontispiece: St Ives, by Alfred Wallis, *c.* 1928

Publisher's Acknowledgements: Pallas Athene would like to thank Stephen and Ruth Alexander, Polly Hudson, Ian and Joanna Panton, Demi Ross and Mike at Olympic Press. Particular thanks are also due to Andrew Ellis for his meticulous revision of the text, and to Barbara Fyjis-Walker, for her devoted ferretting out of errant quotations. David Henry Wilson, as well as making an inspired and exemplary translation, remains the rock on which the English editions of these books are built.

This book is part of the Pallas Guides series, published by Pallas Athene.
If you would like further information about the series, please write to:
Pallas Athene, 59 Linden Gardens, London W2 4HJ
Series editor: Alexander Fyjis-Walker
Series assistant: Barbara Fyjis-Walker
Series mentor: David Elliott
Series designer: James Sutton
Editorial assistants: Jenny Wilson, Andrew Ellis

German edition first published by DuMont Buchverlag GmbH & Co, Cologne, 1996.
English edition, with updatings and revisions, first published by Pallas Athene, 59 Linden Gardens, London W2 4HJ, 2000.
© 1996 DuMont Buchverlag, Köln
Translation, adaptation, revisions, updatings and all additional material © Pallas Athene 2000
All rights for all countries reserved. The moral right of the author has been asserted.

ISBN 1-873429-08 8

Printed in Italy

Contents

For Elle and Laura

Foreword

This is a personal portrait of a unique region of Britain. In drawing it, I have tried to emulate the very best portrait artists by capturing not just the surface features of my subject, but also its inner nature. For this reason I have occasionally included descriptions of people you may not meet, and even of places you may not see, because I feel that in some way they contribute to the character of the West Country.

I have followed a route from east to west, beginning in Dorset and ending in Cornwall, and only in my yellow pages have I resorted for the sake of convenience to an alphabetical presentation.

This book would not have been possible without the wholehearted support of many people. I should like in particular to thank the painter Patrick Heron – one of many English friends whose readiness to talk about their country helped me to gain a deeper insight into it. On the road, *The Buildings of England* by my compatriot Sir Nikolaus Pevsner proved to be a constant source of information and pleasure. The British Central Tourist Office in Frankfurt, and particularly Claudia Ritsert-Clark, gave me invaluable assistance, as did Catherine Althaus of the British Tourist Authority in London. Bob Koenig in Surrey and Inge Hesel of Scandinavian Seaways in Hamburg were a great help with my travel arrangements.

For this English edition I am especially indebted to Alexander Fyjis-Walker, a scrupulously thorough publisher and editor, Barbara Fyjis-Walker and Andrew Ellis who undertook much painstaking research, and my translator David Henry Wilson, who shaped and sometimes even reshaped my text with fine flair. Above all, I thank my wife Else Maria and our daughter Laura, and it is to them that I dedicate this volume with all my love.

Peter Sager

Wiltshire

Wiltshire, say the locals, consists of two thirds chalk and one third cheese. Chalk hills run through the county from east to west, and the cheese is the flat meadowland in the north, on the banks of the Avon. The cottages are made of limestone, and also of flint, and sometimes – for instance, in the villages of Wylye Valley – you find the two together in a lovely chessboard pattern.

Wiltshire's villages are idyllic. Cecil Beaton, the photographer, spent his whole life here, ending up in a Queen Anne house near Salisbury. In Lake, a hamlet south of Stonehenge, there is an Elizabethan country house owned by the pop star Sting. The composer Sir Michael Tippett, the artist Joe Tilson and the novelist V. S. Naipaul all have or had houses in this county. Even the government, in case of war or some other dire emergency, chose Wiltshire for the site of a giant bunker, codenamed Burlington, which lies 120 feet beneath a field near Hawthorn and is large enough to accommodate 55,000 – yes, 55,000 – people.

If you look at a map of Wiltshire, you will find a big bare patch in the middle. That is Salisbury Plain. In reality, it is a vast green expanse undulating on and on as far as the eye can see. The fields stretch out into the swelling hills, the sky arches broad and high above them, there are hardly any people, hardly any trees, and between the evening sun and the fields of rape, you can see a white shape galloping: the White Horse of Westbury, one of the more modern figures carved in the chalk of Salisbury Plain (1778). Around 1900, over half a million sheep grazed on the plain, which then covered three fifths of the county. The erratic blocks of sandstone on the Marlborough Downs are called the Grey Wethers, and the terraces on the hills are called Shepherd Steps – both names testifying to the importance of sheep here over the centuries. Bastard toadflax and bedstraw and rare orchids grow here. And you can see stone curlews, Montagu's harriers, and long-eared owls. No larks ascending in Larkhill, though: whizzbangs and shells, the roar of the Royal Artillery.

Henry Moore: Cyclops, *from a set of lithographs of Stonehenge, 1971-73*

Icon and National Scandal: Stonehenge

Once the bare and chalky heights of Wiltshire were a favourite residential area. Stone Age settlers felt safer on the dry, treeless plain than they did down in the marshy valleys. There is no county in England with so many prehistoric remains as Wiltshire, even though the Ministry of Defence has done its best to plough up the monuments with its tanks. *Stonehenge* has fortunately managed so far to resist such military invasion. This monumental stone circle does not look especially impressive from a distance – it's like some game abandoned by giants. Close to, however, it grows into something mighty and mysterious (col. pl. 2).

The best guess is that Stonehenge is a fragment of some strange temple. Two sets of stones in the shape of a horseshoe are surrounded by two concentric stone circles, and in the centre of this cromlech is the so-called Altar Stone. The outer ring, with a diameter of 97 feet, consisted of thirty stone pillars arranged in pairs, each one capped with a lintel. Seventeen of these trilithons are still standing, and six of their lintels are still in place. These were what gave the structure its name of 'hanging stones'. The inner circle was formed by sixty smaller unhewn stones without lintels. Inside this circle, opening to the north-east, was the large horseshoe of five trilithons – three of which are still standing along with their architrave stones – and this in turn was lined with a smaller horseshoe consisting originally of nineteen monoliths. The sandstone sarsens of the outer circle and of the larger horseshoe come from the nearby Marlborough Downs. The rest are bluestones, and in 1922 it was proved that their place of origin was the top of Carn Meini, on the eastern slopes of the Preseli Hills in Pembrokeshire (now Dyfed). Could this have been a sort of Welsh Olympus in prehistoric times? Why else would the megalith builders have transported these holy stones – more than eighty blocks, each weighing up to 4 tons – over a distance of some 200 miles from the Welsh hills to Salisbury Plain? And how did they do it? On rafts across the Bristol Channel and up the Avon, then on sledges and rollers to Stonehenge? If so – and this would seem to be the most plausible explanation – it was a truly astonishing feat of transport. Equally astonishing, however, is the manner in which these stones were worked on. The lintels were lifted onto the upright stones with levers and wooden ramps, and they fit as precisely as timber frames. (There was an earlier, wooden counterpart of Stonehenge – Woodhenge – not far away, at Durrington.) Mortise and tenon were chiselled out beforehand, and the rounding of the individual lintels follows the curve of the actual circle itself. The sense of harmony and perspective possessed by the artist-engineers of Stonehenge is evident also from the rectangular blocks of sandstone which taper upwards in a convex curve much like the entasis of Greek columns. No less an expert than the 17th-century architect Inigo Jones was the first to point out the mathematical beauty and precision of this stone circle, and he thought it must have been built by the Romans. Just like medieval cathedrals,

Stonehenge went through different phases of construction. The earthworks and the ditch date from the Late Neolithic period (c. 3050 BC), together with the heel stone at the opening to the road and the 56 holes – partly filled with the remains of cremation burials – around the inside of the earthworks; these are known as the Aubrey Holes, after the man who discovered them in the 17th century, the anti-quarian and writer John Aubrey (best known for his *Brief Lives*). The second phase of construction (2900-2600 BC) was the erection of timber settings within the earth-works. No one knows what these wooden structures were, though an extremely complex pattern of post-holes has been found. The third phase was the stone phase, beginning with the arrival of the bluestones from Wales c. 2600 BC. This phase reached its zenith with the erection of the sarsen circle and the processional avenue c. 1600 BC.

The first time I saw Stonehenge was in the mid 1970's. At that time there were no barriers at all, and we wandered around between these mighty stones, touching them with all the tentative curiosity of a child stroking an elephant. Indeed the stones seemed almost to be alive. They are not just grey. Depending on the light and the time of day, they change colour, from green to blue, from grey to ochre. Lichen

Stonehenge: lifting a cap-stone. The sarsen is brought on a sled and turned out onto a pair of piers. A wooden scaffold is constructed around this, and is gradually used to raise the stone. When it has reached the height of the standing stones it is levered up and onto them. Other theories, involving more use of levers, or turning the monoliths into giant wheels have also been proposed

13

An engraving of Stonehenge made in 1575. The caption reads: This showeth the order and manner of the most ancient monument in England called Stonehenge situate in the plain of Salisbury being first brought out of Ireland by Uther Pendragon brother to Aurelius Ambrose then king of the Britons through the help and counsel of Melin, so there erected for a memory of certain noble Britons in the place slain by Hengist and his Saxons AD 490. A showeth the greater called course stones, of weight supposed 12 tons, in length 28 foot in breadth 7 foot, in compass 16 foot. B showeth the lesser called coronets. C showeth where great bones of men are found

and moss grow on their cracked and grainy skin – biologists identified 66 different types in 1994, though there had been 84 twenty years earlier. The losses may have been caused by the growth in traffic, with up to 20,000 cars a day roaring close by Stonehenge.

The more you gaze at these stones, the more mysterious they become. It is assumed that they were a place of worship, but worship of which gods? Definitely not those of the Druids. Almost certainly the stones were connected with observation and perhaps worship of the sun or moon, or both, and their position is linked to a sophisticated calendar system which enabled the Stone Age astronomer-priests to work out the future course of the stars and the optimum times for planting and harvesting. Seen from the Altar Stone, the sun on the day of the summer solstice is directly above the 16-foot high Heelstone a few minutes after sunrise. Along this axis runs the broad, though now barely visible processional path (rudely crossed by the road), which goes as far as the Avon, two miles away. In the opposite direction, the sun during the winter solstice sets through the once complete arch of the central trilithon – as if it were descending through the gate to the Underworld. This observatory was also used for the cult of the dead, as is shown by the 500 or so barrows all around (though many of these have been ploughed under). The precious grave goods that have been found indicate that many generations of Wessex nobility were buried here (2000-1000 BC). No doubt some of them were responsible for the building of Stonehenge.

The megalithic stone circle may have witnessed an ancient cult of the dead, and it has most certainly witnessed the modern cult of the reproduction. Washington has a replica of Stonehenge, standing as a memorial to the dead of the First World War. In Nebraska there are cars stuck upright in the ground to form a Carhenge; New Zealand has a ring of old refrigerators, Fridgehenge; and a few years ago the annual Spam sculpting competition in the States was won by a Spamhenge. The most original, however, is a version commissioned by the American government: in 1982, at the behest of the Office of Nuclear Waste, a lady archaeologist investigated ways of marking the sites of dumped waste so that the warning symbols would still perform their function 10,000 years from now. Of all existing monuments, she concluded that only Stonehenge and the Pyramids of Giza would be able to survive the ravages of time, Nature, and human interference. For financial reasons, it was decided to build stone circles – the Stonehenge solution.

Like the Mona Lisa, this is an icon that has found its way into the collective pictorial memory. For centuries it has inspired people's imaginations. We may see it through the eyes of many artists (assuming we can see through anything other than our cameras and videos). For the Romantic William Blake Stonehenge was a purely mystic symbol; for Turner it was an archaic sign, as much a part of Nature as the plain itself; John Constable painted it as a primeval drama of light and time, with a double rainbow striking the stones like meteorites (col. pl. 1). In his 1836 description of this mythical vision Constable wrote: 'The mysterious monument ... standing remote on a bare and boundless heath, as much unconnected with the events of past ages as it is with the uses of the present, carries you back beyond all historical recall into the obscurity of a totally unknown period.' Henry Moore must have had a similar impression when he first saw Stonehenge on a moonlit night in September 1921. Fifty years later he created a series of lithographs that capture the mood of these Cyclopean sculptures – their material together with their abstract spaces of light and shadow and mystery.

Between 1988 and 1997 a sad spectacle took place on June 21 every year on Salisbury Plain. For four miles all around, the police erected barriers to keep out the very people to whom the stones meant most. The Neo-Druids, hippies old and young, wanted to celebrate the summer solstice there. Thousands of New Age travellers regard Stonehenge as a symbol of their particular culture. For these travellers, and for diviners, witches, pagans and their ilk, there are lines of force proceeding from these stones – powers that have yet to be taken into account by the conservationists. No matter how obscure the different rites may be, they nevertheless pick up the traditions for which these stones were erected in the first place. At the summer solstice in 1998, English Heritage and the police invited more than 400 people to Stonehenge to conduct their ceremonies; and everything passed off very happily for all concerned.

At the halfway mark between London and Cornwall, Stonehenge is a crucial stopping-off place for the coach-trippers: here they can stretch their legs, go to the loo, have a look at the stones, and buy their trilithon sandwiches, sarsen pies, stone age gingerbread men and other prehistoric delicacies. The magic stone circle stands at the intersection of two major roads. As well as those 20,000 cars, about 1000 lorries a day pass along the A303, right beside Stonehenge. From the car park, there is a modern-day processional path to the stones – a concrete pedestrian tunnel like a suburban underpass. More than 700,000 visitors a year buy this product under the trade name of Stonehenge. This sacred place, a national treasure, has become a national disgrace, and in 1993 the matter was even raised in Parliament. UNESCO regards Stonehenge as part of the world's cultural heritage, yet it is now the 'Stones of Shame' according to *The Times*.

English Heritage owns Stonehenge itself, while the surrounding land belongs to the National Trust. Both have been trying for years to improve this scandalous status quo. Stonehenge should be entirely traffic-free, and there should be no roads, car parks or modern buildings in its vicinity. Instead it should be made into an archaeological park that would restore its isolation and its dignity – and would also bring in 1.4 million visitors a year. Less traffic, more trouble? There have been countless studies, meetings, planning committees, protests from farmers, from archaeologists, from Druids, hikers, the military, and the sun-worshippers. Never can a pile of stones have created so many problems. Some want to see the A344 covered with grass, others want the A303 to be diverted but broadened to two lanes. A recent plan was to build an 2790-foot tunnel to avoid the monument entirely. The Department of Transport rejected that as being too expensive. Now English Heritage are mounting a national 'Save Stonehenge' campaign. Pat Johnson, a mathematics teacher from Kent, has a novel plan: she suggests a lifesize glass replica with two artificial rainbows over it. Then we could all go there instead, and leave the stones in peace.

Twenty-two miles north of Stonehenge lies the megalithic circle of *Avebury*, which John Aubrey considered to outshine Stonehenge by as much as 'a cathedral does a parish church'. I went there on a misty morning, and as I stepped onto the grass between the houses, it was as if I was suddenly confronted by a horde of large, grey figures – the petrified gods of Avebury. The circle was badly damaged in the 14th and 16th centuries, and indeed depredations continued into this century. In the 18th century, the stones were used as a quarry for the village that had grown up in the middle of this religious site. By the beginning of the 20th century there were only six of the original 98 stones left standing in the outer circle. Alexander Keiller re-erected as many as possible in the 1930's.

Older, and less well known than Stonehenge though it covers a much wider area, Avebury stone circle originally comprised some 600 stones, with its two processional avenues and two more circles in the middle. The whole site is enclosed in an earthwork wall up to 55 feet high, and an inner ditch, with a circumference of half a mile. The two through roads still use the old entrances. Heading south-west from Avebury Circle, an impressive avenue leads across hills and fields – a processional path which originally comprised about 100 pairs of monoliths guarding the way to the sanctuary of Overton Hill, a mile and a half away. There was also once an equally impressive north avenue; today only two stones remain.

The surroundings of Avebury constitute one vast prehistoric ritual landscape. Here you will find the classic Neolithic site which gave its name to the earliest agriculture: *Windmill Hill*. One of the biggest burial sites of this time was the long chamber tomb at *West Kennett* (c. 3250 BC), south of the mysterious *Silbury Hill*. This hill, sometimes called the greatest pyramid in Europe, stands on the A4, and is a man-made chalk hill 125 feet high with a diameter of more than 550 feet at the base. It dates from around 2750 BC. Bearing in mind all the centuries of English rain, who else could be buried here in this gigantic barrow but Sil, the Sun King himself? Other scholars have interpreted its contours as representing the figure of some pan-European earth-mother. The only suggestion that archaeologists can make to counter this legend is that Silbury Hill was a monumental sundial – a calendar like Stonehenge. Notwithstanding all the theories, present-day Druids assemble here on the first of May and dance around the green hill. But they celebrate the longest night, the winter solstice, in Avebury Circle, where the authorities leave them in peace. When Druids get married there, they sing this hymn:

> Earth, air, fire and water,
> Weave your web of dark and light;
> Earth, air, fire and water,
> Mother, make your circle bright!

Salisbury: Cathedral on the Village Green

It is 1220, and a whole town is on the move, leaving behind a completed cathedral while a new one is being built two miles away. Bishop Richard Poore is leaving *Old Sarum* to found Salisbury. In the prehistoric hill fortress, the clergy had been permanently at loggerheads with the royal garrison – they simply lived too close to one another. It was also too windy up there, and there was not enough water; in the words of a contemporary gleefully reported by Pevsner, it was 'ventis expositus, sterilis, aridus, desertus'; altogether a 'mons maledictus'. If you go to Old Sarum today, you will find the ruins of the Norman castle and the foundations of the old cathedral behind the double earthwork. The stones of Old Sarum were reused to build the walls in and around the new cathedral. At the foot of the abandoned hill, the cattle graze, the cricketers chase their little red ball across the grass, and New Sarum stretches out over the plain, in the shadow of the great cathedral spire.

With its 'Chequers' – houses laid out in a grid pattern around their gardens – *Salisbury* was a model of 13th-century town-planning. Everything is organically connected, tastefully related, and now tastefully modernised. You feel at home here in a manner all too rare these days. There is a Gothic market cross, a broad market-place, a new cinema on the new Canal with a neo-Tudor façade (behind which is a 15th-century hall with open roof trusses), and on the same premises the house of John Halle, cloth merchant and mayor. Until the 18th century, Salisbury was the centre of a flourishing wool industry. Fronting the Old George Shopping Mall is what was once the George Inn, where Samuel Pepys spent the night of 11 June 1668: 'a silk bed and a very good diet'. But he found the bill 'exorbitant'. If you turn off Crane Street into the fields beside the (Wiltshire) Avon, you will suddenly find yourself confronted by John Constable's picture *Salisbury Cathedral from the Meadows* (now in the Tate Gallery; col. pl. 12). If the horse and cart were to come from the left, it would ford the river at precisely the same spot as it did in 1829. The wooden bridge in the foreground has long since been replaced, but it is still made of wood; the bushes on the banks have now dwindled to mere green spaces, but the trees in front of the cathedral have grown so tall that they almost conceal the nave and the west front. Constable would have been pleased about that, as he found it boring just to paint buildings. Nevertheless, he continued to paint different views of Salisbury Cathedral – from the garden of the Bishop's Palace, or with the famous rainbow – because it was so beautifully situated on the river and amid the fields. There was and is nothing quite like it in England. Constable's friend and patron John Fisher was Bishop of Salisbury, and his nephew (also John Fisher) was archdeacon. The Bishop was not, however, too keen on the dark clouds painted over his church. 'I wish to have a more serene sky,' he complained, and so Constable painted the sunny version now in the Frick Collection in New York.

'Life's but a walking shadow': so says Macbeth, and so says the sundial on

Malmesbury House as you walk past and enter *Cathedral Close*. In its atmosphere and architectural variety, Salisbury's Cathedral Close is unique. There are houses dating from the 13th to the 18th century – the homes of the dean, the canons, and the teachers at the Cathedral School. But surpassing them all, despite its innate modesty, is Mompesson House (1701), a Queen Anne house of perfect proportions and elegant interior. As for the Cathedral itself, it does not emerge dramatically from the usual cluster of close knit medieval houses, but instead rises serenely from a wide expanse of green. The cathedral on the village green – a very rural, very English scene. Equally English is the long ground plan, though construction began in precisely the same year as that of Amiens Cathedral (1220), the high point of French Gothic, with its emphasis on unified vertical effects. At Salisbury there are two carefully delineated sets of transepts and a rectangular choir closed off by the Trinity Chapel (A), which is a simple extension, rather than the mighty, vertical climax one would expect in France.

Only the crossing tower (D) soars slenderly and majestically into the heights, with a grace that belies its weight. In the interior, the slim Purbeck columns stand firm under the burden of the 6400 tons of masonry that go to make up this, the tallest spire in England (404 feet). Christopher Wren made an inspection in 1668, and noted the swampy foundations and the fact that the tower was leaning; as in Wells Cathedral, the problem was solved by buttresses in the crossing and by the use of iron tie-rods. In his novel *The Spire* (1964) the Nobel prizewinner William

Salisbury Cathedral, plan
A. *Trinity Chapel*
B. *Cloister*
C. *Chapter House*
D. *Crossing*
E. *West Front*
F. *Nave*
G. *Main transept*
H. *East transept*
I. *Choir*
J. *Grave of William Longespée*

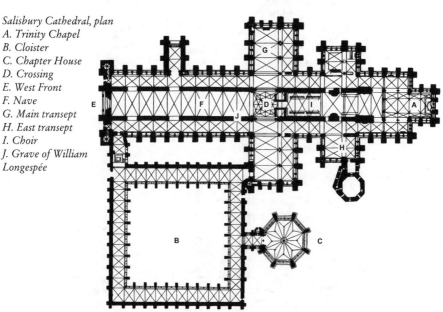

Golding describes the drama accompanying the building of this tower, and the fascinating mixture of technology and faith, with all Dean Jocelin's religious ardour, doubts and ambitions.

The grey nobility of the Chilmark stone – a local limestone – and the triple lancet windows all around help to create a sense of unity throughout the great edifice. It was built very rapidly, and the consecration took place as early as 1258, in the presence of Henry III. Apart from the spire itself (1315), Salisbury Cathedral was completed in just 64 years. It is pure Early English and it has to be said that this uniformity does lead to a certain dullness. The nave is as tall as it is broad, as clear as it is cool. Right up to the clerestory it is filled with slender columns of polished black Purbeck marble – 8760 in all, one for every hour of the year.

On a wood and stone sarcophagus lies a stone knight: William Longespée (J), 1st Earl of Salisbury, who laid one of the foundation stones. This is the earliest English monumental sculpture of a knight at arms. His chainmail coat was originally gilded, and his cape red, while his shield was blue with gold lions. The power of the Bishops of Salisbury in the Middle Ages can be seen from the brass of Bishop Wyville, the largest to survive in all England. Bishop Wyville owned seven manor houses, which he crenellated, and the image he left of himself on his memorial slab (1375) in a fortified tower that was certainly not merely symbolic. It commemorates his recovery by armed combat of the castle of Chevy Chase; his champion, seen at the gate, was disqualified the first time round for cheating, as the Bishop's side had stuffed his breastplate with prayers. The rabbits are a reminder of a valuable warren that Wyville also repossessed.

The new Trinity Chapel window – very modern and very colourful – dominates the entire 449 feet length of the cathedral. Unveiled in 1980 and made by Gabriel Loire, it is called the Prisoners of Conscience window. The cloister (B; col. pl. 13) – never needed, since Salisbury was not a monastery – and the octagonal chapter house (C) date from c. 1275, and were modelled on Westminster Abbey. The tracery windows, fan vault and slender central pier make the latter both unusually high and unusually harmonious. In the cloister, the Library holds among other treasures one of the four copies of the Magna Carta. The first Earl of Salisbury, who was a half brother of King John, was a witness to the signing, and took the historic document back to his home town in 1215.

On the green in front of the Cathedral is Elisabeth Frink's *Walking Madonna* (1981) – Mary as a worn out, middle-aged lady on her way to the town. There was once a bell-tower next to the Cathedral, but now the clock of 1386, one of the oldest in the country, ticks away in the north aisle. The choirboys – and now choirgirls – still take turns to come to evensong, day after day, year after year, century after century. Their voices ring out young and clear, as uplifting and as timeless as the stones of Salisbury.

Salisbury Cathedral: Brass to Bishop Wyville (1375)

V. S. Naipaul

Home and Away: Naipaul in Wiltshire

Far away in the Caribbean on the island of Trinidad, which was still a British colony, an Indian boy dreamed of England. The very first English town that Vidiadhar Surajprasad Naipaul ever saw was Salisbury – or, to be more precise, Constable's painting of Salisbury Cathedral, as illustrated in a third form reader: 'a four-colour reproduction which I had thought the most beautiful picture I had ever seen'. Over thirty years later, V. S. Naipaul was living just a few miles north of the city, writing the story of an uprooting and a rebirth, a novel about a long farewell: *The Enigma of Arrival*. This was his own story.

Naipaul came to England in 1950, when he was eighteen, with a scholarship to Oxford and a burning ambition to be a writer. His arrival was the fulfilment of a dream and the beginning of a trauma. From that moment on, the great literary theme of his life was alienation: the loss of one's home, the search for a new, multi-cultural identity. For years he travelled from London all over the world, and with every book his fame grew. But he found no peace and no identity until he was in the very heart of ancient England, a place, as he said, to which he was utterly foreign – a tiny village in Wiltshire. In 1969 he rented a cottage on an old country estate, Waldenshaw, in the Avon Valley. In the midst of a personal crisis related both to his writing and to life itself, he experienced 'the second, happier childhood as it were, the second arrival'.

During long walks over the Downs, he learned to see anew, as through the eyes of a child: things along the way, in Nature, in the garden of Jack, his neighbour. 'So in tune with the landscape had I become, in that solitude, for the first time in England.' The stranger walked through the fields by the river, as if he were walking through Constable's paintings. 'The past was like something one could stretch out and reach; it was like something physically before one, like something one could walk in.'

Along the paths round Stonehenge and over Salisbury Plain he felt 'the impression was of space, unoccupied land, the beginning of things.' But even there, nothing remained the same. The paths were concreted over, the old estate was in decay, Jack died and then so did his garden, casual workers arrived, a company took over the little farm but then went bankrupt.

No one has described the changes in the English countryside more vividly and more unemotionally than Naipaul. He shows the beauty of the land, and the perils that threaten it. He describes the end of traditional farming, the decline of a whole way of life and an order that had lasted for centuries. The changes he experienced in his little Wiltshire valley mirror the vast upheavals throughout Europe. *The Enigma of Arrival* is the home-loving work of a homeless man, an epic account of the life and death of gardens, people, and cultures. Since 1982, he has lived in his own house in the Avon Valley. In 1989 the Indian Brahmin from Trinidad was given a knighthood; all that's missing for Sir Vidiadhar now is the Nobel Prize for Literature.

Wilton House: Museum and Salon

According to that intrepid traveller Defoe, you have seen nothing until you have seen *Wilton House*. Who, though, would ever imagine that the plain and simple façade of this country house on the outskirts of Salisbury would harbour the most magnificent interiors of the time? For Inigo Jones, who designed them, such contrasts were a matter of style as well as of taste. The architecture, he believed, is the man, and he was all in favour of the sober exterior enclosing the wild fires of inspiration. The Wilton House estate, former site of a Benedictine convent, was given by Henry VIII to William Herbert, a politician and general who had married the sister of the King's last wife, Catherine Parr. His Tudor house was destroyed by fire in 1647, and only the tower in the middle of the east façade survived, together with the so-called Holbein portal, which was originally the entrance to the Great Hall but now stands in the park. Around 1632 the south façade had been taken down and rebuilt by the Flemish landscape gardener Isaac de Caus, an associate of Inigo Jones.

Wilton House

His new design had two floors plus an attic storey, a balustrade and corner pavilions. The original plan was a front of twice the length. Behind this classical
simplicity façade lies the Baroque splendour of the seven state rooms, designed by
Jones himself, and completed by his pupil John Webb (c. 1653).

Grace and grandeur, space and art combine together in the Double Cube Room
to quite stunning effect. True to its name it is as high as it is broad, and the length is
twice the height and breadth (60 x 30 x 30 feet). The walls are of spruce varnished
white, with flowers and garlands of fruit in various shades of gold, and luxuriantly
crowned with mythological paintings on the ceiling. Even if Inigo Jones did not
paint these himself, the whole room is a vivid reminder of the fact that at the start of
his career, Jones was a stage designer at court, much admired for his extravagant
Baroque costumes and sets. William Kent's gold-painted furniture, designed a hundred years later especially for the Double Cube Room, fits in effortlessly. All the
pictures, with the exception of one by a pupil, are by van Dyck (c. 1632-35). They
were not painted for the room, but on the contrary the room was designed for the
paintings. Van Dyck's largest family portrait (col. pl. 3), commissioned by the 4th
Earl of Pembroke, is flanked by two frequent guests at the house, King Charles I
and his wife Henrietta Maria. An enchanting portrait of their three children hangs
over the fireplace.

There is a counterpart to the Double Cube Room, the Single Cube, which is 30 x
30 x 30 feet. Here the painted ceiling shows *Daedalus and Icarus* by the Cavaliere
d'Arpino, and below the dado rail on all four sides are paintings reflecting the literary taste of the time – scenes from Philip Sidney's romance *Arcadia*, which was a
best-seller among the aristocracy until well into the 17th century. *The Countess of
Pembroke's Arcadia*, to give it its proper title, was written at Wilton House, which
Sir Philip Sidney's sister Mary – married to Henry, Earl of Pembroke – made into a
rural literary salon. 'In her time,' observed John Aubrey, 'Wilton house was like a
College, there were so many learned and ingeniouse persons.' The guests included
John Donne, Ben Jonson, who dedicated his *Epigrams,* 'the ripest of my studies' to
the Earl, and perhaps even Shakespeare himself; Shakespeare's editors later dedicated the First Folio to Lord Pembroke's sons William and Philip. This country
house, with its glittering past and present, was Stanley Kubrick's choice for the set
of his amazingly authentic historical film *Barry Lyndon* (1975), based on
Thackeray's first novel *The Luck of Barry Lyndon, a Romance of the Last Century,
by Fitzboodle* (1844).

The artistic treasures include Rembrandt's portrait of his mother, Lucas van
Leyden's *Card Players*, busts by Roubiliac, and works by many other masters such
as Hugo van der Goes, Frans Hals, Lorenzo Lotto, Rubens, Terborch, Reynolds
and more. A particular rarity is the set of 55 gouaches of the Spanish Riding School,
painted by Baron d'Eisenberg, riding instructor to the Emperor Francis I. James
Wyatt, 'the Destroyer' whose restoration of Salisbury Cathedral included the

demolition of its bell-tower, also modernised Wilton House – one of his additions being a two-storey Neo-Gothic cloister round the inner court (1801-14). The 9th Earl of Pembroke built a Palladian bridge across the Nadder (1737), and its perfect rhythm of arches and columns so delighted his contemporaries that imitations sprang up in many different places (including Prior Park, near Bath, see p. 101). Today Wilton belongs to the 17th Earl of Pembroke, a film director. To a lock of Elizabeth I's hair, and Napoleon's dispatch case, he has added a vital new exhibit: Fred Astaire's dancing shoes.

Wilton on the River Wylye was once the capital of Wessex, and is an important centre for carpet manufacture. It profited greatly from its local wool and from the immigration of Huguenot and Flemish weavers in the 17th century. William Morris designed several patterns for the factory, which made its name with handwoven worsted carpets. It is now known as the Royal Wilton Carpet Factory, but its products are much simpler and machine-made. If you hate Victorian architecture, put your judgment to the test by visiting the church of St Mary and St Nicholas. The campanile and the round-arch style are far more reminiscent of a Romanesque church in Italy than a 19th-century parish church in England. The mosaics in the choir and apse, the Cosmati inlay work on the twisted columns, the medieval stained glass – these imitations together with original details are executed with the utmost skill, and combine to great effect. Another Wyatt, Thomas Henry, cousin of the destroyer, designed this basilica in 1843, and it is a wonderful example of the revival of early Christian architecture more frequently practised on the Continent.

The Nadder and the Wardour Valley connect Wilton House to *Wardour Castle*. This was built in 1393 around a hexagonal inner court – a ground plan which is as beautiful as it is unusual, and which met the new desire for domestic comfort rather than any military requirements. Nevertheless, Wardour Castle played a valiant role in the Civil War, since which it has lain in ruins, romantically framed by cedars, cypresses, forest and lake. Indeed so perfect are these ruins that their 18th-century owners did not wish to restore them, but left them as a picturesque feature of their landscaped park, and instead had a new Palladian house (1769-76) built a mile away by James Paine, a popular architect of the time. The chapel, decorated by Italian plasterers, is magnificent, as is the staircase of this Georgian building: it leads to a gallery of Corinthian columns, crowned by a Pantheon-style dome. For a time, this house was an expensive girls' boarding school, but it is now divided up into luxury apartments.

'I do not drink, I build': Beckford at Fonthill

A few miles north of Wardour Castle, William Beckford – 'England's richest son' (Byron) – built himself a country house in the years around 1800 which made his contemporaries seem like beggars and dwarfs. This was *Fonthill Abbey*. It was the palace of his fantasy and the mausoleum of his isolation. It was a folly, not a house – a great piece of architectural theatre. 'Like a dream it arose,' as his biographer James Lees-Milne wrote, 'and like a dream it was extinguished.'

From the Beckford Arms in *Fonthill Gifford*, a road leads all round Beckford country. He loved animals and hated those who hunted them, so to keep the hounds away, he surrounded the woods of Fonthill with a wall almost twelve feet high and seven miles long. The road is lined with its fallen, overgrown ruins.

An empty brick gatehouse, Great Western Avenue – the dead straight approach – and a wide lawn: this was the site of Fonthill Abbey. Imagine a gigantic palace, with nothing left except parts of the north wing, a gallery, and a tower. Between the battlements, a swarm of bees buzzing, and rhododendrons blooming at the edge of the wood. Three urns, on three grey socles. William Beckford (col. pl. 13) lived here.

He was born in 1760, the year King George II died, and he inherited an immense

Fonthill Abbey: View from the southeast, by John Britton, 1823

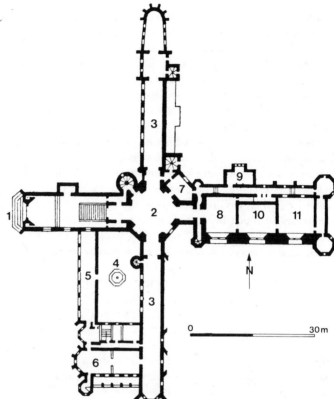

Fonthill Abbey, plan

1. Hall
2. Octagon
3. The Gallery
4. Well
5. Cloister
6. Salon
7. The Porcelain Room
8. Banqueting Room
9. Breakfast Room
10, 11. Drawing Rooms

fortune which his family had accumulated through the slave trade and sugar planta-tions in Jamaica. When he was five years old, he had (or claimed to have had, for he was a splendid fibber) piano lessons from the young Mozart, and his art teacher was the water-colourist Alexander Cozens. When Beckford's father died in 1770, William Pitt the Elder became his guardian – the same William Pitt who pursued England's colonial policy so successfully against the French. In his father's country house at Fonthill Splendens, Beckford celebrated his coming of age in 1781 with a legendary Christmas party: Philippe de Loutherbourg, stage designer at Drury Lane Theatre, transformed the rooms with his 'Eidophusikon' – a moving panorama of transparent pictures illuminated with coloured lights, music, and thunder and light-ning effects; the multimedia succession of scenes was accompanied by songs from the most famous castrati in Europe. Shortly afterwards, Beckford wrote the book which Byron called his Bible and which influenced the darker Romantics all the way through to Mallarmé and Huysmans. The book was *Vathek* (1783), an oriental Faust story, with a magnificent scene of the inferno awaiting the lover of material wealth. It seemed that Beckford was on the verge of a glittering social, literary and political career, but then his homosexual relationship with the handsome youth 'Kitty', William Courtenay, was made public and a vicious campaign was waged against him. Rejected by society for the sixty remaining years of his life, he fled abroad, and then returned to build his ivory tower at Fonthill.

'Some people drink to forget their unhappiness. I do not drink, I build.' He had James Wyatt design him a Neo-Gothic phantasmagoria to replace his father's Palladian house, which he demolished. The new palace was to rival Horace Walpole's Strawberry Hill, which he called a 'Gothic mousetrap'. Wyatt planned a cruciform building with excessively long arms, a central tower 300 feet high, and exactly as long as the nave and sanctuary of Westminster Abbey. 'Twas a mad and diabolic undertaking,' confessed Beckford. 'What has been done passes belief and seems more than anything else to be the result of some pact and wager with Satan. Never has so much brick been used except at Babylon.' From 1796 onwards, the work dragged on. 'Don Cloaca' – as Beckford called his architect, the heavy-drinking, overworked Wyatt – did not supervise things properly, and twice the half-finished tower collapsed. Work then continued day and night by torchlight, sometimes with as many as 500 people. Fonthill Abbey became a legend even before work stopped on it after Wyatt's death in 1813. In the centre was the six-storey octagon with arches over 50 feet high; proceeding from this, in a breathtaking per-spective, was the King Edward Gallery, with a gilded coffered ceiling, and the fan-vaulted gallery of St Michael; the east transept housed Beckford's paintings and treasures in compartments lined with blue damask. There were Persian carpets, and decoration in purple, gold and crimson – an oriental colour scheme later adopted for the Prince Regent's Royal Pavilion in Brighton. Beckford refused to allow the Prince to see Fonthill, and totally rejected the society which had so painfully rejected him. His lost honour had turned him into an eccentric par excellence. The only people he welcomed were artists, and they were fascinated by Fonthill. Turner, John Martin, and Constable all came, and the latter raved about this 'Fairyland', even comparing it to his beloved Salisbury Cathedral, though Beckford, who despised Protestantism, also despised everything about Salisbury Cathedral apart from its spire. His own was not so tall, but being built on a hill stretched 100 feet further into the sky. Beckford dedicated the chapel to his favourite saint, patron of lost causes, Antony of Padua.

In the gigantic banqueting hall, Beckford ate virtually alone. Apart from an army of servants, his only company was a doctor from Strasbourg, a French specialist on heraldry, his Italian confidant Gregorio Franchi, and the Swiss dwarf Perro, whose job was to open the 35-foot high oak door for the few visitors. Beckford in Fonthill Abbey was a figure of immeasurable melancholy, bored and lonely, unable to find peace or satisfaction. Instead, what he found was rheumatism, for although there were always sixty fires burning, even in summer, Fonthill Abbey remained an impractical and uncomfortable place, as cold as the grave. When the price of sugar fell, and the slave trade was abolished in 1807, Beckford's income rapidly dwindled. In 1822, Christie's announced the auction of Fonthill Abbey, and hundreds came every day to view this strange palace. Fonthill Fever gripped the nation. The following year, to Beckford's unbounded relief, a gunpowder millionaire from Scotland bought the folly for £330,000. Two years later, the tower collapsed. Beckford wished he had been there.

He lived on for another twenty years in Bath (see p. 100) and went on collecting. Today his various art treasures are scattered all over the world, from Hampton Court to the Metropolitan Museum in New York. The largest collection of Beckfordiana is at Brodick Castle in Scotland. The National Gallery in London has at least two dozen masterpieces from his collection, including Raphael's *St Catherine* and Bellini's portrait of Doge Loredan. Beckford's palace, just like Henry VIII's Nonsuch Palace, was simply too huge to survive as a romantic ruin. The tower was used as a quarry, and its grey-green Chilmark stones were recycled into farmhouses. Only the underground maze of grottoes east of the lake is still there. But there is a modest copy of Fonthill Abbey to be seen at Hadlow Tower, near Tonbridge in Kent (1838-40).

Stourhead: Paradise Overflowing

East Knoyle is the village next to Fonthill, and there the Arts & Crafts architect Philip Webb built one of his masterpieces: Clouds (1885). This late Victorian country house was the meeting place of the Souls, a circle of aesthetes and aristocrats, that included Edward Burne-Jones and Prime Minister Arthur Balfour. Today, Clouds is a treatment centre for alcohol and drug dependency. Not far away, on the site where Knoyle House now stands, Christopher Wren was born.

Wren's father was rector of East Knoyle, and himself decorated the choir of the village church with stucco reliefs of Jacob's Dream and the Resurrection – pictures which were regarded as politically provocative during the Civil War, and led to Dr Wren being fined and removed from office in 1647. Christopher himself, as a surveyor of the royal buildings, also took sides politically – namely, with the Tories. When the Whigs came to power in 1714, under George I, he lost his position as court architect (though as he was by then 82 years old, perhaps he took it philosophically). His Baroque style contrasted with the stricter, classical architecture of Neo-Palladianism, as introduced into England by Inigo Jones. The latter style was based on the villas built by Andrea Palladio in the 16th century for Venetian noblemen; these villas were the models used by Colen Campbell in 1721, when he designed *Stourhead* in Stourton for the London banker Henry Hoare, son of Richard Hoare, Lord Mayor of London in 1712.

Alfred the Great, by Michael Rysbrack

The house was given two flanking pavilions by Sir Richard Colt Hoare, who also commissioned the satinwood furniture that gives the interiors such grace. from Chippendale. The great man also designed candelabra, wine coolers and flower stands for the Hoares. Other commissions were given to the naturalised Flemish sculptor Michael Rysbrack, and to two German artists: Angelica Kauffmann and Anton Raphael Mengs. The picture gallery, cool and elegant, not to say earnest, has a superlative collection.

Far more famous than Stourhead's pictures, though, is its garde (col. pls. 5 & 6). This is a picture in itself, the most perfect landscaped park in England, with the possible exception of its near contemporary at Stowe in Buckinghamshire. Though visited by 250,000 people every year (up to 2500 a day in the peak season), it is a truly edenic garden and one of the National Trust's crown jewels. We walk round a lake whose banks trace an irregular line of beauty that confronts us with one surprising vista after another: temples, grotto, bridges. Thus quite naturally and spontaneously we fulfil the artistic dreams of William Kent, creator of the English garden. But Kent was not the designer of Stourhead. Astonishingly it is the work of an amateur, the banker Henry Hoare the Younger (or, as he is usually known, Henry the Magnificent), son of the man who built the house. He created the park shortly after 1740, observing Kent's ground rules and Horace's axiom: 'Beatus ille qui procul negotiis' (happy the man who lives far from business). Though Henry Flitcroft, an architect and close associate of Kent, is listed as 'adviser' at Stourhead, he was certainly responsible for the design of all the buildings in the garden and probably deserves more credit than he is usually given.

Wherever you look, there are views like paintings. On the far bank, surrounded by beeches and rhododendrons, there is a garden temple in the form of the Pantheon, with Rysbrack's statues of Flora and Hercules in the rotunda. From there you can look back at a five-arched bridge, the old village church, and the Temple of Flora – 'a charming Gaspard picture,' enthused Henry Hoare, who of course was a Poussin collector. When he went to Italy but failed to acquire an original Claude Lorrain, he had copies painted. According to Alexander Pope, all gardening is landscape painting, and quite possibly Hoare had in mind Claude's *Aeneas on Delos* (now National Gallery, London) while he was designing Stourhead. It is a garden of quotations, and there are lines from Virgil's *Aeneid* in the Temple of Flora and from Pope in the Grotto. In this watery shrine lies the sleeping nymph Ariadne, and the Stour runs forth from a river god's urn. Heathen and classical, poetry, painting, natural philosophy, landscape and architecture are all blended here into a rich and masterly work of art. On Apollo's hill stands his temple, a domed rotunda with Corinthian columns (inspired by the original temple at Baalbec). The incorporation of such antiquities as the Gothic Market Cross, brought from Bristol in 1765, and the rustic cottage near the Pantheon mark the end of the Palladian style and the beginning of the Neo-Gothic.

Stourhead: map of the gardens
1. *Entrance from house*
2. *Temple of Flora*
3. *Paradise Spring*
4. *Boathouse*
5. *Grotto*
6. *Gothic House*
7. *Pantheon*
8. *Iron Bridge*
9. *Dam*
10. *Waterfall*
11. *Rock bridge*
12. *Site of the Hermitage*
13. *Temple of Apollo*
14. *Grottoes*
15. *Stone bridge*
16 *Gothic Cross*
17 *Church*
18. *Obelisk*
19. *St Peter's Spring*
20. *Monastery*
21. *Alfred's Tower*

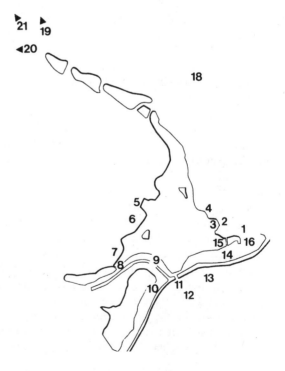

Henry Hoare also planned a hermitage, which was very much in fashion at the time. The banker even played with the idea of putting himself on show in this hut as a live recluse – isolation as a work of art, the English gentleman as a garden gnome. Ornamental hermits were a popular idea in the 18th century, and quite a few were engaged to look solitary and wise for a wage; but none ever saw out the full term of their contract. Tom Stoppard plays with the idea in *Arcadia*.

The yellow azaleas smell like honey, and the rhododendrons flower dark purple, salmon pink, crimson, scarlet, and snow white. This is what most people come to see, but Henry Hoare would have found such displays tasteless. They were not planted at Stourhead until 1894, because Victorian gardeners preferred the bright and striking colours which to 18th-century eyes were simply vulgar. In those days, people went for more moderate forms of the sublime – different shades of green supplied by different plants, the tender green of spring, the darker tinges of autumn, subtle gradations of light and shade. The woods around Stourhead have hand-kerchief trees, deciduous cypresses, and some of the finest tulip trees in England – *Liriodendron tulipifera*, for dendrophiles the king of deciduous trees.

South-east of Stourhead is another extraordinary garden (sadly private and never open to the public), created by one of the great 20th-century garden architects, Sir Geoffrey Jellicoe. *Shute House* in Donhead St Mary is a waterscape, with lakes, canals and waterfalls. It is an open-air laboratory of garden philosophy, a consumm-ation of Jellicoe's ideas, and a new chapter in the history of English landscape.

Longleat: Kama Sutra with Lord Bath

Heaven's Gate is in Wiltshire, just a few miles north of Stourhead. Sweet-scented azaleas, incense cedars, gum and tulip trees line the way, and from these heights we can look down on *Longleat*: a gently undulating valley of green, the house standing by a serpentine lake, oak trees, sheep, and all the other requisites of the perfect pas-toral setting created by Capability Brown in 1757 (col. pl. 10). Prior to that, the house had been surrounded by a formal Elizabethan garden, which the landscape architect Russell Page partly restored after 1945. If Capability Brown returned to Longleat today, he would get quite a surprise. In the shade of his trees are dozing lions and tigers; antelopes, zebras, giraffes and elephants graze in his fields. Noah's Ark appears to have landed at Longleat. And so it did in 1965. That was when the circus owner Jimmy Chipperfield suggested to the 6th Marquess of Bath that he should put lions in his park. His Lordship thought the cages would have to be awfully big if cars were going to drive into them. 'That's the whole point,' replied Chipperfield. 'We'll put the people into cages – their cars – and let the lions out.' When England's first safari park opened in Longleat at Easter 1966, the *Times* thun-dered against this 'dangerous folly'. But people came in their thousands, and the

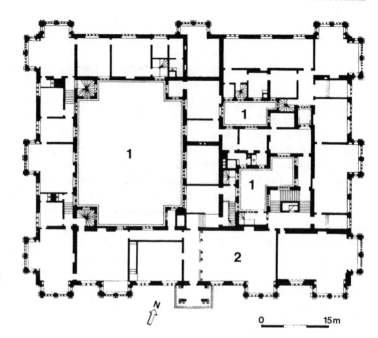

Longleat, plan
1. Courtyards
2. Great Hall

Lions of Longleat became a household name. They brought the Marquess publicity, cash, and dung. Lion dung, he swore, kept the deer away from his roses, and for that reason alone, every Englishman should keep a pet lion.

'Lordy', as his friends called him, had inherited a rather run-down, 118-room house plus astronomical death duties. The stark choice was between selling the family silver and putting it on display. Longleat was the first of the great British houses to open itself up permanently to the public (Easter 1949). Since then, over 700 have followed suit in England, attracting some 50 million visitors a year. The Marquess of Bath, once an object of ridicule, is now regarded as the pioneer of the stately homes business – the supreme salesman of historical mothballs.

Longleat is a magnificent example of the early Renaissance English country house: it is a rectangular building, constructed around two inner courtyards, with uniform façades all round and large bay windows with vigorous mullions and transoms. The expanse of glass is reminiscent of 'Hardwick Hall, more glass than wall', but the emphasis on the horizontal and the right-angle is also typically English; the rectangular bays jut out firmly from the walls, making strong vertical accents and strengthening the corners, but without disrupting the horizontality. The classical pattern of Doric, Ionic and Corinthian pilasters between the windows of the three storeys is an Italian motif. The model for this symmetrical façade is believed to have been Somerset House in London (the predecessor of the current Somerset House), where Sir John Thynne, faithful adjutant of the Lord Protector, Duke of Somerset, was working when he acquired the dissolved Augustinian monastery of Longleat for £53. In 1547 he started building a country house of Bath stone in a manner befitting his high rank and station, and never ceased to work on it until his death in 1580. His master mason was Robert Smythson, who created a similar great Elizabethan house in Nottinghamshire, Wollaton Hall, and almost certainly the incomparable Hardwick Hall itself.

Longleat was one of the 'prodigy houses' of its time. Today, however, the main attractions lie outside it, with such lordly entertainments as the science fiction world of Dr Who, Pet's Corner, Postman Pat and a tethered hot air balloon. In the stables stands Churchill's shining black Austin Ten, and outside are the giant castle and the narrow gauge railway – children's (and Dads') delight. You can also visit Pets' Corner, where all the noble darlings rest in peace: the Pekinese Potiphar and Pansy, the greyhound Drake, the terrier Jenny Wren, Homer the Dove, and the green parrot Jew Süss, buried in 1933. Pansy's death inspired Lady Weymouth to verse:

> Brave little huntress ever true,
> Engraved upon my heart are you.
> No one can fill your special place,
> My Pansy with a sooty face...

> And when I stand, alone and grey,
> Outside the forest, Lord I pray
> That I may hear her little bark
> To lead me through the unknown dark.

Of the original Elizabethan interior, only the Great Hall with its hammerbeam roof has survived. The other rooms were totally transformed in the 19th century, particularly by the Victorian designer J. D. Crace. The rooms positively glow with their coffered ceilings in Italian Renaissance style, and their wall coverings of Genoese velvet and Spanish leather. Together with Flemish tapestries and John Wootton's monumental hunting scenes (c. 1740), the highlights include paintings by Jacopo Tintoretto and Jacob Isaac van Ruisdael. There was also a Titian, but it was stolen in 1995.

In the mid 1950's, the 6th Marquess of Bath moved into a smaller house on his estate, and gave the whole west wing to his eldest son. The young Alexander Weymouth believed (and still believes) himself to be an artist, and the results – all over his private rooms – are to be gazed at in wonderment: a cycle of murals on a Baroque scale, offering 'keyhole glimpses of my psyche'. The walls of the library, the billiard room, the children's room, the dining room – they are all covered with satirical scenes, as if the Expressionists had come pouring out of Jackson Pollock's tubes. The paint is piled on thick, mixed with sawdust to create a plastic effect. 'Never exhibited anywhere else,' the guide assures us. We are not surprised.

A third of the wall space at Longleat has been covered, with the climax coming in the Kama Sutra room. Phallic trees all around are hung with 33 aphrodisiac apples, each one filled with juicy love scenes showing lots of highly instructive positions derived from the Tree of Knowledge. True to form, there is a four poster bed complete with large mirror in the canopy – for variations which he might perhaps have omitted from his paintings, because as he writes in the catalogue, 'one can't think of everything, you know!' From this centre for sexual acrobatics we make our way to the spiral staircase. Here, like hunting trophies, hang the portraits of his 'wifelets', all his mistresses up and down the stairs, in chronological order. The guide calls them his 'Bluebeard Collection'. The names are on the back of the pictures – 68 of them as of April 1999. Art-lovers are not always impressed; one wrote in the visitors' book: 'Number 13 looks like my mum. Please explain!'

There is no doubt about it, the wildest lion of Longleat is Lord Bath (col. pl. 8). A few days after my first visit, I was granted an audience. A giant of a man in a patchwork pullover, with long grey hair, a shaggy beard, a benevolent smile, a gold ring in his right ear, and a hearing aid in his left, Lord Bath is in his sixties. As always, he was barefoot, for he only wears shoes, collar and tie when he takes his place in the House of Lords, which England's old hippie does surprisingly often. He has a penthouse suite on the third floor of Longleat, 'in the style of the 21st century'. His desk is like the control deck of a spaceship, and there is other futuristic paraphernalia all around. 'My father never accepted that it was sensible for me to become a painter and writer. Those were not jobs he respected. I was supposed to realize his vision of Longleat, and I was refusing to do that.' They were constantly in conflict, not least on political matters. By the end of his life, the old Lord Bath had the biggest collection of Nazi souvenirs and Hitler watercolours in England. In Derek Jarman's *Jubilee*, Hitler, still alive in the era of punk, is kept as a kind of pet at Longleat. 'Yes, my father was very right wing, deriding democracy, praising Hitler. He was converted to fascism by an American general. But one must always weigh against that the fact that he also collected Churchilliana on the basis that he was about the most ruthless bastard we had in this country. He admired ruthlessness.' A small part of this grotesque collection can be seen in the stables, including Churchill's singed siren suit and cigar stubs, Hitler's cutlery from the bunker in Berlin, and the skin of the very first lion of Longleat, whose name was 'Marquess'. This exhibition is the son's memorial to his dead father, and he has even managed to throw his father out of the house posthumously: Graham Sutherland's portrait of the old Lord Bath, the one noteworthy piece of 20th-century art in the whole house, now has a place of honour in the stable, along with the Hitler collection. Honi soit qui mal y pense.

Since he inherited the house and title in 1992, the Kama Sutra artist has run

Longleat much more professionally than many people expected. The father set up a safari park, and the son has built a Center Parcs holiday village. This £80 million leisure centre has brought Longleat more and more visitors, and more and more profit. It is a stroke of genius. 'My father gambled on lions, and I'm gambling on mazes. It's my main interest now. I want to plant a new maze every year – go to Longleat to get lost!' (col. pl. 9). The Maze of Love is a love garden of box hedges and rose arches curved into hearts, under which the lost visitor is supposed to linger and to kiss his sweetheart. Sex, please, we're British. Longleat employs 200 people, welcomes half a million visitors a year, and has a turnover of several million pounds. His Lordship is more of a businessman than he seems. He makes skilful use of his image as a hippie and an artist. All the rows with his father, all the love affairs, all the 'bad boy' headlines – great publicity for Longleat. 'What my father invested in me has paid off.'

Lord Bath, his bare feet in direct contact with the forces of the earth, is a practising pantheist. 'I celebrate solstice. My wife celebrates Christmas. Sometimes that leads to a bit of confusion.' How does Lady Bath react to her husband's Bluebeard image? 'Well, she knew me a long time before we were married, so nothing comes as a a a surprise to her.' For nearly thirty years he has – he says – been happily, if distantly married to Anna Gael, originally from Hungary. 'She lives in Paris, but comes over here to Longleat once a month for a week.' He sent their two children, Lenka and Ceawlin, to comprehensive school. Why not to a public school like Eton, where he went himself? 'Because I feel that is where class division originates.' But this left-wing lord never wanted to be a Communist: 'That would have been far too much against my self-interest.' He therefore founded his own political party, the Wessex Regionalist Party.

The very mention of Wessex makes his bright blue eyes glow. Wessex is almost as beautiful as the Kama Sutra, though a lot more difficult to put into practice. Wessex was the name of the Anglo-Saxon kingdom between London and Cornwall, and his son Ceawlin is named after the third king. Now it's high time Wessex regained its autonomy in a Europe of regions. His election poster of 1974 still hangs at Longleat. 'I got 521 votes, and later a little under 2000 in the European elections.' He had to admit that he couldn't create a state out of that result, and so from then on he concentrated on promoting regional art, and took himself off to the House of Lords.

What a man! So long as there are still eccentrics like him, England will still be England. Taste? Style? He goes on happily writing, painting, and fornicating, and he even knows that he is no great artist. 'I consider myself a failed preacher,' he says. 'Life is getting more and more centralised. The only way of making that bearable is to promote a philosophy of individualism within it.' Every morning he sits at his spaceship writing desk in Longleat House and works on his autobiography. Three million words so far. 'I'm only on Volume 9. By my calculation, I'll catch up with the present in 2008, with Volume 25.' That is something a lot of us will look forward to. No publisher has accepted it, as yet, but Lord Bath will be publishing on his own website.

Lacock Abbey: Fox Talbot Invents Photography

There are many beautiful old villages in England, but if the National Trust takes over a whole village and preserves it intact, then it must be something special. The National Trust took over *Lacock* in 1944. It is situated on the Avon, south of Chippenham. No new buildings, no posters, no television aerials are allowed to intrude on this cluster of houses dating from between the 13th and the 18th century. All the more eagerly, then, do the film-makers descend on this museum-piece of a village when, for instance, they want to do another Jane Austen. *Castle Combe*, on the edge of the Cotswolds, is another favoured film set (*Doctor Dolittle*), a picture postcard tourist attraction basking under full listing.

If you want to see a normal village, as opposed to a showpiece, and you also want to see how the classic English village has changed over the years, then go to *Kington Langley*, just a few miles further on. It was the model for the fictional village of Kington Borel in the book *Wiltshire Village*, written in 1939 by the artist and engraver Robin Tanner and his wife Heather. Even then it was an idealised view of country life in the old days, a eulogy to the rural world of the birds and the bees: 'small things, flowers, birds, and the sweet air, with gentle hills and smiling valleys.' But let us return to Lacock.

On the edge of the village, in the meadows by the Avon, stands *Lacock Abbey*, founded in 1232 by Ela, widow of the Earl of Salisbury. This Augustinian abbey did not escape the Reformation, and was duly converted into a mansion. The abbess' hall underwent a remarkable renaissance. A gentleman-architect Sanderson Miller, hitherto known only for his construction of ready-made ruins, changed this medieval hall into one of the earliest and noblest pieces of Gothic Revival in England (1754/55). In niches all over the walls, below Neo-Gothic canopies, stand terracotta figures by a virtually unknown sculptor called Victor Alexander Sederbach. Lacock Abbey is famous for another reason, too. It was here that William Henry Fox Talbot invented photography. The glory of being the first was also claimed by Daguerre, who certainly gained greater publicity and was indeed the first to publish (in Paris, 1839) what Fox Talbot had discovered independently and at the same time in the remoteness of his

William Henry Fox Talbot by James Moffat, 1866

37

country house in England: namely, a method of enabling Nature to copy itself. Fox Talbot had enjoyed a typical upper class upbringing, having been educated at Harrow and Cambridge, and he was the heir to Lacock, which had been the family home of the Talbots since the 16th century. He had time and he had money, so he travelled, and studied. He translated *Macbeth* into Greek verse just for fun, published an Assyrian dictionary, and gained academic honours for helping to decipher the cuneiform inscriptions at Nineveh. In October 1833 he went to Lake Como. The landscape so enthralled the classical tourist that he wanted to draw it as accurately as possible with the aid of his camera obscura. 'This led me to reflect on the inimitable beauty of the pictures of nature's painting which the glass lens of the camera throws upon the paper in its focus – fairy pictures, creations of a moment, and destined as rapidly to fade away. It was probably thus that the idea occurred to me: How charming it would be if it were possible to cause these natural images to imprint themselves durably and remain fixed on the paper!'

From his desire to give permanence to these fleeting masterpieces of Nature arose his major contribution to the invention of photography: the negative, out of which light-proof, positive copies could be made. The future belonged to these infinitely reproducible paper pictures – the Talbotype – and not to the Daguerrotype, which could produce only one picture per copper plate. This must have been the most inconspicuous sensation in history: near the central oriel window in the south gallery of Lacock Abbey hangs a tiny photo which Fox Talbot took of this same window in August 1835. Exposure time: 30 minutes. This indoor photograph was so clear that, as he proudly recorded, each of the 200 or so leaded glass plates could be counted through a magnifying glass. The original, which is now in the Science Museum in London, is the oldest known negative. In 1841, Fox Talbot patented the so-called Calotype, his method of making pictures visible on paper, which he considered to be the only one with a future, and upon this rests his claim to be the inventor of photography. But it was Daguerre who triumphed. All his life, Fox Talbot remained in the Frenchman's shadow, and he grew increasingly embittered. Nevertheless, he continued to experiment in his laboratory at Lacock Abbey and in a studio in Reading, which was the first photographic studio in the world. If he could not have the glory, at least he wanted the money. He charged huge licence fees, and ruthlessly exploited even the discoveries of his great rival. His photos, however, make one almost overlook the more grasping side of his character: the delicate pictures of moss and lace, the detailed yet ghostly negatives of Lacock library or of the Neo-Gothic hall, still lives, chess-players, a picnic, an open door. Many of these pictures appeared in his book *The Pencil of Nature* (1844), the first annotated book of photographs. He wrote pragmatically, as only an Englishman could write

Lacock Abbey, the Hall

The Open Door, from The Pencil of Nature

about such an invention. In one picture 'a whole forest of chimneys borders the horizon; for the instrument chronicles whatever it sees and certainly would delineate a chimney pot or a chimney-sweeper with the same impartiality as it would the Apollo of Belvedere.' William Henry Fox Talbot died in 1877 on his own estate, and is buried in the village churchyard. Precisely what photography is, and who pioneered it in England, and how he worked, has all been explained by the National Trust in the former barn of Lacock Abbey, which is now the Fox Talbot Museum of Photography.

Along with Lacock Abbey and the Benedictine Abbey of Amesbury, Malmesbury Abbey was one of the three biggest monasteries in Wiltshire. The little town of *Malmesbury,* birthplace of the philosopher Thomas Hobbes, is on the edge of the Cotswolds, situated on a hill overlooking the Avon. The fragmentary remains of the abbey church bear witness to its former beauty, as does J. M. W. Turner's watercolour of 1792. When the abbey was torn down after the Reformation, only the nave of the Norman church survived, and this was bought by a rich cloth merchant who gave it to the community as a parish church. The south porch (*c.* 1160-70) is a biblical arch of triumph: a broad round arch with eight archivolts, which unfold their stories and spread their decorations uninterrupted from one end to the other, from the Old to the New Testament. Anyone stepping through this entrance will find a second, narrower doorway, and in its tympanum is Christ in His Glory. In two lunettes in the porch, the Apostles sit opposite one another, six on either side, with an angel flying over their heads. The rich folds of the garments, the animated expressions and gestures, the elongated figures – all these make it one of the finest pieces of Norman sculpture in England.

Here the monk Elmer achieved legendary fame as an 11th-century English Icarus when he made himself a pair of wings and jumped off the church tower; despite the strong wind and his even stronger faith, he broke both legs. The chronicler William of Malmesbury, whose *Gesta Regum Anglorum* is a rich source of anecdotes about the period after 1066, was pupil, teacher, monk and abbot here. In his day, the monastery library of Malmesbury was famous throughout Europe. In the treasure chamber above the church portal is a magnificent illuminated Bible of 1407, the work of Flemish artists.

According to William of Malmesbury, it was Abbot Aldhelm who founded an *ecclesiola* in *Bradford-on-Avon*. Whether this 'little church' was St Lawrence is not certain, but what is beyond doubt is that St Lawrence is one of the most important Anglo-Saxon churches in England; it was built around 700, extended by a storey *c.* 1000, and has survived virtually intact ever since. Until well into the 19th century, its true nature was unknown. It was used as a charnel house and as a school for the poor; a gardener lived in the chancel, and houses and stables had been built all around it. Today we can see its structure quite clearly: it consists of a single nave and a rectangular chancel, and originally there was a portico on either side of the nave. Each of these additional, almost separate sections is reached through an unusually narrow doorway. Equally unusual are the proportions of the rooms: the nave and chancel are very narrow and very high, with the height exceeding the length. The stonework is rough, even clumsy, but nothing is wasted here – everything is compressed and concentrated, and the modesty and simplicity are what give the church its serenity. There are just two angels hovering high above the chancel arch, probably the remains of a rood like the one in Romsey. The simplicity of the interior is matched by that of the exterior: a frieze of blind arches runs all the way round with flat pilasters as the only (typically Anglo-Saxon) decoration; there are just a few vertical and horizontal bands on the walls, rather like the beams of a timber-framed house. The architecture is primitive in the very best sense of the word, straightforward and powerful, totally different from the contemporary, richly decorated chapels at Aix-la-Chapelle or Oviedo in Asturias. St Lawrence is a little gem in a jewel-box of a town – Bradford, the Broad Ford of the Avon, once a centre of the wool industry. On the nine-arched Avon Bridge (13th/17th century) is a little house. Could it have been a detention cell, or a little chapel for pilgrims? Both, apparently. Wherever you look in Bradford, you'll find sights to treasure, like the monumental 14th-century Tithe Barn in the south-east, or The Hall at the end of Woolley Street – but I like best strolling through the lanes of the Shambles.

Malmesbury Abbey, the tympanum

There is one town in Wiltshire, the biggest, that everybody used to avoid if they could: *Swindon*, the industrial centre on the M4. It owes its existence and our attention to one man – Isambard Kingdom Brunel. In 1843 this engineering genius opened the Great Western Railway locomotive and wagon works here, halfway between Bristol and London, and for the workers he built houses, shops, pubs, and indeed a whole Railway Village which became the early Victorian nucleus of this railway town. The 300 or so buildings are now all listed, and they constitute the biggest architectural ensemble that Brunel built in England. In the 1950's there were still 40,000 people employed in these Great Western workshops, but by 1986 they were closed. That left plenty of space for a Railway Museum, as well as for the National Monuments Record Centre, which houses more than six million photographs of England's architectural heritage. Swindon is also now home to one of the biggest 'attractions' in the West Country – the Designer Outlet Shopping Village in the old Brunel sheds. Coachloads of shoppers visit it every day of the year from as far afield as Swansea and London.

Brunel's 20th-century successor, the engineering artist Sir Norman Foster, has also left his mark on Swindon. Standing on high, bright yellow piers linked by girders hanging from steel cables, and covered with a folded roof, is his Renault Parts Distribution Centre (1982/83), crouching on the edge of the town, like a giant yellow insect about to hop into the green fields of Wiltshire (col. pl. 11).

Dorset

Behind the green hills, you will meet the Huntsman in his red coat and black riding cape, and rejoice in his motto: 'Hardy Beer from Hardy's Country'. In Dorset, everyone knows about the great writer, even if they don't all know his books. Hardy and Dorset go together like Devon and cream teas, and Dorset itself is the epitome of the rolling English countryside – a vast landscape park, where industry has scarcely dared to show its ugly face. Hardy's enduring popularity with a conservative public is due not least to the fact that in the age of industry, commerce and the cash nexus, he invoked the eternal power of Nature, describing the passions – often tragic – of the countryfolk in the villages he knew so well. How can anything good come when the shepherd Gabriel Oak falls in love with the farm-owner Bathsheba Everdene in *Far from the Madding Crowd*, a title ironically borrowed from an earlier version of pastoral, Thomas Gray's romantic *Elegy Written in a Country Churchyard*?

Dorset has remained far from the madding crowd. It is too remote for London commuters, and tourists generally hurry through it on their way to Cornwall. Bournemouth and Poole are its only towns with more than 100,000 inhabitants, and the rest consists of quiet little towns and villages where church and pub, vicarage, manor house and farmhouses stand together much as they did in Hardy's novels. This is provincial life at its purest, where even a stranger is made to feel at home. Here the great author could live and write in peace, and there was also room for T. E. Lawrence – Lawrence of Arabia – to find refuge far from the hurly-burly of his desert adventures. Dorset is a county of international repute. You will find Worldwide Butterflies Ltd (also marketed as Lullingstone Silk Farm) in Over Compton near Sherborne, and Dorset's stone quarries helped to build medieval cathedrals in Normandy and the UN building in New York.

The Cerne Giant

Garden Cities by the Sea: The Dead Souls of Bournemouth

The little harbour town of *Christchurch* would long since have been joined to the seaside resort of Bournemouth were it not for the fact that they are separated by the mouth of the Rivers East Avon and Stour. Christchurch owes its name and its importance in the Middle Ages to its priory church, which the Augustinians found here in 1094, when they established their monastery, and which they extended to its present cathedral dimensions. Norman architecture is rarely so light and so lively as the outer wall of the north transept, with the trellis design round the top of its stair turret, the fish-scale decoration in its spandrels, and the columns with their overlapping, almost dancing arches. In the chancel is a wondrous reredos, depicting the tree of Jesse, towering up into the Perpendicular vault – a monumental example of Decorated sculpture (*c.* 1350). Down below the west tower is a white marble monument to the poet Shelley (1854) and his wife, as a Pietà. The sailing boat is a reference to the fact that he was drowned while sailing in the Mediterranean. Beneath are lines from his poem *Adonais*, written a year earlier on the death of his friend Keats:

> He has outsoared the shadow of our night.
> Envy and calumny and hate and pain,
> And that unrest which men miscall delight,
> Can touch him not and torture not again.

Shelley's ashes are buried at the Pyramid of Cestius in Rome, but his heart lies in *Bournemouth*, in the churchyard of St Peter's. That is where, after life's fitful fever, all this literary family now rest in peace: Shelley's wife Mary, whose novel *Frankenstein* (1818) brought a new dimension to Gothic horror and spawned some thirty films, the latest by Kenneth Branagh (1994); her father William Godwin, initially a minister, then an atheist and anarchic pamphleteer, and author of the propagandist novel *Caleb Williams* (1794); and her mother Mary Wollstonecraft, who in her book *Vindication of the Rights of Women* (1792) demanded the right of women to self-determination, and indeed lived her life accordingly.

The dead souls of Bournemouth: they sit upon the park benches, pensioned off, trying to make up for a lifetime of rain with a final flourish of southern sun. And they watch the antics of the young folk, who have come from all over the world to take language lessons, play on the pier, and bathe on the miles of beach that stretch out beneath the cliffs. Deep valleys cut through the hills – these are the 'chines', filled with pines and rhododendrons. This is a garden city by the sea, predestined to be a spa and holiday resort. In the middle of the 19th century, Bournemouth had barely 700 inhabitants; today it has nearly 160,000. In 1883, William Morris found the Riviera style villas 'simply blackguardly', suitable only for 'ignorant purse-proud digesting machines' But his contemporaries came not for the architecture but for the climate, and some brought to Mediterranean Bournemouth a touch of *morbidezza*. The tubercular illustrator Aubrey Beardsley, a leading figure of the Decadents in the 1890's, was converted to Catholicism here in the winter of 1896, shortly before his premature death. Paul Verlaine, the great French poet, also came here after two years in prison (he had shot his lover Arthur Rimbaud in the wrist) and a temporary conversion to Catholicism; while trying to put his shattered life together again, he spent 1876-77 teaching at St Aloysius School, until he couldn't stand it any more and went back to France (to teach English). For three years, 1884-1887, Robert Louis Stevenson vainly sought a Bournemouth cure for his tuberculosis, and the Lord of the Rings J. R. R. Tolkien died here in 1973.

Bournemouth's fame, however, does not rest on the reputation of its dead writers. It has two leg-saving lifts between its upper and lower promenades, two symphony orchestras, and several museums. The Russell-Cotes Art Gallery is on East Cliff – a Victorian mixture of Italian villa and Scottish castle, with a decor that is Japanese, Moorish and French. This is where in 1884 Sir Merton Russell-Cotes, a successful hotelier, housed his collection of Victorian paintings and Japanese and Burmese art,

Norman blind arcading at Christchurch Abbey

as well as a theatrical collection in memory of his friend the Shakespearian actor Henry Irving. Since then it has been enlivened by modern art and craftwork and a well-designed extension.

If you look beyond the tourist attractions, you will find damning evidence of the ever increasing social divide in England's so-called 'classless society'. The West Cliff bulges with elegant old hotels and new shopping precincts; Boscombe, to the east, is riddled with empty, boarded-up shops and former guest-houses now housing guests on social welfare, while the streets are home to beggars, addicts, and the homeless. Pompous conference centres in the west mock the soup kitchens of the east, and the Council boast that Bournemouth is a 'modern, European, cosmopolitan' resort. Perhaps they think Boscombe is simply on another planet.

For centuries the focal point of Poole Bay was not Bournemouth but the trading port of *Poole*. The natural harbour is said to be the biggest in the world apart from Sydney; its bays are as popular now with yachtsmen as they once were with pirates, smugglers, and the Newfoundland sailors who made Poole a major fishing market in the 18th century. Of this golden age, nothing remains except the Custom House, known as the Harbour Office, and a few old warehouses and merchants' houses on the quay. *Brownsea Island*, in the middle of the bay, was the setting in August 1907 for Baden-Powell's very first Boy Scouts' camp – the Boy Scouts movement that he founded shortly after was so phenomenally successful that it held the first worldwide Jamboree in 1920. This island resort, complete with one of Henry VIII's castles, is a nature reserve, and as such has so far escaped exploitation by the oil predators always circling here, for beneath the romantic bay lies one of the biggest oilfields in Western Europe.

The best view of Poole's splendour is from Canford Cliffs, when the flowers are blooming in *Compton Acres*. Before 1914 there was nothing here except moorland, but today it is an open-air museum of rare plants and sculpture – a garden made of seven gardens. These are terraces full of optical and botanical surprises, from the symmetrical Italian garden to the animal sculptures, temples and pagodas of one of the most authentic Japanese gardens in Europe.

Wimborne Minster is a small town on the Stour, named with understandable pride after its minster church. This is a veritable school of styles: Norman round piers, tower and arches in the nave, Early English lancet windows in the chancel, a Perpendicular clerestory, a Decorated crypt. In the choir, encased in Purbeck marble, is a collector's item for the brass enthusiast: the half-figure of King Ethelred, who was defeated by the Danes in 871 (though the brass mistakenly says 873); it is the only known brass of an English king (*c.* 1440). Long before there was any such thing as a public library, Wimborne had its own Chained Library above the sacristy. This was the private collection of a Presbyterian who opened it up to the public in 1686, but installed his own anti-theft device by fastening the books with chains. What did the educated layman read in those days? A nine-language edition of the

Bible, Plato, Plutarch, Erasmus, Raleigh's *History of the World*, and the best-selling *Anatomy of Melancholy* by the Anglican clergyman Robert Burton (1621).

But now, without further ado, let us go to *Kingston Lacy*. This house is filled right up to its hipped roof with the most wonderful paintings: Titian, Rubens, Sebastiano del Piombo. Outside is a park of laurel paths and lime avenues. It is an English Arcadia. Here, between Tarrant Crawford and Wimborne, there lived for over 300 years one of the great landed families of Dorset, the Bankes, and when the last of them died, childless, in 1981, the house, garden and 16,000 acres of prime land (including Corfe Castle, Studland Bay and Badbury Rings) fell into the more than willing and ever reliable hands of the National Trust.

Kingston Lacy is a Restoration house, built between 1663 and 1665 by the Cavalier architect Sir Roger Pratt. It is the most important of his few surviving buildings. The classic proportions combine with a fluent elegance in a kind of Baroque neoclassicism. Between 1835 and 1846 Sir Charles Barry covered Pratt's brick façade with Caen ashlar, and even more magnificently, he created a majestic stairwell of Carrara marble. The lords of Kingston were royalists and Members of Parliament, who had themselves painted by Lely, Lawrence and van Dyck, and of course collected many other paintings, though none did so with greater acumen than William Bankes, a friend of Lord Byron's. The rooms are filled with souvenirs from his many journeys: pictures from the schools of Raphael and Murillo, a Velázquez, an early ceiling fresco by Guido Reni. Egypt was an especially rich source, and the treasures include a pink obelisk in the park, which the Isis priests of Philae had erected *c.* 150 BC to celebrate the fact that they would never ever have to pay any more taxes. Even the clergy nowadays would scarcely be able to believe in such miracles.

Crossword Puzzles in Green: Amazing Mazes

In *Hurn*, right beside Bournemouth Airport, lies Russell Lucas-Rowe's Wonderland. Tired of wrestling with milk quotas laid down by Brussels, this young farmer decided to sell his cows and to change his dairy tales for fairy tales. He opened Wonderland in 1992, and now welcomes more than 100,000 visitors a year – a magic example of how to overcome the current crisis in British farming. The great attraction of *Merritown Farm* is its Alice-in-Wonderland maze. The entrance is a rabbit-hole, and the exit is a cascade of playing cards, as at the end of Alice's dream. The main characters of Lewis Carroll's immortal story appear in the style of Tenniel's classic illustrations, planted in the beech hedges which line the mile of paths.

If you really want to get lost, England is the best country in the world for you. There are more mazes in England than anywhere else in Europe. According to

Julian Barnes, the maze combines two national passions: gardens and crossword puzzles. The new golden age of this esoteric art, in which the greatest confusion is created within the smallest area, reached its peak in 1991, when the Hampton Court maze celebrated its 300th birthday. The Year of the Maze was promoted by Adrian Fisher, a business consultant, who in 1979 joined forces with Randall Coate, a retired diplomat, to set up the firm of Minotaur Designs. Their labyrinths are labours of love, and each one is a masterpiece of systematic chaos. Together they have designed over 40 mazes worldwide, in the parks of castles, manor houses and leisure centres, for private citizens, companies and towns; their themes are heraldic, mythological or symbolic, and their materials are yew, boxtree, brick or even marble mosaic. The Alice maze is their design, too. Fisher says that mazes are ideal for modern mass tourism, for they create an oasis of peace amid beautiful surroundings, where people of all ages can meet and play together.

Ever since Daedálus created a labyrinth for Minos, King of Crete, in which to keep the Minotaur, the monster who was part bull and part human, we have looked for playful parallels to the problems of the real world. For people in the Middle Ages, the maze symbolised the tangled paths of life – the world's confusions on the road to salvation. Even in Tudor times the mythical thinker had become a garden ornament. Today, mazes are popular entertainments, decorative puzzles that have lost their meaning. But with their combination of geometry and symbol, of fun and mystery, they retain their fascination – anachronistic shoots of fantasy in the age of the computer game.

Alice Maze at Merritown Farm

Redevelopment 1780 Style: Milton Abbas

Milton Abbey, north-west of Poole, can probably boast of the most eccentric land-lord that any abbey ever had. You can see him in the north transept, just as he wished to see himself: Joseph Damer, Lord Milton, first Earl of Dorchester, ideal husband, nobleman, gazing out over his beloved wife Caroline towards the end of himself and all things. This is a touching monument, personal but at the same time universal, so typical of the Enlightenment in its combination of clarity, pathos and sentiment, designed some time after 1775 by the top man of the time, Robert Adam, and carved by Agostino Carlini. Caroline's clothes, skin and hair are so beautifully, delicately modelled that she seems neither dead nor of stone. Here in his church, Lord Dorchester is lily-white. And outside as well, on the estate that once belonged to him, everything looks perfect. The idyllic lake nestles comfortably in the idyllic valley. But for centuries the idyllic landscape had been a town, and the demolition of that town was in full swing when the destroyer was having himself carved in marble and was forcing his tenants to move to the model village of Milton Abbas, three-quarters of a mile away from the big house.

Milton Abbas was an example of redevelopment and compulsory resettlement 1780-style. How did it come about? Lord Dorchester's manor was the abbey, which had been altered, renovated and extended; but he was still an unhappy man, and for two reasons. The old town of Middleton – over 100 houses, four pubs, a brewery and a school – blocked his view; and the young people were noisy, stole his fruit, and threw stones down his chimney. In other words, Lord Dorchester wanted to be far from the madding crowd. Since he was not prepared to move himself, he moved them. He forced his tenants out of their old houses, promising them new and better accommodation; he got rid of the last but one, a lawyer, by opening a sluice gate; he demolished all their cottages but the very last, Green Walk Cottage, standing by the edge of the forest near the church. He shifted the school far away to Blandford Forum. By a gloriously ironic stroke of fate, his manor house is now a boys' school.

Lord Dorchester destroyed a town and built a ruin. He built it on the other side of the lake, quite in accordance with the picturesque taste of his time and of his landscape gardener, Capability Brown. The latter also created the initial plans for the model village of Milton Abbas, with its thatched houses designed by William Chambers and built in 1780. Of course, His Lordship did not dispossess his tenants without compensation, but the family houses we see today, with lawns in the front and woods at the back, were often inhabited by four families, which in those days might mean up to thirty people. Lord Dorchester himself lived in what his architect Chambers later described as 'this vast ugly house in Dorset'. Chambers resigned in 1774, and his successor as interior designer, James Wyatt, did his best to make up for the vast ugly neoclassical exterior with plaster ceilings in the style of Adam. Of the old Abbey, all that Lord Dorchester left standing was the Abbot's hall (1498).

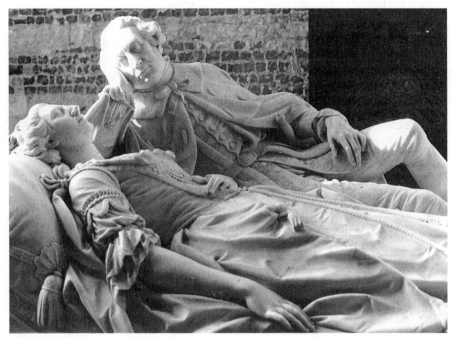

Tomb of Lord Dorchester, Milton Abbey

The chancel and transepts of the uncompleted Abbey Church (15th century) give some idea of the magnificence of this Benedictine monastery. It was founded *c.* 935 by King Aethelstan, to mark his gratitude for victory over the Danes.

The Stones of Purbeck

Even if you have never been to the Isle of Purbeck, you are sure to have seen its marble – for instance, in Westminster Abbey. It's not really marble at all, but a conglomerate rich in shells. Polished, it can be black, as in the columns of Salisbury Cathedral; unpolished it remains silver-grey, as in the arches of Exeter. It was used for the piers in Ely and Durham Cathedrals and many medieval churches, and it is still used today for decorations and monuments (as, for example, around Kingston).

Anyone wandering through the heaths and woods of Purbeck's hills to the rocky slopes of *Kimmeridge* will find traces of a much older stone industry that goes back to Roman times. It was because of these quarries, and not for the fine view, that a 17th-century businessman named William Clavell built the manor at *Smedmore*.

The most curious stone of Purbeck, however, is the 40-ton 'Great Globe' (1887), a 'chiselled map of the world' on the cliffs of *Durlston Head*. This is not Purbeck but Portland stone, from a rival concern nearby. It is only one of many stone mementos which George Burt left behind as architectural riddles to be solved by the people of his birthplace, *Swanage*, and their holiday guests. No other English town has as many reminders of Olde Englande as this Dorset *lapidarium*, Old-London-by-the-Sea. Burt was the nephew and partner of John Mowlem, who ran a stonemason's yard, and Burt reconstructed in Swanage what the Victorians tore down in London: Doric columns from the Custom House on Waterloo Bridge, Wellington's clock tower, and the Baroque façade of the Mercers' Hall in Cheapside (1670), which since 1882 has endowed Swanage's townhall with a disproportionate splendour. Diagonally opposite in the High Street, Burt collected more Londoniana around his own Purbeck House: a gateway from Hyde Park, cast-iron columns and railings from Billingsgate Market, and three blocks of granite from London Bridge which had been erected by his own firm Mowlem & Co in 1831, and was taken down in 1968 and shipped off to an oil millionaire in Arizona as a de-luxe souvenir of Olde England.

The Isle of Purbeck is only small, but it has a remarkable variety of landscape features: high limestone cliffs, old pastures, forests, chalk hills, and between them all that ever rarer biotope, moorland. Purbeck has been designated an Area of Outstanding Natural Beauty, but this only gives it limited protection. The rich flora and fauna are less important to industry than the rich minerals. Stone, sand and gravel have always been quarried here in quantity, and this ceaseless exploitation cannot help but destroy the delicate balance of nature. China clay is another of the island's resources – a particularly fine clay which Josiah Wedgwood was already extracting back in the middle of the 18th century.

Where the English coast is at its most beautiful, there you will find the oak-leaf sign of the National Trust, or the designation Heritage Coast. On Purbeck you will find them both. South of Corfe Castle is a no-through-road to *Worth Matravers*, and from the village pub, the 'Square and Compass', you can follow a path to the chapel on the clifftop at *St Aldhelm's Head*, then all the way round again to the pub. The cliffs here are called Dancing Ledge, which was the title Derek Jarman gave to a chapter of his autobiography where he describes a cold night in a nearby quarry, filming *The Angelic Conversation* (1985): Shakespeare's sonnets with Judi Dench, a series of enigmatic scenes shot on the Dorset coast.

Amongst the stones of Purbeck one must include the fossils of *Lulworth*. Between the almost circular coves of Lulworth and Mupe, halfway up the cliffs, is a whole half-mile of drowned and petrified *Fossil Forest*. The expert eye can detect the giant cycads and other tropical plants that grew here millions of years ago.

East Lulworth has a ruined castle (17th century), but far more spectacular is *Corfe Castle*, right in the middle of the island. The village is older than its castle, whose history is part of England's history. After William the Conqueror built the Norman keep, Corfe Castle, like its counterpart in Dover, was enclosed in walls and bastions that withstood weeks of siege and were only breached and captured by the Parliamentarian troops (1646) through an act of treachery. It was not the first such act. In 978, at Martyr's Gate (where you now pay your entrance money) Elfrida, lady of the castle, had her stepson King Edward murdered. After what was supposed to have been a 'hunting accident', with true medieval logic she became a nun and her son was crowned king. But Ethelred the 'Unraed' (= ill-advised, and not unready) gave England a miserable time, though he did sire two better quality princes in Edmund Ironside and Edward the Confessor. King John, also known as John Lackland, who managed to lose most of England's French possessions, at least held onto Corfe Castle, which was his favourite residence. Here in this remote and secure place, the King who had been forced by the barons to sign the Magna Carta in 1215 kept various precious items, including the crown jewels and his State prisoners, such as the daughters of the Scottish king and – even more important for his peace of mind – his own wife. Corfe itself is a grey, slate-roofed village in the midst of Purbeck's green hills. In the 13th century it was the centre of the island's stone industry, and it is still the seat of the Company of Marblers and Stone-Cutters, the oldest union in the country.

On the Green Edge of the World: Lawrence and Hardy

On the northern edge of Purbeck lies *Wareham*, a thriving port before Poole took over. This is a little town in the marshes, surrounded by ancient green earthworks, its streets laid out like a chessboard: the Anglo-Saxon heritage has left its mark on Wareham. In the Middle Ages, the town had no fewer than seven churches, three of which have survived, and two of which are still worth seeing. In the Church of Lady St Mary is a hexagonal Norman font of lead, with the twelve apostles standing beneath twelve arches. St Martin's is not so old, but has typical Anglo-Saxon 'long-and-short work' in the nave and chancel, and is much the better preserved of the two churches. In the north aisle, a man lies on a sarcophagus that was never his. He is dressed in Arab robes, with his head on a camel's saddle, his hand on an Arab dagger, his pose that of a medieval crusader – doubly incongruous in this Anglo-Saxon setting. His name is Lawrence of Arabia, and this monument by Eric Kennington (1935) smacks more of Hollywood than of holy stone. Lawrence was never just make-believe, even in his most adventurous campaigns and disguises.

Moorland, military training ground, a tank museum, and a writer's house: it was along this short stretch of road between polar opposites, which he found in no way contradictory, that the 46-year-old T. E. Lawrence crashed on his motor-bike on 13 May 1935. He was on his way home from Bovington Camp to his cottage *Clouds*

Hill. Who was this man, to whom King George V sent his personal physician, and whose funeral in Moreton village churchyard was attended by the King of Iraq, Winston Churchill, Mrs Thomas Hardy, Siegfried Sassoon and Lady Astor, among others, and whose coffin bore the inscription: 'To T.E.L., who should sleep among kings'? He had ended his days serving as an ordinary soldier and using an assumed name. Officer Lawrence, the British government's most highly decorated agent in the Middle East, had demoted himself because his campaign to gain independence for the Arabs had failed through what he regarded as political betrayal by the English. As a close friend of the Emir Faisal (later King of Iraq), he had organized the Arab uprising against the Turks (1916-18), and was the last of the great adventurers in the days of the British Empire, which actually owed him its last colonial acquisition, the Palestine Mandate. But Lawrence was a conqueror who had no desire for power: he was first and foremost a writer, and unlike Kipling did not dream of British supremacy. After reading *The Seven Pillars of Wisdom* (1926), the great Austrian man of letters Hofmannsthal described Lawrence as 'a true hero, of incomparable elegance and inner grace – and furthermore, wondrously, as great a writer as Sallust'.

Clouds Hill lies hidden behind rhododendron bushes. It's a simple cottage which Lawrence bought in 1923. 'As ugly as my sins,' was his description of it, 'bleak, angular, small, unstable: very like its owner.' This was where he hoped to find peace and quiet after the years of guerilla warfare, and to establish himself as a writer. Once adviser to Winston Churchill at the Colonial Office, he joined the RAF in 1922 as aircraftman John Hume Ross, and when his identity was discovered, enlisted in the Royal Tank Corps in 1923, transferring back to the RAF in 1925. He

Lawrence of Arabia

was now known as T. E. Shaw, or alternatively No. 338 171. During his last years of service he designed motor boats, listened to Mozart, and translated the Odyssey into English prose. The rooms at Clouds Hill are small and spartan, 'no pictures and no ornaments'. In the churchyard in *Moreton* I saw a withered laurel wreath on a narrow grave, at the foot of which lay an open book with the words 'Deus Illuminatio Mea' (God is my light). This is the motto of Oxford University, where the archaeology student T. E. Lawrence wrote a thesis on the influence of the crusades on medieval military architecture in Europe.

Lawrence died on Thomas Hardy's heath, where it is at its most beautiful, between the rivers Frome and Piddle. There, in the little hamlet of *Higher Bockhampton*, on the edge of the blackberry-filled woods, stands the thatched cottage where Hardy was born in 1840, the son of a stonemason. He was a local writer, but his work was universal; he wrote at a time of radical change, and he captured its problems in great symphonies of rural life and tragedy. *Far From the Madding Crowd* and *Under the Greenwood Tree* were two of the most popular books he wrote in this cottage. With their precise descriptions of places and countryside, they are like coded, literary guidebooks to Wessex, from Sandbourne (Bournemouth) to Shaston (Shaftesbury) and on to Budmouth Regis (Weymouth). The Anglo-Saxon kingdom of Wessex, which under King Alfred embraced the whole of Wiltshire and Hampshire (though not Dorset), has recently been revived as a political concept by the regionalists. But Hardy was not writing about this historical kingdom. His Dorset was 'a partly real, partly dream-country'. There he spent most of his life, apart from a few years in London.

The popular image of Hardy Country can easily make one lose sight of present-day realities (and tourist guides certainly do). For instance, Egdon Heath is not to be found on any map, because this was Hardy's made-up name for a whole collection of Dorset heaths. One in particular inspired him: Canford Heath, which was then a huge area of low hills between Bournemouth, Poole and Wimborne Minster – a mysterious, black and brown desert of ferns and gorse. Egdon Heath is the gloomy setting of *The Return of the Native* (1878), an untameable wasteland, though 'civilization was now its enemy'. Little remains of Egdon Heath, save for the music of that name by Hardy's friend Gustav Holst. *Canford Heath* is just an arid relic, under constant threat from the ever-advancing armies of road-builders. Perhaps Dorset's heaths will soon have disappeared altogether.

In the middle of the 18th century, the heathland around Poole covered an area of 150 square miles. Today this has shrunk to 20. Agriculture, military training, clay and gravel pits have all dug into the heath; it has been covered with trees, with houses, with roads. The process that began in Hardy's day has been dramatically accelerated in ours, and of the three heaths that he put together under the name of Egdon, Puddletown is now a conifer planation, and Bovington has been taken over by the Tank Corps. Only *Winfrith Heath* has remained relatively untouched. To the west of Wareham, it is a unique ecological oasis, home to such rare species as the crested newt, natterjack, sand lizard, Dartford warbler and smooth snake. Pale butterwort and blue lungwort still bloom around *Winfrith Newburgh*. The one good thing that has come out of military manoeuvres on the heathland hills of Purbeck is that they have kept away the bungalows, caravan sites and supermarkets.

If you take a Hardy tour of Wessex, sooner or later you will go along Wareham Road, and shortly before you reach Dorchester you will stop at 'The Trumpet Major'. That was the title of one of Hardy's love stories, written in 1880, and you can fall in love with Hardy's Ale as well, sold here in old, numbered bottles, and as good as his description of it: 'It was of the most beautiful colour that the eye of an artist in beer could desire; full in body, yet brisk as a volcano; piquant, yet without a twang; luminous as an autumn sunset, free from streakiness of taste; but, finally, rather heady.'

On the eastern outskirts of Dorchester, the trained architect Thomas Hardy designed himself a brick house (1885), which Pevsner dismisses as having no architectural quality whatsoever. Hardy's brother (a professional builder) constructed the house, and there Hardy lived until he died in 1928. Today, the ring road passes close to *Max Gate*, but in Hardy's day the house still lay in pastures green. His favourite dog Wessex lies buried in the garden – a terrier that terrified all the guests, but nevertheless had a fine sense of discernment: it liked T. E. Lawrence, but cut John Galsworthy down to size by biting him in the leg. In Max Gate, Hardy wrote *Tess of the D'Urbervilles, Jude the Obscure* – his last novel – and many of his finest poems. 'Poor old Hardy is perfectly ordinary, nice, conventional, never says a clever thing; says commonplaces about his books; has tea at the Rectory; is very healthy; objects to American visitors; & never mentions literature. How am I to dress for this Obituary?' asked Virginia Woolf in her diary of 27 September, 1922, six years before Hardy's death.

He asked to be buried in the churchyard at *Stinsford*, and there it is written in stone that his ashes are in Poets' Corner, Westminster Abbey, but his heart lies here. The inscription does not mention the fact that, according to rumour, the village cat also lies here, having managed to eat Hardy's heart before it was buried.

If you wish to take the A35 direct from Bournemouth to Dorchester without making any literary diversions, at least stop in Bere Regis and Athelhampton. In the parish church at *Bere Regis*, the twelve apostles – carved almost lifesize in oak, and dressed in 15th-century costumes – gaze down from the dragon beams on either side of the open roof trusses (col. pls. 21 & 22). This solemn assembly is part of a magnificent roof on the painted bosses of which Cardinal Morton, Archbishop of Canterbury, left his coat of arms, for it was he who footed the bill. It was also Cardinal Morton who presided over the marriage in 1485 between Elizabeth of York and Henry of Lancaster, thus bringing to an end the thirty-year Wars of the Roses. The roof of the Great Hall at *Athelhampton* dates from roughly the same time, *c.* 1500. So do the linenfold wood panelling and the high bay window with its heraldic glass: this is a late medieval room of quite exceptional character. Originally Athelhampton was a much larger country estate belonging to Sir William Martyn, Lord Mayor of London, and it is one of the finest specimens of secular Perpendicular architecture in Dorset. The windows of the residential quarters are like rows of grilles, but the effect is both striking and homely. Today, tea is served and antiques are sold in the former stables, to help the present owner preserve his house and his Elizabethan gardens.

Dorchester's Disneyland: Prince Charles Builds a Model Town

Hardy readers know it as Casterbridge: 'It is huddled all together; and it is shut in by a square wall of trees, like a plot of garden ground by a box-edging.' Dorchester, the Roman Durnovaria, may be England's smallest county town, with some 20,000 inhabitants. It is, however, expanding, though most people are in white collar jobs now rather than on the land. All round the heart of the old town, along the banks of the mill stream, are The Walks, laid out in the 18th century over the levelled Roman walls. The principal church is St Peter's, in front of which is a bronze statue of the great dialect poet William Barnes, but I found St George's more impressive: this is an Edwardian church with a Norman tympanum over the south portal, and two stained glass windows by William Morris (1903-13) in the transepts. Outside, on a street corner, a group of lifesize bronze figures by Elisabeth Frink recall the Catholic martyrs who were hanged, drawn and quartered in Dorchester in the 16th century.

Near the former County Court is the local museum, vigorously old-fashioned and bulging with various collections. The main room is a museum piece in itself – a Victorian exhibition hall of 1883, with cast-iron columns, arches, galleries, and a glass roof. On display is a reconstruction of Hardy's study, and there are household objects from olden times, including cabinets of fossils. Here Alfred Stevens, Dorset's Victorian sculptor and designer, found a refuge for his work, after he had lost his room at the Tate Gallery. At least in the provinces he was still a big fish. On the southern outskirts of the town, the Romans created an amphitheatre out of Maumbury Rings, a Neolithic place of worship, and their mini-Colosseum of lime-stone and grass was big enough to hold 10,000 people. In the Middle Ages it became a jousting-field, in the Civil War it was a bastion, then it turned into a place of execution, and today it is a children's playground. *Mutatis mutandis.*

On the western outskirts of Dorchester, just ten minutes' walk from the centre, a new town began to raise its roofs in 1992. It is called *Poundbury*, and it is being built by Prince Charles. As Duke of Cornwall and owner of these 400 acres of arable land, he is willing and able to play a leading part in this project. Britain's king-in-waiting has many interests, including polo, organic farming and water-colours, but the relevant passion in this case was and is architecture. For years he has campaigned against modern 'carbuncles' and the culture of concrete. In 1992 he opened his own school of architecture in London, and in the same year he began to realize his dream of creating a new and better type of town. For his master planner he chose Leon Krier, born just two years before him in 1946, and a major international figure in the theory of town planning, though he has hardly built a thing. The paper of his unfulfilled projects, by his own admission, probably weighs more than all the building material he has ever used. In his drawings and essays, Krier shows himself to be equally influenced by Le Corbusier and the neo-gothic Pugin, but the major trend is towards a form of neoclassicism . His attack on the brutalism of post-war architecture, and his campaign for a renewal of society through a return to traditional architecture and urban culture, both blend perfectly with the Prince of Wales's desire to revive communal and urban life, and with his vision of a national rebirth.

Krier's Poundbury will eventually consist of four independent quarters, each different in character, each about 100 acres in area and surrounded by parks. Each will contain its own public buildings, homes, shops, pubs, offices and workshops. The idea is to create a variety of occupations within a single zone, instead of that zone being confined to offices or being a mere dormitory. The houses themselves will be close together, rather than scattered all over the countryside. Poundbury will bring back the concept of urban life in a country setting, as was perfectly normal for centuries with the traditional market towns, like Dorchester itself. In such urban villages, all the necessities of everyday life are within walking distance. It is an ideal that is certainly eco-friendly, but perhaps in this day and age unrealistic: no one should live more than ten minutes away from his or her workplace. 'Commuting is polluting,' says Krier.

This return to a traditional way of life is to be accompanied by the use of traditional architectural forms and local materials, to fit in with the surrounding countryside. Poundbury's houses have mullion windows and saddleback roofs, and the walls are of brick, plastered or clad with Purbeck stone. Aerials and satellite dishes are banned. If the outside is 18th- or 19th-century, however, the inside is fully wired and equipped with all the latest energy-saving and environmentally friendly devices. The Prince of Green Thinking is as concerned with ecology as he is with craftsmanship, and he discusses the type of brick, the style of chimney and streetlight, and even the street names (from Hardy's novels, of course) with everyone involved. No detail is left to chance in this great quest for a truly beautiful English experience.

'God bless the Prince of Wales, God protect us from his architecture.' So say even some of his friends. This smalltown royal Utopia merely imitates ancient traditions instead of creating new ones. 'Disneyland approach' is the verdict of Richard

Rogers, one of the country's greatest modern architects. A technologically advanced pastiche like Poundbury is no substitute for contemporary architecture. Poundbury has become a showpiece for both sides in the current debate on Neo-Neoclassicism and a 'natural', native English style. As another example of historical mimicry, critics of this new revivalism point to a building that Prince Charles opened at the beginning of the 1990's just up the road from Poundbury: a supermarket in the style of a gigantic barn, Tudorish Tesco, the ultimate disguise. There are three other new shopping developments around Dorchester, all part of the country-wide, systematic destruction of old town centres and individual shops. Even in Poundbury, the little family business will not be able to compete, because people are used to buying cheaply and in bulk. They will therefore drive off in their cars to the supermarkets, thereby increasing the volume of traffic and pollution, and neither Leon Krier nor the Prince of Wales will be able to stop them.

For all its craftsmanship and all its humanitarian and environmental ideals, Poundbury is merely an echo of the 19th century, and will not become a blueprint for the 21st. The plan is for around 25,000 people to live here, though development will take a good 25 years. By then it will be clear whether Charlestown has become a British theme park, a model for provincial urban life, or a provincial suburb.

If you look to the south-west from Poundbury, beyond the ring road, you will see 'an enormous many-limbed organism of an antediluvian time, lying lifeless and covered with a thin green cloth, which hides its substance while revealing its contour'. This is Thomas Hardy's description in *Return of the Native* of the prehistoric hill fort of *Maiden Castle*. What was begun by the settlers of Windmill Hill around 3000 BC was continued by the farmers of the Stone Age and the Celtic migrants of the Ice Age: they fortified the place for man and for beast. But when Vespasian's legions marched into these fields in AD 44, the farmers of Maiden Castle did not stand a chance. Their bones were discovered at the end of the 19th century, outside the fortifications, whose fourfold earthworks still tower up to 90 feet in height, and in those days were reinforced with stones and palisades. The people who survived were resettled in Durnovaria, and in the 4th century the Romans built a little temple in Maiden Castle. Then followed the Dark Ages. Today we can stand amid the grazing sheep and drink in the atmosphere of those bygone times, surrounded by history that is sculptured in waves over the countryside.

The 2625-foot long oval of Maiden Castle is the largest of England's prehistoric hill forts, but there are other impressive remnants of ancient settlements in Dorset: Badbury Rings near Shapwick (five miles north-west of Wimborne Minster), and Hambledon Hill Fort near Child Okeford (eight miles north of Blandford Forum). But those are nothing, say the people of North Downs, compared to the wonderful giant of *Cerne Abbas*. Between Dorchester and Sherborne, visible for miles around, there stands a naked man, chalk white against the green, with more than just his club stretching high. This is naïve art on a grand scale: a figure cut in the grassy hill,

The Giant in c. 1100 AD (left) and c. 1850 (right); compare with p. 44

perhaps a prehistoric Priapus, or a 2nd-century Roman or Celtic Hercules. Over 180 feet long from his toes to the tip of his club, the Cerne Giant and his proudly erected penis certainly fulfil the same fertility function as the standing stones, or menhirs. Local girls looking for potent husbands, and women wanting children are still drawn to this giant symbol – a heathen relic which evidently did not bother the Benedictine monks at the foot of the hill, so long as the weddings and baptisms took place in their church. Their 10th-century monastery suffered the usual fate of monasteries after 1538, but not an inch of the giant was touched. Only in Victorian times was it deemed necessary to cover his private parts with bushes, though late in the 19th century they were uncovered again and joined to his navel. It is to this bold enlargement of his organ that the giant owes his positively superhuman erection of no less than 22 feet.

Lyme Regis: Louisa Musgrove Falls, and What is Meryl Streep Up To?

If you head for the coast, you will find a much younger hill man south of Dorchester – George III in chalk, mounted on the White Horse of Osmington (the horse was cut in 1807, and George III added later). On the promenade in *Weymouth* you'll see him again, in full regalia, flanked by a lion and a unicorn. The grateful townsfolk celebrated the 50th year of his reign by erecting this monument in 1809, for King George had made the resort of Weymouth almost as popular as his son the Prince Regent made Brighton. He slept at the 'Gloucester' on the Esplanade, and in 1789, while the French were busy storming the Bastille on the other side of the Channel, he was happily splashing away in his blue serge toga, accompanied by women wearing purple sashes that were comfortingly inscribed in gold lettering: 'God Save The King'. His Majesty would change in a cabin drawn by horses, and when he emerged to test the waters, the town band – housed in another bathing machine – would strike up the National Anthem. Bathing has often been a favourite royal pastime. Queen Victoria, however, preferred the Isle of Wight, and therefore the not-quite-so-grateful people of Weymouth only celebrated her Golden Jubilee in 1887 by erecting a clock tower without a statue. The present Queen will get neither clock tower nor statue in Weymouth, since she spends her holidays in the Scottish highlands. Truth to tell, English seaside resorts are no longer everyone's cup of tea.

The bright Victorian clock tower, pleasant Georgian architecture, a few Tudor houses, and a little port – that is Weymouth, and charming it is too. Constable painted the broad bay in 1816 while he was on his honeymoon here, and Weymouth was also the birthplace of James Thornhill, the first successful English history painter. Better known than his altarpiece (1721) in St Mary's are his frescos in the dome of St Paul's, London. Thornhill was MP for Weymouth for twelve years (1722-34), following in the footsteps of Christopher Wren, MP for a year (1702). As court painter, he worked at Hampton Court, Blenheim Palace and Windsor Castle. He was knighted in 1720, and was even able to buy himself a country house: Thornhill House in the Blackmoor Vale in north Dorset. The young William Hogarth could scarcely have found himself a better match than Jane Thornhill, his master's daughter.

For St Paul's Cathedral, Christopher Wren used limestone – originally white – taken from the *Isle of Portland*. To reach this 4½ mile-long peninsula from Weymouth, you have to go across a dam and past a natural harbour which served as a naval base from Tudor times until 1995, when the Royal Navy closed it down for financial reasons. Hardy called it the 'Gibraltar of Wessex'. Portland is one vast stone quarry, and has been so since Charles I set up a royal monopoly here, and Inigo Jones had Portland stone shipped across for his banqueting hall at Whitehall in 1619. The massive façade of the United Nations Building in New York is made of the same material. Unlike its rival, Purbeck (see p. 52), Portland has little to offer apart from its admittedly beautiful stony view: you can gaze out from the Pennsylvania Castle Hotel, a crenellated villa built by James Wyatt in 1800 for the governor of Portland and grandson of the founder of Pennsylvania; or you can scan the horizon from Portland Castle, a coastal fort built by Henry VIII, at a cost in 1539 of £4964, 19 shillings and 10 pence farthing.

Between Portland and Lyme Regis, you can hear the song of the sirens along *Chesil Bank*. This is the grinding, sighing crescendo and decrescendo of millions of pebbles, sending out messages to all the water sprites in the English Channel. Chesil Bank is 23 feet high, up to 510 feet broad, and almost 16 miles long, and it is one great bank of shingle that has no equal anywhere in Europe. Seafarers avoid the area, and ornithologists stick to the harmless lagoon behind the great bank. The mixture here of salt and fresh water makes the long lagoon an ideal breeding ground for little terns, ringed plovers, grey herons, cormorants, goldcrests and other birds. Mink and weasels are also at home in these shallow waters, as are two hundred mute swans. Starting in 1393, the Benedictine monks of *Abbotsbury* bred them in their own swannery to provide meat. Today the swans provide the quills that have been used since time immemorial by Lloyd's of London to register the names of sunken ships in their official insurance records. Only these quills can ensure calligraphic continuity.

The stones of Chesil Bank, with their infinite variety of forms, and the broader shapes of the landscape itself were a constant attraction for the artist Paul Nash (col. pl. 14), when he wrote his guide to Dorset in 1935. The author and poet John Cowper Powys, who grew up in Dorset and Somerset, found lifelong inspiration in the countryside around Dorchester. His novels *Weymouth Sands* (1934) and *Maiden Castle* (1936) are full of references to the prehistoric sites of a mythical childhood. Although he died in Wales and regarded himself as 'obstinately Welsh', he had his ashes scattered in the sea at Chesil Bank. There, in the madness of youth, he had done something that no one else should ever try: he had swum out into the currents – 'one of the most daring things I ever did'.

A coastal path leads west along Lyme Bay, and in the fields on top of the cliffs you will find primroses and wild orchids in early May, and knapweed, buttercups and daisies in the summer. This Heritage Coast between Bridport and Charmouth is truly spectacular, with its glowing *Golden Cap*, the highest cliff on the Channel (617 feet). The fact that the fields and hills of the hinterland have remained untouched is due entirely to the National Trust, which owns more than 2000 acres of land along the Golden Cap. However, the extension of the A35 threatens even this showpiece, and the planned Morecombelake bypass east of Lyme Regis would certainly ruin a substantial area of this beautiful countryside. The environmentalists are putting up strong resistance: 'This is a fight to save the jewel in the crown.'

A 'sweet retired bay' was Jane Austen's description of *Charmouth* and *Lyme Regis* at the beginning of the 19th century, but by the end of that century things had already changed, as the Victorians – including Alfred Lord Tennyson – made their pilgrimages to the spot where Louisa Musgrove had fallen into the arms of her rescuer. This dramatic event took place on the Cobb, the ancient stone breakwater, in Chapter 12 of Jane Austen's *Persuasion*. Another visitor to Lyme, in autumn and winter 1895, was James Whistler who, as his wife was dying of cancer, painted the beautiful but melancholic portrait of a girl, *The Little Rose of Lyme Regis*, now in a Boston museum, and, even finer, *The Master Smith of Lyme*. Lyme has a picture postcard beauty. It's a tiny town in which every lane exudes a Regency atmosphere, disturbed only by the hordes of visitors who come here all year and every year. Those on the beach will be seen with eyes down, as if there were some mysterious game of bingo being played on the sands. Others may be hammering at the rocks, as if trying to release a hidden Prometheus. The object of their search: fossils. This is the fossil-seeker's El Dorado, and the best time for discoveries outside the souvenir shops is after the winter storms and before the tourist floods. And if your only find among the Jurassic limestone rocks is an empty Coca-Cola bottle, then comfort yourself with the thought that even King Frederick Augustus II of Saxony, some 150 years ago, had to go and buy what he was looking for: a fossilized Icthyosaurus. He got it from one of the leading experts in Europe, a local lady named Mary Anning who, as a twelve-year-old in 1811, had discovered the very first such fossil. That can be admired today in the British Museum, while little Mary is to be seen in Lyme's Dinosaurland. One of the nicest exhibits in the local museum is a bonnet 'reputed to have been worn by Jane Austen'. Today's literary luminary of Lyme is John Fowles, who arrived in 1965 and made the town the setting for his most famous novel, *The French Lieutenant's Woman*. In the film, the hero (played by Jeremy Irons) is – inevitably – searching for fossils when he catches sight of the heroine (Meryl Streep) on the beach. Then later, like Louisa Musgrove, she stands upon the Cobb, wrapped in a long black cape. She does not, however, fall, at least, not here.

Art School in Wood: John Makepeace in Parnham House

England's manor houses are furniture fossils. Around 1900, so it would seem, the

owners must have decided never to buy any new furniture. Only the nouveaux riches, the social climbers, the parvenus need to buy, while those who really count inherit their furniture (and their house and title as well). The exception to this is *Parnham House*. Here virtually every item you see is new. The Lord of the Manor, however, has not bought it. He has made it. John Makepeace is England's leading furniture designer, and Parnham House is a college of cabinet-making.

Deep in the country, north-east of Lyme Regis, Parnham House is Elizabethan with later extensions, including some by John Nash (1810). There are terraces with balustrades, and pavilions and colourful herbaceous borders round the north side of the house. Long rows of tall, skittle-shaped yews parade across the lawn like evergreen sugarloaves.

John Makepeace

John Makepeace bought this rural idyll in 1976, as a home and a workshop. 'There's no reason,' he says, 'why a bowl made of wood shouldn't be just as valuable as a bowl made of silver. Because every piece of wood has its own intrinsic beauty and uniqueness.' Anyone seeing his work will recognize his love for his material, and his feeling for its sensuous qualities. Look at his 'Obelisk' of curved, silken yew, with drawers of scented cedar of Lebanon. Or 'Eclipse', a tall, elliptical drinks cabinet with a golden red yew veneer, frame of black oak, and interior of white ilex. Makepeace creates masterly blends of ash, maple and elm, wood and polished aluminium, leather, or slate, conjuring perfect forms out of contrasting materials, or at the other extreme transmuting a single yew tree into a magnificent four-poster bed.

The Knot Chair

The craftsmanship, elegance and imaginative flair of his work are matchless. Just look at the different varieties of chair: the Gothic, whose curves consist of more than 2000 chips of ebony; the Knot, with a seat and back of elm, carved in the shape of a cushion, and 'knotted' to an oak frame – a *trompe-l'œil* piece of furniture. With effortless ease, Makepeace combines a Baroque imagination with the mathematical precision of an engineer, the purism of Ove Arup with the virtuosity of Grinling Gibbons. You can sit on a bright chair of vineleaves at a slate-black table of oak. The latter stands on stones of limewood, inspired by the pebbles of Chesil Bank. Furniture mannerism, made in Parnham, sold all over the world.

In 1977 John Makepeace set up the Parnham Trust and his School for Craftsmen in Wood. Twenty-two students live and work there. 'First they have to learn how to make simple things well. Only then can one start to play creatively with this ability. You can only design things if you know yourself and your own values.' It is largely to this college and its exemplary workshops that England owes her Renaissance in cabinet-making. Some of Makepeace's former students have already opened their own studios: Ronald Emett in Beaminster, Ben Brooks in London, Verena Wriedt in Hamburg. The most illustrious of his disciples is David Linley, the Queen's nephew. His speciality is intarsia furniture and cigar boxes in the form of historic houses. Like William Morris, John Makepeace is acutely aware of the social aspects of his work. 'Ecological questions change everything, including aesthetics. If you change your philosophy, the whole object changes.' Instead of importing tropical woods, he uses native hardwoods, but making politically correct furniture is still not enough for him. In 1983 he bought some 400 acres of woodland east of Parnham and began a pilot project: Hooke Park College. 'We're trying out methods of making more productive use of the first harvest, which until now has only been good for sawdust.' His 'House of Trees', the training centre of this new school, shows just how the thin and flexible young wood can be used to make a brilliant roof. Research programmes bring together material scientists, engineers and architects to create a new, ecologically sound way of using timber. A handful of buildings by Edward Cullinan, show some of this philosophy in practice. Without a doubt, John Makepeace is producing far more than just the antiques of tomorrow.

'All beauty is truth': Sherborne and Shaftesbury

Forde Abbey, in a park on the western edge of the Dorset Downs, was a monastery with a house fit for a prince. Thomas Chard was the last abbot, and the home that he built for himself (to the greater glory of God) was of such opulent splendour that it is little wonder Henry VIII decided the time had come for Reformation. Chard was still busy setting the last capitals on the columns of his cloister when, in 1539, he had to join his colleagues on the way out of Paradise. The great entrance is in mature Perpendicular style, with oriel tracery over the portal. The Hall is baronial. The crypt (where tea is served) and the dormitory above it are both 13th-century, and these and the 12th-century chapel (which used to be the chapter house) are the oldest surviving sections of the abbey, which was founded by the Cistercians of Waverley in 1141. Sir Edmond Prideaux, Cromwell's Attorney-General, bought Forde Abbey in 1649 and extended it, building a saloon above Abbot Chard's cloister. The showpiece of the house is the magnificent series of Mortlake tapestries that cover the walls of the saloon, made in the reign of Charles I by weavers from Flanders after cartoons by Raphael that the King had bought (now in the Victoria & Albert Museum). The borders were probably designed by Rubens, who gave a Baroque frame of columns, putti and garlands to these monumental Renaissance scenes from the lives of the apostles. It was in this great room that Jeremy Bentham, the philosopher and social reformer who rented Forde Abbey for three years (1815-18), developed his ideas on utilitarianism. His basic creed was that all actions are right and good if they promote 'the greatest happiness of the greatest number', and so he would certainly have been delighted to see the crowds gathering on a summer's day to visit the house and garden.

Sherborne and Shaftesbury are the only towns in the north of Dorset, the former on the Somerset border, the latter next to Wiltshire. They are small towns with a great past. They were both focal points of southern England's medieval monastic culture, the richness of which is still to be seen in Sherborne, whereas we can only reconstruct that of Shaftesbury. Nowhere else in Dorset have I seen such a perfect medieval picture as in *Sherborne*: abbey church, school, alms-houses, and terraced houses clustered round the church green. In Anglo-Saxon times, this was the seat of

Sherborne Abbey, vaulting

the bishopric of Wessex. The monastery school has long been a leading public (now called independent) school, with John Le Carré one of its most famous old boys. The mainly medieval buildings are grouped round a wide courtyard, and border on the northern walls of the parish church, which in Saxon times was a cathedral, and from 998 was a Benedictine abbey.

Like Forde Abbey, Sherborne Abbey glows in the golden brown of Ham Hill stone, quarried twelve miles away in Somerset. If you go past the rubble-built exterior west wall, which was once part of a massive Anglo-Saxon 'westwork', you will enter the church through the Late Norman south porch (*c.* 1170): this is a broad round arch with a double zigzag motif, each section being supported by two columns with demon capitals. Inside, the fan-vaulted roof of the nave is one of the glories of English Gothic. It is amazing how light great masses of stone can seem, almost like crochetwork, while the fanned ribs and liernes seem as flimsy as gossamer. The fan-vaults begin unusually high up, and are flat rather than ogival. This enhances the impression of height, while the continuous transverse ridge-rib emphasises the depth. Apart from the cloister of the former Benedictine Abbey of Gloucester (*c.* 1360), the fan-vault of Sherborne (*c.* 1450) is the first great one of its kind in England, its breadth and elegance exceeded only by the magnificent roof of King's College Chapel in Cambridge, built a few decades later.

High up – too high even for the Puritan iconoclasts – are about a hundred huge bosses decorated with foliage and coats-of-arms. On one of them, a mermaid is combing her hair. Down below, on the misericord of one of the choir stalls, a father is beating his son (15th century). The different phases of the abbey's construction are clearly visible in the interior: the doorway in the north aisle is Anglo-Saxon; the crossing is Norman; the arches of the Lady Chapel are Early English; the rest is Perpendicular. In a baroque triumphal gateway John Digby, Earl of Bristol, stands face to face with Death; near him, on low plinths, are his two wives, holding their inflamed hearts in their hands (1698, by John van Nost).

So princely a death could only be died by one who had lived like a prince. *Sherborne Castle*, in an idyllic park outside the town, is still the residence of the Digbys. Their predecessor was Sir Walter Raleigh. When he fell into disfavour, Elizabeth I took away from him in 1603 what she had given him in 1592: Sherborne Castle. This, however, was the Old Castle built by Bishop Roger of Salisbury (1107- 35). Raleigh wished to live in a more modern manner, and so he discontinued the renovations of the once impressive Norman palace, and in 1594 built a new house on the other side of the Yeo valley. This was Sherborne Court. He thus proved to be something of an architectural pioneer, because under James I such lodges became very fashionable as hunting or weekend residences. In 1617, after his downfall, Raleigh's summer home – a simple rectangle extended *c.* 1600 by four corner turrets – was taken over by Sir John Digby, England's ambassador to Spain and later first Earl of Bristol. Without losing the stylistic continuity, Digby added four

1. *Stonehenge, by John Constable, 1836*

2. Stonehenge

3. *The Family of Lord Pembroke, by van Dyck, c. 1632*

4. *William Beckford,*
by Romney

5. River God, in the grotto at Stourhead

6. Overleaf, the lake at Stourhead

7. Merritown Farm: Russell Lucas-Rowe in Wonderland

8. The Marquess of Bath

9. Maze at Longleat

10. Longleat

11. Renault factory, Swindon, by Sir Norman Foster

12. *Salisbury Cathedral in the Meadows, by Constable, c. 1829*

13. *Salisbury Cathedral in winter*

14. Equivalents for the Megaliths, by Paul Nash, 1935

15. *Affpuddle, parish church*

wings with balustrades and four more corner turrets. Based on a symmetrical H-groundplan, with a bizarre gallery of chimneys, Sherborne Castle now stands in a landscaped park which no one but Capability Brown could have laid out in so picturesque a fashion (1756/1776-79). Raleigh's formal Elizabethan garden disappeared beneath the waters of the Yeo, dammed to form a serpentine lake, but the cedars which Raleigh himself had planted were spared. The castle near them, where the Digbies held out for Charles I, suffered as a result; as Pevsner notes drily, 'Fairfax's incapacitating of castles was nothing if not thorough.' In 1723 Alexander Pope, poet and gardener, found the ruins 'inexpressibly awful and solemn' but could not forbear to improve. 'The open courts from building to building might be thrown into circles or octagons of grass or flowers; and even in the gaping rooms you have fine trees grown, that might be made a natural tapestry to the walls, and arch you overhead, where time has uncovered them to the sky. Little paths of earth or sand might be made up the half-tumbled walls, to guide from one view to another on the higher parts; and seats placed here and there to enjoy those views, which are more romantic than imagination can form them.' The 'ruinous taste', as he called it, required a great deal of ruining.

Life is sweet in the West Country, and what could be sweeter than clotted cream, the indispensable ingredient of teas from Dorset to Cornwall? Go to the 'Three Wishes' in Sherborne, and have them all fulfilled at the same time: scones, strawberry jam, and lashings and lashings of glorious clotted cream. The best clotted cream is made from the milk of Jersey or Guernsey cows, lovingly and slowly separated from the milk. 'For use with Tarts, stewed Fruits etc it is unrivalled,' a Victorian advertisement reads, 'and to Coffee, Cocoa and Chocolate it gives a richness and flavour unapproachable. Children and persons requiring a nutritive diet are by the free use greatly benefitted, while as a rival to Cod Liver Oil and in care of debility and consumption, it is highly commended and prescribed by the Medical Profession. To be kept dry and cool, NOT ON ICE, OR IT TURNS FUSTY.'

On to *Shaftesbury*, through parklike pastures and the orchards of Blackmoor Vale. Shaftesbury stands high on a sandstone hill, and as the only hilltop town in the county, it is an event in itself. Historically, however, it is a seat of melancholy. Once it was a centre of monastic life, but today it is merely the place where the A30 and the A350 intersect, and of its Benedictine abbey (Park Walk), the only remains are a few fragments and foundations. Alfred the Great founded it in the last quarter of the 9th century for his daughter Abbess Aethelgifu. Her canonization, and the burial here of King Edward the Martyr in 979, made Shaftesbury into a popular place of pilgrimage. At that time, the Abbot of Glastonbury and the Abbess of Shaftesbury between them owned more land than the King of England. Of the twelve medieval churches, only one has survived: the Perpendicular St Peter's. Near it, a cobbled road makes its way down the hill, offering a romantic view over Blackmoor Vale. The name of this beauty spot is Gold Hill, but don't start

Sherborne Abbey:
detail of carving
on the portal

prospecting – the name is a corruption of Guild Hall Hill (col. pl. 17).

The great German poets Goethe and Schiller, during the Storm and Stress period of German Romanticism, were enthusiastic about Shaftesbury – not the town, but the philosopher. St Giles House, family home of the Earls of Shaftesbury, lies between Shaftesbury and Bournemouth. In the village church at *Wimborne St Giles* the allegory of a mourner commemorates Anthony, Earl of Shaftesbury, the moral philosopher, who maintained: 'All beauty is truth'. Perhaps this will not suffice to get you through life, but it will certainly get you through Dorset.

A few houses, a little church, and a manor house: that is *Chettle*, a remote hamlet in the hills of Cranborne Chase. With its rounded corners, you feel you could almost pick Chettle House up like a cake tin. It's a cosy, slender, elegant house of reddish brick, with window dressings and capitals of Chilmark stone. Pilasters and balustrades give it a kind of refined nobility. This is one of the very few surviving houses (1710-15) built by Thomas Archer during his short career as court architect to Queen Anne. He was the only major English Baroque architect to visit Rome, where he was able to see for himself the works of Bernini and Borromini.

When I visited this little gem, Patrick Bourke, the owner, was hard at work on restorations. His beard was grey, and his feet were bare. 'He can't afford shoes,' joked the caretaker. 'He needs all his money to repair the roof.' There is a croquet lawn, a pond, cedars, a little vineyard, garden walls and urns gently crumbling away.

Somerset

Cider, Cheddar cheese, Mendip snails – Somerset is a county with flavours all its own. It has windy heights and cold stone caves up on Dunkery Beacon and down in Wookey Hole, and Exmoor's rivers are full of fish, and the Bristol Channel is full of seasiders. You can see King Arthur three times over, even before you have had your pint of scrumpy: here he's keeper of the Holy Grail, there he's a Roman commander, and everywhere he's King of Britain. What the poets have joined together let no man put asunder. Was Cadbury Castle simply Somerset's biggest Ice Age hillfort, or was it Arthur's legendary Camelot? John Steinbeck stood on this hill, gazed at the panorama, and felt 'a gentle rumbling earthquake of the spirit'. In order to do his research on Arthur, the American Nobel-prizewinner rented a cottage near Bruton in 1958, and found the peace of which he had always dreamed.

It is not knights-at-arms, however, that give Somerset its character. If anything, that honour must go to sheep. The county has few castles, but a lot of wool churches with splendid Perpendicular towers which, even in the tiniest villages, bear witness to the golden age of the wool trade. Very few of these church towers have fewer than six bells, and Somerset is indeed the county of the bell-ringer. By the end of the 14th century, it was producing a quarter of England's wool. Today you have to specialize in order to capitalize. For example, in Wensleydale sheep, the largest British breed, whose soft mohair-like wool is much in demand among fashion designers such as Katherine Hamnett. In the whole of Britain there are no more than 1300 of these rare animals, and one in six of these can be found on Foxhollow Farm near Norton sub Hamdon.

If you haven't got sheep to crop your lawn, you need a lawnmower. Andrew Hall in Ilminster has over 600 of them – vintage lawnmowers dating from 1847 to 1940, the largest collection of these most English of machines. There is another record held by Somerset (if you discount the cricketing feats of Ian Botham, Viv Richards et al.): the best bagpipe-makers in the world, David Naill & Co, are not to be found in Scotland, but in Minehead. Indeed Somerset has played its full part in the spread of British culture. The Franciscan Roger Bacon (c. 1214-1294) left Ilchester for

Door at Sharpham

Oxford, and with his scientific experiments sent shock waves through the ranks of the theologians. His great successor in the Age of the Enlightenment was John Locke (1632-1704), founder of British empiricism, who began life in Wrington, where Hannah More was to end her days. She was a bluestocking in London, before going to work among the lead-miners on the Mendips, for whose children she set up the first Sunday School; she was an emancipated woman of action, and the fact that she set up home with her four sisters had even Dr Samuel Johnson gasping: 'What, five women living happily together?' All five remain happily together in the churchyard at Wrington, and in the south porch of All Saints Parish Church, Hannah More and John Locke make a fine couple, brought together by courtesy of the sculptors who carved their memorial busts.

Somerset is the Cider County, but here as elsewhere in England the orchards have dwindled so much that the countryside itself has changed character. Instead of the large and beautiful apple trees of old, the growers now prefer the short, bush-like varieties which yield three times as many apples and take up far less space. More and more cheap apple concentrate is being imported from abroad, and the result is the insipid taste of mass production. Fortunately, the traditional farmhouse cider is still being made, for instance at Pass Vale Farm in Burrow Hill, where Julian Temperley even distils his own cider brandy, called Somerset Royal.

Somerset Royal cider brandy label by Elisabeth Frink

Somerset Royal

CIDER
BRANDY
1991
Distilled from
cider made
entirely with
Somerset apples
Aged for three years in oak barrels
70cl   42% vol

Attempted Murder on Exmoor

It is said that there are more ponies on Exmoor than people. About 10,000 people live in this area of approximately 265 square miles, where the climate can at times be pretty harsh. That is no problem for the tough, long-haired Exmoor ponies, which are directly descended from a race of wild horses that survived the Ice Age in northern Europe. They have mealy muzzles, shining frogs' eyes, and skin that varies from reddish to dark brown. Not a single white hair is allowed on a pure-bred Exmoor. These animals were probably here even before the first Beaker People and Bronze Age settlers built their stone circles and barrows on the moor. Such prehistoric relics – at Withypool, for instance, and south-west of Simonsbath – are less common here than on Dartmoor, and many a menhir now serves merely as a rubbing-stone for an itchy Exmoor pony.

In 1724 Daniel Defoe found the moor 'a filthy, barren ground'. Today it is a National Park full of paths for walking and riding, and well marked with the sign of the black stag's head on a green background. Instead of the stark granite rocks of Dartmoor, there are hills that curve gently from one valley to another, covered with a carpet of primroses and cowslips in the spring, and yellow gorse and purple heather in autumn. Nature lovers will find about 800 different species of plants and 245 of birds. And in the little village of *Selworthy*, just off the A39, I came across another unusual species: a party of retired folk displaying their watercolours. On their painting holidays they were capturing (on a modest scale) the sights of the moment. In Selworthy these are the white-walled thatched cottages that descend the hill on which stands All Saints, a Perpendicular gem (col. pl. 43). On the other side of the valley stands *Dunkery Beacon*, the highest point on Exmoor (1707 feet).

Exmoor is the smallest of the ten National Parks in England and Wales, and like all the others it is mostly private land. Only about a fifth belongs to the National Trust or the National Parks and Forestry Commission. Most of the moor is grazing land, but more and more of its barns are being converted into holiday homes, particularly as a result of the Common Agricultural Policy. The loss of traditional jobs has accelerated the rate at which young people leave the land, but in its natural state it has plenty to offer the tourist. You can catch salmon and trout in the River Exe, and you can ride, hike or hunt. In the densely wooded valleys, deer can still run wild and get themselves pursued by the English hunting classes. Local farmers are not averse to getting on their own high horses, and showing the foxes how fast their hounds can run.

But the hunt is no longer the idyllic pursuit depicted by the popular engravings of Henry Alken. As like as not, any meet will also be joined by the sabs – the hunt saboteurs – out for their favourite sport of countryfolk-sticking. Blood sports of all kinds (except, as yet, fishing) are subject to increasingly militant protest. There is a profound irony in this situation: the very fact that for so long much of Exmoor has remained a wilderness, providing a habitat for so many different species, is due not to the lovers of Nature and animals, but to the hunt-loving private owners. Does this, however, give them a licence to kill? The argument rages on. Perhaps the best place to pursue it is in one of the pubs where hunter and hunted end up nicely balanced – the former stuffing himself at the bar, and the latter already stuffed on the wall. Go to the Black Venus Inn in Challacombe (over the border in Devon). There are leather straps hanging from the oak beams, in case you find yourself overstuffed.

Tarr Steps are between Winsford and Hawkridge. They are not a folk dance, but a bridge – to be precise, the longest clapper bridge on Exmoor and indeed anywhere else. You walk for 180 feet on large stone slabs supported by stone pillars three feet above the River Barle, crossing from a wooded bank to open meadows. Those who know about these things say that Tarr Steps have been there since the Iron Age.

As you follow the river valleys along the border between Somerset and Devon, you come to Doone Valley and the church of *Oare*, to which literary pilgrims come from all over the country. 'The sound of a shot rang through the church.' What happened next, every Englishman knows – or has done since the TV film. Lorna Doone, in bloodstained wedding dress, collapses by the altar at the feet of her lover, John Ridd. Whodunnit? The dastardly Carver Doone. But justice prevails. Carver Doone perishes, Lorna recovers, and she and John live happily ever after. Richard D. Blackmore based his ever popular thriller of a love story (published in 1869) on local 17th-century tales of thieves and murderers. The son of a clergyman, Blackmore wrote many poems and novels, but this was his only best-seller. Some of the chapters were written, it is said, in the Royal Oak near Withypool.

From Lynmouth to Xanadu: Coastal Paths and Romantic Dreams

Just two miles north of Oare, Exmoor falls steeply down towards the Bristol Channel over a distance of some thirty miles. The coastal path from Minehead to Ilfracombe is a literary route *par excellence*, especially between Combe Martin and Woody Bay. In the little resort of *Lynmouth,* just over the border in Devon, Shelley

Shelley

spent a turbulent summer in 1812 with his wife, the 17-year-old Harriet Westbrook, in one of the cottages on the harbour's edge (now part of the Rising Sun Hotel). He wanted to set up a radical commune of 'like spirits' here, and he completed *Queen Mab*, a blank verse epic which waged furious battle on church and crown, marriage, capitalism '& the Devil knows what'. In their place, the revolutionary romantic advocated atheism and a republic, free love and vegetarianism. The legend goes that Shelley put his inflammatory ideas in a bottle, and threw it into the sea at Lynmouth.

Romantic Lynmouth did not enjoy real popularity until the Victorians began to discover the charms of Germany, and realized that the atmosphere of the Rhine and the Black Forest could be found here too: forests, cliffs and a Rhenish Tower, though the latter is 'none too Rhenish', as Pevsner pointed out, who enjoyed the Germanically 'tidy footpaths and frequency of conifers', not to mention the cog railway that still heaves its way up to *Lynton*.

Shelley's friend Robert Southey, the Poet Laureate from Bristol, also enjoyed the Exmoor coast. One rainy afternoon in 1799, he took shelter in the Ship Inn at *Porlock*, where he sat 'making my sonnet by the alehouse fire'. 'Thy wooded glens the traveller with delight/Recalls to memory.' The crooked shingle tower of Porlock's church looks down on the graveyard, where a devoted couple lie forever united: 'She first deceased him; he a little tried/To live without her, liked it not, and died.' There are many variations on these lines inscribed on 17th- and 18th-century graves, but the original author is believed to have been Sir Henry Wotton, writer and diplomat, who was born in Kent in 1568. On a visit to Augsburg he wrote his famous definition of an ambassador in an album of apothegms: 'An Ambassador is an honest man, sent to lie abroad for the good of his country.'

Between Porlock and the Valley of the Rocks near Lynton (rocks rejoicing in such names as White Lady and Devil's Cheesewring), along the clifftop path 1310 feet above the sea and running parallel to the present-day A39, S. T. Coleridge, William Wordsworth and his sister Dorothy wandered together during the autumn of 1797. It is to this romantic experience that we owe Coleridge's immortal *Rime of the Ancient Mariner*, in which the old seaman recounts his crime of killing the albatross, and the penance he had to suffer on board the ghost ship. In *Watchet*, a tiny sailing and fishing

Coleridge

harbour, Coleridge watched his mariner set out on that fateful voyage which was to end in the safe haven of literary history. These paths between heaven, earth and water are still such stuff as dreams are made on (if you can avoid them at peak season).

> In Xanadu did Kubla Khan
> A stately pleasure-dome decree:
> Where Alph, the sacred river, ran
> Through caverns measureless to man
> Down to a sunless sea.

Even the greatest poetry, however, is earthbound. Let us therefore comfort ourselves by trusting that Coleridge's biographers know precisely where Xanadu lies, and precisely why *Kubla Khan* remained a fragment. The location was Ash Farm, in isolated *Culbone*, and there Coleridge had an opium-inspired dream; 'on awakening he instantly and eagerly wrote down the lines that are here preserved. At this moment he was unfortunately called out by a person on business from Porlock.'

Further along the coastal path is *Minehead*. Most people go there to enjoy the typical facilities of an English seaside resort, but those of a more esoteric bent might admire the illuminations of the Fitzjames Missal (15th century) in St Michael's Church, which towers like a lighthouse over the town and bay, and for centuries was used for that very purpose. A short drive away from Minehead is the beautiful medieval village of *Dunster*, on the edge of Exmoor. St George's Church contains the longest screen in England (54 feet), which was built after a quarrel between the priory and the townspeople in 1498, and served to separate the monks' choir from the parish church. According to Arthur Mee it is 'one of the most impressive pieces of craftsmanship the Flemish artists ever made for an English church'; and he, having covered the whole of the King's England, should have known. The originally Norman castle of the Luttrells has a magnificent plaster ceiling (1681) in the Inner Hall, and a bedroom used by King Charles II. At the entrance to the little town is the octagonal Yarn Market (*c.* 1589), and at the other end is the romantic Packhorse Bridge. Dunster is a delightful place for wandering and for gazing. It also has an architectural-cum-culinary rarity: the Dovecote. This medieval structure has a much admired and very practical revolving ladder (col. pl. 25), by means of which you can easily gain access to the 500 clutches of eggs and up to 200 squabs a week – sufficient to feed succulent pigeon pie to generations of gourmets in the castle and the neighbouring Benedictine priory. But alas, we are 100 years too late. The birds have flown.

The Quantock and Mendip Hills: Poets and Other Cave-Dwellers

'There is everything here: sea, woods wild as fancy ever painted, brooks clear and pebbly, villages so romantic.' The *Quantock Hills*, described so rapturously by Dorothy Wordsworth when she came here in 1797 (from the Lake District, which is not without its own charms) have changed very little since that time. They stretch over twelve miles from Watchet on Bridgwater Bay as far as Taunton. 'England's loveliest hills,' I was told by the locals, and my scepticism soon disappeared when we left the A39 at Holford, and climbed the twisting road to our hotel at *Alfoxton Park*.

Dorothy Wordsworth

This is a two-storey country house with a colonnaded Tuscan porch, Georgian through and through, apart from the swimming pool. William and Dorothy Wordsworth lived here and enjoyed the view of Wales across the Bristol Channel. The privilege and pleasure of sleeping in Dorothy's bedroom will now cost you a great deal more than the £23 Wordsworth paid in 1797 for a whole year's rent. Of course the Wordsworths had no desire to play golf or tennis, or to hunt deer. All they wanted to do was wander around with Coleridge, write poetry, and savour the 'wild simplicity'. Wordsworth worked hard nevertheless. One of the fragments from his notebook (known, from an earlier spelling, as the Alfoxden Notebook) has as fine a description as he would ever write:

> ...lovely as the fairy day
> Which one hour after sunset the sea gains
> From the bright sunset when, on the bare hill-top,
> Scarce distant twenty paces, the sheep bleats
> Unseen, and darkness covers all the vales.

Alfoxton was the birthplace of the *Lyrical Ballads*, the foundation stone of English Romanticism; Wordsworth also wrote *The Borderers* here, a tragedy in verse about the harsh government of the Jacobins in France. The wild behaviour of these arty folk must have put the neighbours in fear of their lives, for they were denounced by a spy as 'a set of Violent Democrats', and after one year were given notice to leave.

William Wordsworth

This short and explosive stay has left no mark on Alfoxton Park – not even a display case of mementoes. All the more gratifying, then, to find so many in a much simpler environment: Coleridge's once thatched cottage in nearby *Nether Stowey*. At the age of 24, he came here with wife and child, not as a holidaymaker, but as a poet and farmer. For two years, he spent the early morning working in his garden, and then alternated between reading, writing poetry, and working. 'So jogs the day, and I am happy,' he wrote, and given the choice between becoming a self-sufficient gardener and a Milton, he would have chosen the former. This lyrical back-to-the-land movement of English Romantics has been on display to all in Coleridge's Cottage since 1908: the contemporary portraits of his family and friends; the bookshelf made from the beech tree at Woodlands Farm where Coleridge and Wordsworth used to meet; the drawing of Heidelberg Castle, a souvenir of their trip together up the Rhine in 1828; four differently coloured locks of the poet's hair; his cavalry sword; his desk with three quills. But even in idyllic Nether Stowey, the poet suffered from 'Fears in Solitude' and, in particular, fear of a Napoleonic invasion. This was in 1798, and in the same year Coleridge and Wordsworth travelled together to Germany in order to study philosophy.

A few miles south-west of Nether Stowey and its 'Ancient Mariner' pub, another writer spent the last ten years of his life (1956-66): Evelyn Waugh, coruscating author of such novels as *A Handful of Dust* (1934) and *Brideshead Revisited* (1945). His son, Auberon Waugh, writer and journalist, who now lives at his country seat at *Combe Florey*, gave memorable descriptions of Evelyn in his autobiography, *Will This Do?*

Not far away, in the southern foothills of the Quantocks, is *Hestercombe*. This Edwardian garden (1904-08) is the best preserved of all those designed by the legendary partnership of Edwin Lutyens and Gertrude Jekyll. Here architect and gardener, working on equal terms, combined together to create a perfect example of horticultural art (col. pl. 26).

Bench end, Spaxton

Lutyens used the slope below the old mansion to form a series of symmetrical terraces, with a square parterre in the centre, long, narrow rills running along the sides as in Elizabethan gardens, and a long pergola closing off the southern side. This main garden is linked by a rotunda on the east side of the house, almost like an elbow, to a narrow side section which leads to an orangery (in Lutyen's typical 'Wrenaissance' style) and ends in a little Dutch rose garden. The lay-out is clear and simple, and the details are exquisite. The rotunda alone is a gem: a circular pond set in stone lozenges, like a garden eye reflecting light and clouds. For the paths and walls, Lutyens used plain grey slate, and for the balustrades, niches and other ornaments he used smooth, golden Ham Hill stone. Within this richly textured, geometrical framework Gertrude Jekyll unfolded the full range of her plant repertoire, like a painter with her palette.

There are grey beds of sweet-scented lavender, rosemary, catmint, globe thistles and sea holly lining the Grey Walk. Valerian and cotton lavender cascade over the drystone walls, and in the side-terrace rills, Gertrude Jekyll planted irises, arum lilies, water plantain and arrowhead, with red poppies and orange-coloured lilies on the borders – the glowing colours of summer. Sometimes the paths are overhung with broad-leaved saxifrage (one of her favourite plants) and sometimes with silver-grey hare's-ear. As you stroll through the pergola, your nostrils and eyes will be filled with intoxicating scents and sights; you will pass alternating round and square pillars bedecked with honeysuckle and clematis, climbing roses and Russian vine, and when you reach the end of this 250-foot long pergola, you can gaze out at the landscape through grandiose round windows.

After the war, Hestercombe became headquarters of the Somerset Fire Brigade. The gardens have been superbly restored by the County Council. Another Somerset garden designed by Gertrude Jekyll, at *Barrington Court*, a Tudor house south-east of Taunton, is being reconstructed by the National Trust. In 1917 Jekyll had drawn up plans for a garden divided into nine different areas. Three of these – the lily, iris and rose gardens – are taking shape once more.

Meanwhile, the head gardener at Hestercombe, David Usher, is busy on an even more difficult project. In the undergrowth behind the house, he found traces of an older landscaped garden, covering some 35 acres, with four lakes, waterfalls, and the remains of at least nine buildings and seats. This is *Combe Park*, which was designed in 1750-90 by a gentleman rejoicing in the name of Copplestone-Warre- Bampfylde. Another exciting piece of England's garden history comes back to life.

From Hestercombe you can look south across Taunton Vale as far as the Blackdown Hills. *Taunton* is the

Bench end, Spaxton

county town, famous for its cider and infamous for Judge Jeffreys and the Bloody Assizes. It was here in 1685 that Jeffreys tried the followers of the Duke of Monmouth. The favourite illegitimate son of Charles II and his mistress Lucy Walters, and Protestant, Monmouth saw an opportunity with the accession of the Catholic James II, and had himself proclaimed King in Taunton. Shortly afterwards, in July 1685, his attempt to win the crown ended in the marshy fields of Sedgemoor. This was the last battle fought on English soil, and together with Judge Jeffreys' bloody sequel it is fully documented in the County Museum. Much more enjoyable escapades are those of Jeremy James, the hero of several popular children's books by David Henry Wilson, who lives in Taunton. And another most palatable adventure to be had in this town is dinner at the Castle Hotel, which under its manager, the food critic Kit Chapman, and its well-known chef Phil Vickery, has made no small contribution to the culinary revolution in England.

There are many Somerset folk who would say that Sedgemoor was not the last battle fought on English soil. In the early 1980's, the County Cricket Club was one of the most glamorous in England, with its success built round the great all-rounder Ian Botham and the two West Indian stars Viv Richards and Joel Garner. But in 1986 it all turned sour, when after a poor season the Committee decided to sack Richards and Garner. A disgusted Botham announced that if they went, he would go too, and all hell broke loose in Somerset. It was a triumph of mediocrity over greatness, and not until 1993 did the bitter taste finally fade, when a new committee offered honorary life membership to all three, which they graciously accepted.

The Perpendicular tower of St Mary Magdalene rises high over Taunton. It is a typical wool church, and there are more remnants of Somerset's great wool industry at St Margaret's in *Spaxton*, where a richly carved bench-end depicts a fuller with his bat cleaning and thickening the cloth. Such bench-ends date mainly from the 15th century, and are to be found in many of Somerset's churches. They are as much a speciality here as fonts in Cornwall or choir screens in Devon. As well as tools, flowers and figures, there are carvings of windmills (Bishop's Lydeard), cock-fighting (Hatch Beauchamp), and even mermaids and naked dragon-killers (Crowcombe). If you have time to turn off at *Brent Knoll*, you will find three literally fabulous benches in the nave of St Michael's. This is a polemic comic-strip in wood: Reynard the Fox, disguised as an abbot, is preaching to the geese; two benches further on, the geese are stringing the villain up. There is another curiosity on the wall, where a monument to John Somerset and his two wives sports the biggest hat you will ever see on an English monument. Outside, visible for miles around between the seaside resorts of Burnham and Weston, is *Brent Knoll Camp*, an Iron Age hillfort. Here the Devil is believed to have thrown his shovelful of earth when he dug out Cheddar Gorge. The Devil also cooks with water, and history proves it: *Cheddar Gorge*, 425 feet deep at its lowest point, was created millions of years ago, when an underground river ate away at the chalky Mendip Hills until they collapsed. The result was another flood, which has grown ever more voluminous: the tourists. If you want to get away from them all, you can either go up on the Mendips by climbing the 236 steps of Jacob's Ladder, or you can go down below them into Gough's Cave. Discovered in 1877, this dripstone cave is a completely natural phenomenon. An Ice Age skeleton was found here at the beginning of the century, one of the original inhabitants of Cheddar, who was ceremonially butchered and probably defleshed. (The visitor's centre likewise; it was once a pioneering piece of modern English architecture, built by Geoffrey Jellicoe in 1934). Now Cheddar is more of a vegetarian's place. 'The best cheese that England affords, if not, that the whole world affords' asserted Daniel Defoe. If you can find a farmhouse that makes it properly, you will agree. The world knows Cheddar because the first great steps in scientific cheese making were taken by Joseph Harding, who published his wife's perfected methods in 1859. Not content with issuing a pamphlet, the whole family issued forth to spread the Cheddar gospel (systematic method, hygiene, temperature control) over the world. 'The result may not always be happy,' as Jane Grigson says 'but the original impulse was a generous one.'

Wookey Hole, two miles north of Wells, is another spectacular dripstone cave in the Mendips, some sixty thousand years old. The poet Alexander Pope is said to have been so impressed by the cobalt-blue and copper-green minerals, when he came here at the beginning of the 18th century, that he took home a complete dripstone curtain for his garden grotto in Twickenham on the Thames. One of the three large caves hollowed out by the River Axe is the Witch's Kitchen, and here sits the Witch of Wookey Hole, one of Nature's little jokes, carved in limestone. Nature's contribution to the tourist value of Wookey does not go unaided, however, since the caves and the whole valley were bought in 1973 by Madame Tussaud's. The old papermill (once used to store some 2000 moulds and disembodied waxwork heads) now houses a mirror maze, 'Neptune's Kingdom' made of distorted mirrors, and, more appropriately, demonstrations of traditional paper-making.

Wells Cathedral

Don't go straight into the Cathedral. First have a good look round the city. The approach alone is worth the trip, whether you're coming from Bath or down from the Mendips. Town and country are in complete harmony, and there are cows grazing behind the Bishop's Gothic Palace. The Cathedral City of *Wells* sounds grand, but in fact it's a tiny town, always was, and no doubt always will be. In the 13th century there were 4000 inhabitants, and now there are 10,000. The 170 or so figures on the front of the Cathedral seem like a vast crowd. In the Middle Ages Wells, halfway between Glastonbury and Bath, made architectural and ecclesiastical history. It is a history that lives in the present, can be read on every building, and has remained intact – yet never ossified – to a degree rarely seen these days.

In Wells the visitor must feel, like God, that a thousand ages are like an evening gone. Morning coffee, 15th century, in the Refectory in the cloister of the Cathedral, where the cakes and biscuits are all home-made; lunch, 16th century, in the Star Hotel, where you eat in the former stables; afternoon tea, 17th century, in the Crown Hotel in the marketplace, beneath whose three half-timbered gables the Quaker William Penn preached just before his arrest; and let us spend the night 600 years back, in the Ancient Gate House Hotel, where the city walls run right through the house, the door is Norman and the stones round the windows Saxon, and there is a bedroom directly above the gatehouse actually *in* the town walls. On the pavement in the market square you'll come across a brass plaque commemorating a more recent bit of history: Mary Bignal Rand won the Olympic gold medal and broke the world record for long jump in Tokyo in 1964. She came from Wells and the Mayor sent her a telegram of congratulations reading: 'Us be proud of ee'.

A few steps further on is the gatehouse called Pennyless Porch, where beggars ask

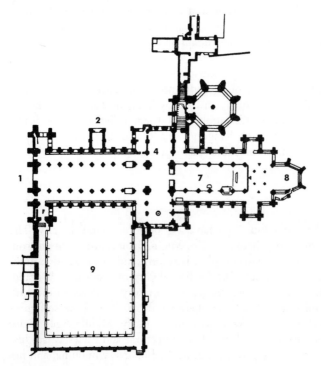

Wells Cathedral, plan
1. West Front
2. North Portal
3. Crossing Tower
4. Astronomical Clock
5. Chapter House steps
6. Chapter House
7. Chancel
8. Lady Chapel
9. Cloister

churchgoers for alms. A few more steps, and there is the Cathedral. You find your-self standing before a massive, grey sandstone wall that soars up into the sky and stretches 165 feet wide. In front of it is a great expanse of green that seems to let the mighty building breathe. The *West Front* (1) (col. pl. 41) is the glory of Wells, like a winged altar opened wide to display its whole host of figures. The two towers are almost stunted (even more so before the upper parts were added), and unlike their French counterparts are not placed at the end of the aisles but beside them. This only re-emphasizes the astonishing breadth of the front, leaving all the more space for the statues, which originally were painted in glowing colours. There is no other church in England with such a gallery of 13th-century sculpture. Here we have the history of salvation and a world theatre all in one, with kings and tyrants, scenes from the Old and New Testaments, angels, apostles, and above them all, enthroned in a niche between the two towers, Christ in His Glory. The local stonemasons may well have been following – though by no means matching – the examples of Chartres and Rheims, but as Peter Kidson says, 'everything about this façade is as wilfully insular as the architecture behind it.' Originally there were no fewer than 366 statues, some lifesize, others larger than life, but many of them have been destroyed or badly damaged. The statue of Christ and several others have been newly carved, 'in the same spirit', but nevertheless they are only copies.

Wells became a bishopric in 909. Bishop Reginald began the new cathedral around 1180, on the site of a Saxon church itself built over a Roman mausoleum, laid out near springs; little survives of the Saxon building beyond a few foundations, the font and some tombs. The church itself was aligned with these 'holy wells' and with the town's street pattern, which still survives, and it was finished *c.* 1348. From the first phase of construction one can discern two different styles: the transepts, the six eastern bays of the nave and the western bays of the chancel (6) are all Norman Transitional; the rest of the nave, the west front (without the towers) and the north porch (2), with its ten orders of columns and array of figured capitals, are all Early English. The second phase was the period of the Decorated, and to this belong the Chapter House, the Lady Chapel (8), the eastern end of the chancel, and the cross-ing tower (3; 1315-22, rebuilt *c.* 1440). The south tower of the west front dates from after 1386, and the north from after 1424. Finally, the cloister and Cathedral Library (9) are Perpendicular (15th century).

Right in the middle of the church is the crossing-arch, on top of which – head down as it were – is a second arch, and in the spandrels on each side of their head-to-head meeting-point are two round eyes which fix us with a stony stare. With the gaping mouth of the arch below, it's as if we are about to be swallowed up by some medieval Colossus. This monstrous figure eight (1338) beneath the square *Crossing Tower* (3) is a defiant, even triumphant answer to a pressing problem: the tower simply had to be shored up, almost as soon as it was finished (col. pl. 42). All around are capitals bursting with buds, while those in the nave and south transept

Chapter House ceiling: the 'finest cone of ribs to be seen in England'

are covered with grotesque figures telling their stories in stone: two men are stealing grapes, and farmers with an axe and pitchfork follow them all round the column, and finally catch up with them; there is a shoemaker at work, a girl with a thorn, and a man with toothache. A richly ornate Bishop Bekynton (*c.* 1452) lies above his own skeleton – a grinning reminder of our common fate.

There are few staircases that bear the footprints of the centuries with more grace and rhythm than the *Chapter House Staircase* (5). It rises straight from the Cathedral, past the corbel figure of a monk bearing, like an Atlas, the weight of a ceiling column, and then curves majestically off into the *Chapter House* (6; *c.* 1290-1306). If the staircase is perfection, so too is the Chapter House. Its central pier fans out into 32 ribs that arch over the octagonal room; eighteen columns of Purbeck marble around the walls reflect the splendour of the centrepiece. The room is like a poem, a triumph of geometry, with proportions that seem to enfold you in a living, human warmth. The vault is reminiscent of the vaults in Exeter and Lincoln, but here it is infinitely more beautiful and more subtle. Wells was the first English cathedral to use the Gothic pointed arch as a motif throughout, from the arcades to the vaults. With its Romanesque cubes and its Gothic curves, its rich alternation of large and small spaces, and especially its hall-like sections (the Lady Chapel, the 'arbitrary, irrational, and exquisitely mysterious' retrochoir), Wells is a truly magnificent example of English Gothic. Its emphasis on the vertical combined with the serenity of the horizontal is as typically English as the blend of size and intimacy.

In the triforium of the northern aisle is a brightly dressed man who uses his hands and feet to work a bell. He does this so skilfully that four knights come riding round inside, and two knights start jousting on the north wall outside, and between them all they inform the people of Wells that another quarter of an hour of their lives has gone by. Ever since 1390, the famous astronomical clock (4) has performed this service, with the tireless Jack Blandifer striking the bell – the most famous Quarter Jack in the land.

Cathedral, Bishop's Palace, and the precincts around them have changed less since the Middle Ages in Wells than in most cathedral cities. *Vicars' Close*, linked to the Cathedral by a bridge, is one of the earliest terraces (1348) – a perfectly preserved medieval street of 42 two-storey houses (No. 22 has been restored with its original groundplan), still used by Cathedral staff and theology students. The 'Bishop's Eye' – one of three surviving medieval gatehouses – still keeps a sharp watch on those who come from the Market Place to the *Bishop's Palace* (13th/14th century). Bishop Ralph of Shrewsbury was responsible for the moat, but his motives were more political than aesthetic, as he wished to keep the ordinary folk at a safe distance. The moat, made in 1340, is famous for its mute swans which, in the 19th century, were trained by the daughter of Bishop Hervey to grab a rope hanging from the gatehouse window and ring the attached bell when they were hungry. A handful of bread would then be thrown to them. The present swans have recently been trained to do the same. In the rose garden at the house is the source that gave the city its name. *Bishop Burnell's Hall* (c. 1280) was deliberately and scandalously made into a 'picturesque' ruin in the 19th century, but is still mightily impressive, as are the windows and the bosses of the tierceron vault in the Chapel. The citizens of Wells may, however, have preferred to stand beneath the carved and painted trusses of *St Cuthbert's* (15th century), the largest parish church in Somerset. And yet in the Middle Ages none of this splendour could match the power and the glory of Glastonbury.

Peace, Pop and Opium Salad: The Holy Grail and Glastonbury

The Abbey Church of *Glastonbury* was 590 feet long – 200 feet longer than Wells Cathedral. But Wells never became a monastery, and so unlike Glastonbury it escaped the marauding attentions of Henry VIII. England's biggest Abbey became its most famous ruin in a little town full of historical superlatives. The new followers of old legends, tourists and New Age travellers, flock to Glastonbury much like medieval pilgrims. This is the place of the Holy Grail and the tomb of King Arthur, and here grows the thorn which sprang from the staff of Joseph of Arimathea when he came from the Holy Land, and which is still sent every Christmas to Her Majesty the Queen. Here the oldest Christian community in England built their first church, and here, drawn by the magic of Glastonbury's past, the newest cults have established their capital.

'No Hippies Allowed' said the signs in the restaurants when I first came here in the 1970's. But today the young flowerfolk have Glastonbury in the palms of their hands. There are shops here called Pendragon and Avalon, even though they only sell shoes. Everywhere you will find candles and incense, runic chains, crystals, Celtic and cosmic charms, herbal massages, courses in meditation, pottery, tarot, astrology, aromatherapy, and all the erapies and ologies you can think of. You will even find 'Spiritual healing for animals and all other living things'. You can put an amethyst on your forehead, or lapis lazuli anywhere you like ... 'Can you feel the vibrations?' Glastonbury is hip and holy, a health farm for the soul. The streets are full of musicians, Neo-Druids, beggars and ancient hippies. A T-shirt urges me to 'Say No To Real Jobs', and a wall informs me that 'Jesus was here – it's the Glastonbury Connection'.

Here the medieval myth and the ersatz myths of modern times come together in a strange spectacle: every year travellers from England and all over Europe meet on Glastonbury Tor, a conical hill whose ruined church tower can be seen for miles around. During his mission to Britain, Joseph of Arimathea is said to have buried the Holy Grail here – the chalice from which Jesus drank at the Last Supper, and in which Joseph caught His blood as it fell from the Cross. And indeed at the foot of the tor, the red waters of the Chalice Well still flow – though the colour is in fact due to the high iron content. Connected with this Eucharistic legend is the Celtic one of King Arthur, who gathered together the Knights of the Round Table in a quest to find the Grail. It may be said that this was the first and the most exclusive men's club in British history. Tennyson, in his *Idylls of the King* (1859-85) – a moral and allegorical retelling of Arthurian legend – described Glastonbury as an island paradise:

> To the island valley of Avilion,
> Where falls not hail, or rain, or any snow,
> Nor ever wind blows loudly; but it lies
> Deep-meadow'd, happy, fair with orchard lawns
> And bowery hollows, crowned with summer sea.

Glastonbury, the legendary Isle of Avalon, was indeed once an island, washed by the waters of the Bristol Channel, which flowed between the Quantocks and the

Mendips. North-west of the town are the sites of prehistoric lake villages, including Meare, and various remains are to be seen in Glastonbury Museum. As far as the legends of Arthur and, especially, Joseph of Arimathea are concerned, historians have long since discredited them as the pious fictions of the monks. In order to rebuild their monastery, which had burned down in 1184, they needed money, and miraculously they discovered two holy graves. The fact that these proved a powerful magnet for pilgrims, thereby increasing the prestige of the Abbey, lay in the nature of miracles. All that is left to us today is a little plaque in the grass, where once there was the high altar. It simply announces that King Arthur and Queen Guinevere are buried there. Sceptics should confine themselves to the authentic tombs of Anglo-Saxon kings buried in Glastonbury: Edmund I, Edgar, and Edmund Ironside.

The Benedictine *Abbey*, of which St Dunstan was made Abbot around 940, and which Erasmus visited in 1510, must have been vast, judging by the magnificence of the ruins. Piranesian pathos on an English bowling green. Despite all the destruction, the layout of the Abbey Church of St Peter and Paul can clearly be seen in the grass, with the width of the nave doubled by that of the two aisles; the height of the building must have been tremendous. The two portals with their archivolt figures – the Annunciation, the Nativity, infanticide, a cow being milked – are finer even than the sculptures in Wells Cathedral, though their condition is still deteriorating. Many generations used the Abbey as a quarry, but with a fine sense of earthly proportion, the plunderers did leave intact one building – perhaps the holiest of holies for the monks: the Abbot's Kitchen (14th century). The ground plan is square, but the four fireplaces rise into an octagonal pyramid roof with lantern. This is one of the biggest

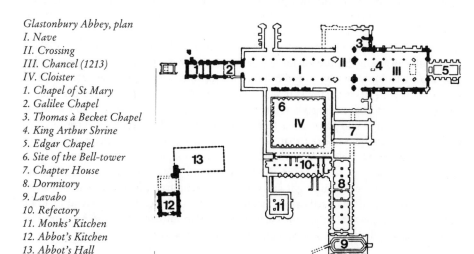

Glastonbury Abbey, plan
I. Nave
II. Crossing
III. Chancel (1213)
IV. Cloister
1. Chapel of St Mary
2. Galilee Chapel
3. Thomas à Becket Chapel
4. King Arthur Shrine
5. Edgar Chapel
6. Site of the Bell-tower
7. Chapter House
8. Dormitory
9. Lavabo
10. Refectory
11. Monks' Kitchen
12. Abbot's Kitchen
13. Abbot's Hall

and best preserved medieval kitchens in Europe.

Anyone not of a nervous disposition can spend the night at the George and Pilgrims in the very room from which in 1539 Henry VIII is said to have watched the Abbey burn. Glastonbury's last Abbot, Richard Whiting, fled to *Sharpham Park* near Walton, two miles away. This former estate of the abbots is now in private hands, but some years ago the lady of the house was kind enough to take me through the labyrinth of fine rooms, and to tell me all about Henry Fielding, who was born there. There is nothing to see of the great novelist, except what he himself must have seen, unchanged through the centuries: across the fields, Glastonbury Tor, where Abbot Whiting was executed, and where the Grail lies hidden.

When the sun goes down over the Vale of Avalon, the farmer Michael Eavis hears heavenly voices: Van Morrison, Johnny Cash and David Bowie, Simple Minds and Stone Roses, Led Zeppelin, Oasis – all of them have appeared live in his fields at *Pilton*, for as well as being a farmer, Michael Eavis is a pop impresario. He started the Glastonbury Festival, mother of all English Rock Festivals, in 1970, one year after Woodstock. About 1500 fans came, and paid £1 each to get in. At the 25th Festival in 1995, over 100,000 came, and they paid £65 a head. It is now the biggest open-air festival in Europe. Its founder was born in 1935, went to Wells Cathedral School, became a sailor, and finally a farmer. He went in for organic farming long before it became fashionable, and it is said that he milks his 250 cows to the latest hits from the charts. Athelstan Joseph Michael Eavis is a Methodist, which again marks him out as different: 'There is a strong anti-establishment tradition in Methodism. I was brought up to think that whatever the Establishment is doing needs to be questioned.' And so the message from Woodstock got through to Worthy Farm, and it fell on the right ears at the right time in the right place. In their search for love and peace, a new generation found its Holy Grail for a few days in Glastonbury, while the farmer Michael Eavis found 'a sort of Utopia'.

While other people tried to get rid of the hippies and later the travellers, Michael Eavis offered them the use of his fields. It was no easy task, however, to get his neighbours to look kindly on radical alternatives in this rural, Conservative part of England. In June, though, the skinheads, punks, rockers and ravers come together in general peace and harmony to listen to the top bands. They congregate in the circus tent, the 'Healing Field', and at the stands of the anti-nuclear and animal rights campaigners. It must be admitted that not all of them confine their intake to popcorn and organic honey. Salads of seaweed and opium, magic mushrooms, aphrodisiac mandrakes – they are all items on the dream menu. Glastonbury is to youth what Ascot is to the oldies. You might call it the Glyndebourne of the alternative world. But even Michael Eavis needs an occasional break, so there was no festival in 1996. He was making plans to stand for Parliament, as Labour candidate for Avalon. Alas even the Labour landslide of 1997 failed to dislodge his Tory rival.

Country of the War Photographer: Don McCullin's House of the Dead

In the hills of Somerset lives a man whose house is full of dead people. They lie in his cupboards, captured in thousands of negatives. The man is a photographer, and his name is synonymous with war photography: Don McCullin. 'At night, if you let your imagination run wild, the archives and the dark room are like Dante's Inferno.' Don McCullin has survived the killing fields not only of Vietnam, but also of the Congo, Cyprus, Northern Ireland, Biafra, Beirut, Nicaragua, El Salvador, Cambodia, Kurdistan, and so on and on. He had had more experience of the front line than any of England's generals in the Falklands War (which he was not allowed to photograph). He has seen every nightmare imaginable: starvation, murder, torture, executions – all frozen in time by his camera. At first photographing war was an adventure for him, a profession that would bring him swift fame. But his pictures of human suffering bear witness to his human involvement; they take sides. 'I was always on the side of the victims.' John Berger wrote that McCullin's photos had 'the function of an eye that we cannot close'. But in the end, even this great visual historian of war had had enough, and went in search of peace.

In 1984 he found it in the countryside, far from the killing fields. He now lives alone in a hamlet south of Bath, his old cottage surrounded by a garden and the gentle sounds of Nature. It is a return to the countryside of his childhood, for when he was five years old and German bombs were falling on London, he was evacuated to Somerset, to the village of Norton St Philip. Now once again he has sought refuge in this rural haven, after all the years as a foreign legionnaire with camera. *Homecoming* was the title he chose for the resultant book, and here on the fringes of English society he was able to take stock of himself and of the world he knows and has known – a world that encompasses all the extremes of war and peace. In 1989 he published *Open Skies*, still lives and landscapes of Somerset. A tired warrior burying his sorrows in the idylls of the country? Like Roger Fenton, the pioneer of war photography, who after the Crimean War also withdrew to the country and composed still lifes. But when in autumn the great Atlantic storms come rumbling in from the West over the Bristol Channel, Don McCullin goes outside with his camera, and captures landscapes like battlefields, with clouds of metallic black, and shadowed continents, and hills shrouded in night, the ever beating hearts of darkness. This is the grim side of his new world, for still he seeks a home: 'I feel that I am sleeping on a bed of nails. Every negative a nail! Then I go off and do my landscapes, because I feel this guilt stifling me. It's like trying to rub away something. I feel like a black man who wants to become a white man. You can never be free of them, these stains of memory.'

Open Skies is dedicated to his wife Christine. For years they had been separated, and in 1988 she died of cancer. 'I took it out on the landscape, I turned sunny days into war.' Dark images from Somerset. But the pathos of these landscapes has another root as well. 'I live here in a hill village, surrounded by the beginnings of English history. Over there I can see a hill fort from the Iron Age, and over there is what was once a Roman camp. Stonehenge isn't far away, and the mythical birthplace of King Arthur. London depresses me. But as soon as I come here, into this magnetic field, my spirit changes.' Heroic landscapes, seen through the Stoic eyes of memory and history, a different, darker Somerset which the visitor rarely experiences. This is a land of magic powers.

'I love the countryside, and I love beauty. I think I'm a good judge of beauty, because I've spent forty years looking at ugliness.' One of his Somerset photos shows a wide slope with hedged-in fields and a ridge crowned with trees. 'The real English countryside.' This is what the warrior is now defending. 'Every day we're losing hundreds of acres of land, for golf courses, so-called leisure parks, or country villages full of town houses that stick to them like limpets.' These too constitute Don McCullin's dark pastorals – images of a new and different menace. He uses them for campaigns to save the environment, for instance the Somerset Levels. 'I want to leave behind in people's minds to say: he really did some beautiful landscapes and some good still lifes. I want to be remembered for that – and not as a war photographer.'

The *Somerset Levels* stretch over 250 square miles north-east of Taunton. They are the remains of a region which was once at the mouth of the Bristol Channel, and to which Somerset owes its name: *somer saeta*, Land of the Summer People, for in winter it used to be flooded and inaccessible. What was left of these marshes after they had been drained in the 18th century is now threatened by intensive farming. The Levels are still one of the largest areas of wetlands in England, and are home to all kinds of waterfowl as well as being one of the last remaining refuges of the otter. Bewick's swans, lapwing, teal and wigeon spend their winters here, and catchfly, marsh orchids and many other wild flowers bloom in the summer. In West Sedgemoor, reed from the *salix triandra* is harvested in November, and in Stoke St Gregory the traditional basket-making industry is flourishing. There is a great demand nowadays for waste-paper, fishing and laundry baskets, picnic hampers, and garden fences all woven from the wonderful willows of the wetlands.

Just as traditional, but far more controversial environmentally, is the peat industry of the levels. Everywhere you go you will see great piles of peat waiting bagging. It has been extracted here since prehistoric times, but now we use such vast quantities, mainly for trivial tasks round the garden, that there is a real danger of this unique environment disappearing. At *Westhay*, near Glastonbury, Somerset County Council has started a Peat Moors Visitors' Centre to explain the issues involved – and even included a replica Iron Age village, to show you how it all started.

'In my end is my beginning': The Golden Stones of Montacute

Just a few miles away from Yeovil are three of the most important country houses in Somerset: Montacute, Barrington Court (see p. 81), and Brympton d'Evercy. The gold medal must go to *Montacute House*, which like the rest of the village glows with honey-coloured Ham Hill stone. Ham Hill itself lies close by; from there comes the stone used for so many buildings in Somerset and Dorset, and ever since the Stone Age this hill fort has towered over the countryside. On the edge of the village, at the foot of the conical hill (*mons acutus*) from which both village and house derive their name, the Phelips built *Montacute House*, probably beginning in 1588, the year of the Armada. They were among the late 16th-century *parvenus* who profited from Henry VIII's dissolution of the monasteries, in this case the Cluniac Abbey of Montacute. *Nouveaux riches* they may have been, but they were people of style and taste. Edward Phelips was Speaker in the House of Commons during the reign of James I, and opened proceedings at the trial of Guy Fawkes following the Gunpowder Plot of 1605. It was he who had the house built – as typically Elizabethan as Longleat House or Hardwick Hall, with its H-shaped groundplan, large Perpendicular windows, curved Flemish gables, and various Renaissance features such as the column-shaped chimneys. All over the gables are stone dogs, and below them, in the window niches the whole length of the Long

Montacute House

Gallery, are the Nine Worthies dressed in Roman armour: Joshua, David, Judas Maccabeus, Hector, Alexander the Great, Julius Caesar, King Arthur, Charlemagne, and Godfrey of Bouillon. They look down over the front court, the original entrance to Montacute, and bear witness to the triumph of Renaissance symmetry and the glory of Ham Hill stone. The seam of gold runs on into the front court, whose flower borders are encased in balustrades, obelisks, elegant lanterns, and two pavilions with roofs that curve as gracefully as the necks of swans. They are empty, and their mezzanine floors are an illusion, for these are decorative follies built in 1588. The garden itself is a Victorian pastiche of formal Elizabethan gardens. On permanent loan from the National Portrait Gallery in London are over a hundred magnificent portraits from Tudor and Stuart times, hung in the Long Gallery and constituting the biggest collection of such works to be seen anywhere in England.

Just a few miles away, on the Dorset border, is *East Coker*, a tiny village of thatched houses in Ham Hill stone. It was from here, in the middle of the 17th century, that the ancestors of the poet T. S. Eliot set out for America. Three hundred years later, their famous descendant returned to East Coker. 'In my beginning is my end. In my end is my beginning.' Thus he begins and ends his autobiographical poem *East Coker*, the second of the *Four Quartets* (1935-42), and this is the inscription on the oval memorial in the village church of St Michael, where Eliot's ashes were buried on Easter Saturday, 1965.

Housing Boom and Hot Springs: The Wonder of Bath

'Bath lies in a laughing valley, completely enclosed in substantial heights that only open up in order to make way for the beautiful River Avon.' Johanna Schopenhauer, mother of the great philosopher, was one of many famous people who came, saw, and were conquered by *Bath*. The view of this town is of a wonderfully integrated beauty. Soon the valley became too narrow for her, and so she raised herself up onto the nearest heights, then higher and ever higher she piled palace upon palace, each competing with the others in beauty and in all the decorativeness of modern architecture.' Love at first sight, expressed by a sensitive visitor some 200 years ago and, it has to be said, one of thousands of rapturous descriptions penned in the 18th century. But if today you turn off the roaring M4 and make your way towards this glorious city, you too will be enchanted by the sheer beauty of the place. It still lies in a laughing valley.

No other town is as welcoming as Bath. It receives us in the open arms of its crescents, and embraces us with the gentle geometry of its circuses and squares; then it lets us go back to our own over-developed towns with images of how things ought to be. Bath is a gift from the comfort-loving Georgian age to succeeding generations of admirers. No other English city has been so perfectly preserved – in spite of the

Georgian arcade, Bath

Baedeker raids by the German Luftwaffe in 1942 – and in 1988 it became one of only four 'World Heritage Cities' to be named by UNESCO, the others being Venice, Vatican City and Valetta.

Bath must have grown up in a period of natural good taste, for the beauty and the quality of its architecture is not confined to individual showpieces; it is everywhere. You get the impression that the whole place was laid out in the midst of a landscaped garden and allowed to grow organically. Not so, as the wonderful *Building of Bath Museum* (13/14) demonstrates. Vision, determination, speculation, riches and ruin were all players, as in any other great building project. The main architects were a father and son, both named John Wood, and what they planned was neither more nor less than a Roman town, with a 'forum' for assemblies and a 'circus' for sports meetings. The English edition of Palladio had been published in 1715, and excavation of the Roman baths began in the middle of the 18th century. The Palladianism of the Woods, however, like that of Inigo Jones before them, turned out to be completely English. And yet their architecture, the Georgian wonder of Bath, was in fact the result of what was largely a speculative building enterprise.

Around 1700 Bath had about 3000 inhabitants. By 1810, the number had grown to 30,000. The flood of prosperous visitors and the swiftly rising population triggered a housing boom which gripped contemporary speculators like the gambling fever which was the other passion of the age. Architects such as the Woods were

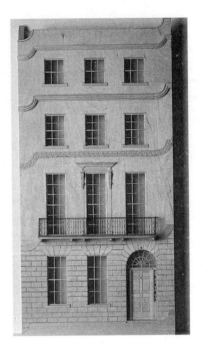

Façades of Bath: models from the Building of Bath Museum

also entrepreneurs, and they invested enthusiastically in the new game. They found building land, leased it from the owners – generally for 99 years – then in turn leased the land to clients, who duly engaged them as architects, and rented or sold the houses they built. Building needed to be swift and economical. The fact that the results are so beautiful and so solid, and that despite the large number of individual speculators the overall effect is so uniform and well integrated, is perhaps the real miracle of Bath.

The Georgian houses which are to be seen all over the town are marvels of common sense. For all their elegance, they are basically very simple, at once both splendid and modest. Most of them have five storeys, with flat windows that are flush with the facades, and closed off by horizontal mansards rather than pointed roofs. Columns, pilasters, friezes and other forms of decoration are used regularly but never excessively. Here we have understatement in stone, the beauty of plainness. The proportions are strikingly harmonious. the gaps perfectly calculated, distance and intimacy exquisitely balanced. And yet these aesthetic delights are largely the result of sound economics. Tall, narrow terraced houses were the most profitable form of architecture, because those who built them had to pay according

Façades of Bath: models from the Building of Bath Museum

to the width of the façade. It therefore made financial sense to build back, up, and even down (with basements). Expensive Bath stone ashlar was mainly used only for the front of the house, whereas rendered rubble sufficed for the rear. The joins on the smooth limestone façades are so fine as to be almost invisible, but even there the Bath stone is often just the thinnest of skins covering walls made of cheaper material. And yet these walls have proved astonishingly durable. Different sized rectangles determine the proportions of the fronts, creating a geometrical harmony that reaches right up to the frames of the sash windows. What a shame that even in this Georgian showtown, many of the sash windows were taken out by modernizing Victorians and sometimes replaced by single panes of plain glass. Fortunately the 1970's-1990's have seen a great many of the original sizes of windows and glass put back, as can be seen, for example, in Queen Square.

The Bath stone, the architect and his pattern books ensured the unified effect of these façades. Choice of individual doorframes was left to the owners. So too was the rear of the house, and even in the finest squares and crescents, the backs are well worth a visit. There you will find a wonderful assortment of balconies, outbuildings, and conservatories. Incidentally, the beautiful iron railings were once resplendent in their Georgian colours of blue, grey and dark green, instead of the widow's black of today.

Most of these houses, which are now divided up into offices and flats, used to accommodate just one family. The average Georgian household consisted of ten to twelve people, with staff generally outnumbering family. The dining and reception rooms would be on the ground floor, the drawing rooms on the grand first floor, and on the third floor were the bedrooms. Servants' and children's rooms would be in the attic, and the kitchen was in the basement. During the building boom, between 1714 and 1830, about 7000 houses were constructed in Bath, and some 5000 are still standing. Over 200 of them were built by the Woods, including some of the finest ensembles of Georgian architecture. And yet when the younger Wood died in 1781, he left his widow nothing but debts.

A stroll through Bath can be quite literally a mounting pleasure: you can start from Pulteney Bridge down at the river, and climb right up to Lansdown Crescent. With shops on both sides, like one long, narrow house on three arches, *Pulteney Bridge* (1) spans the River Avon. It is Bath's Ponte Vecchio, built in 1770 after a design by Robert Adam. *Queen Square* (7) is the first residential area built by John Wood the elder (1729-36), and is as royal as its name. Each side of this square is a spatial unit, and the seven houses on the north side run together to form a single palace front, with rusticated ground floor and attached central pediment, following the example of Covent Garden, which was Inigo Jones's first square in London. Past what may have been John Wood the Younger's own home, the Baroque corner house at 41 Gay Street (1740), you will come to *King's Circus*, which forms a perfect circle of houses. Three streets radiate out of it, and the façades are divided into three orders of twin columns, one on top of the other – Doric, Ionic and Corinthian – which enhance the circular rhythm and at the same time emphasize the gentleness of the horizontal. This was the first circus in England, planned by the elder Wood, begun by his son in 1754 (the year when his father died), and completed thirteen years later. Its influence even spread to Germany, where it was a model for the Königsplatz in Kassel (after 1767). The impression made on Wood's contemporaries by Bath's circus was summed up by the eponymous hero of Smollett's satirical epistolary novel *Humphrey Clinker*: 'like Vespasian's Amphitheatre turned outside in.' In fact underlying Wood's design was the concept of prehistoric stone circles. He believed that Bath was a Druid settlement founded by King Lear's father, the mythical swineherd Bladud, who is commemorated by the stone acorns on the roofs of the Circus. Originally the central area was cobbled. As for the plane trees, they were planted in 1804. If you want to see a typical town garden of 1770, go and look at the restored *Georgian Garden* (9) behind No 4.

King's Circus and *Royal Crescent* (10): Any French or Italian town-planner would have created an axial link between these two showpieces. Wood, however, takes us almost casually along Brock Street before suddenly, without a single

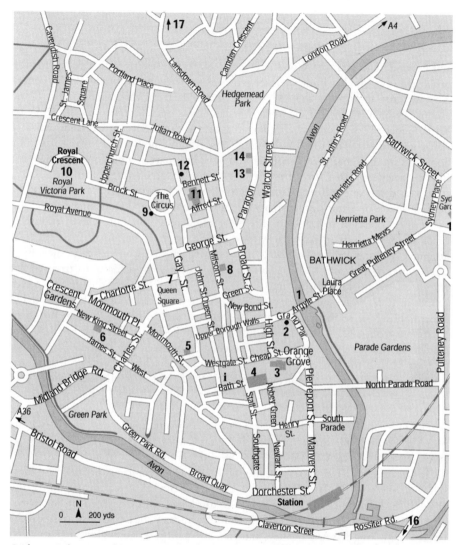

Bath 1. Pulteney Bridge 2. Victoria Art Gallery 3. Bath Abbey 4. Roman Baths and Pump Rooms 5. Theatre Royal 6. Herschel House Museum 7. Queen Square 8. National Centre of Photography 9. Georgian Garden 10. Royal Crescent 11. Assembly Rooms (Costume Museum) 12. Museum of East Asian Art 13/14. Building of Bath Museum 15. Holburne Museum 16 Prior Park 17. Lansdown Crescent and Beckford's Tower

warning sign, confronting us with his masterpiece. The shock makes the beauty all the more breathtaking (col. pl. 29). The houses form a single unit – a sickle-shaped façade, 605 feet long, with 114 monumental Ionic columns. This mass of stone seems almost to be in motion, as it opens out into the encircling frame of the countryside, down the green hill above Bath and the Avon, and as far as Beechen Cliff and beyond. The younger Wood does not seek to impress us with a palace for the privileged few – he has built a terrace which is a palace for everyone. But of course even in those days, only the seriously rich could afford these houses. No 1, for example, which is now the Georgian Museum, was once occupied by the Duke of York, George III's second son. Today an apartment in the Royal Crescent will cost you a good quarter of a million pounds, and a whole house (only seven have not been split up into apartments) will set you back best part of a million and a quarter. If you haven't got that sort of money, but can manage one night of royal luxury, then go and stay at the Royal Crescent Hotel, with a view over Victoria Park and its daily spectacle of picnickers, footballers, courting couples and frolicking dogs.

This first crescent in England (1767-74) has been copied and varied countless times since, not least in Bath itself, most strikingly with *Lansdown Crescent* (17), designed by John Palmer (1789-92). His convex-concave-convex front takes up a Borromini rhythm, and it also affords a magnificent view of Bath. In front of the entrances are the old cast iron lamp overthrows – as old, that is as the Queen's Silver Jubilee in 1977, when they were restored in celebration. (Each house had to provide street lighting for so many hours until a specified time at night.) William Beckford lived here from 1823 – after selling Fonthill Abbey – until his death in 1844. The gardens of this lonely, eccentric man stretched from his house 'Baghdad' for a mile up Sion Hill to the highest point on Lansdown. There he had a new, neoclassical tower built by Henry E. Goodridge, only half the height of Fonthill, crowned by an octagonal lantern of wood and cast iron columns (1825-27). Every morning Beckford used to go riding on his grey Arab, accompanied by five servants and six greyhounds, all the way to his tower. His sole companion otherwise was Perro, the dwarf of Fonthill. He spent his time editing his diaries and collecting more art treasures and rare books. William Beckford lies buried at the foot of his tower, next to his favourite dogs Tout and Tiny, in a pink granite sarcophagus designed by himself. Eccentric to the last, Beckford had himself buried in a tumulus above the ground, in the manner of the old Anglo-Saxon kings whose descendant he considered himself to be. In 1848 his park became a cemetery, beautifully situated on the ridge overlooking the Avon valley, and adorned with weeping willows of stone and other Victorian monuments.

In 1762, long before Beckford's tower, Ralph Allen built a real folly across the way on Bathwick Hill. *Sham Castle* is a wall with turrets and battlements and nothing behind except a golf course. It is a stage set pure and simple, which created a delightfully romantic castle view for Bath's postmaster when he looked out of his window in town. To Ralph Allen, however, we owe a great deal more than this, the craziest prospect of 'England's Florence'. He was the Woods' patron, and they

16. Pavilion at Montacute House

*17. Gold Hill in Shaftesbury, with
a view of Blackmoor Vale*

18. Late Norman south portal, Sherborne Abbey

19. Misericord, Sherborne Abbey

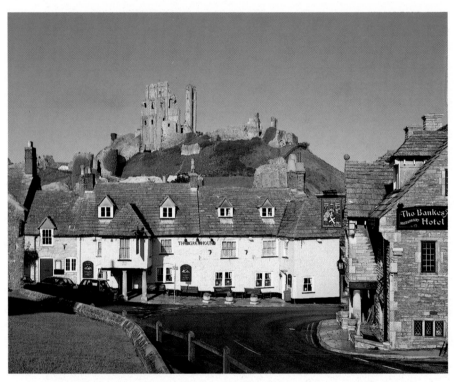

24. Corfe Castle

23. Previous page: Kingston Lacy

25. Medieval dovecote, Dunster

26. Hestercombe

27. Medusa head, Roman Bath Museum

28. Roman bath, Bath

29. Royal Crescent, Bath

30. Abbey Church, Bath

*31. Heavenly ladder,
Bath Abbey*

32. St Lawrence Church, Bradford-on-Avon

extracted their wonderful Bath stone from his quarries in Combe Down. This oolitic limestone, with its soft tinge of yellow-grey, gives the town a special tone. The Woods regarded it an ideal building material, 'fit for the Walls of a Palace for the Greatest Prince in Europe'. Colen Campbell disagreed, sying it was 'as soft as Cheshire Cheese.' This makes it perfect for carving detail, but vulnerable to weathering. As a sort of advertisement for his stone, which he had hoped to sell throughout the kingdom, Ralph Allen built the nearby country house of *Prior Park* (16), a Palladian villa in the grand style, which the elder Wood designed for him (1735-50). There Allen received his many guests, who included writers like Pope, Richardson and Fielding. Henry Fielding, who was married in the village church at Charlcombe in 1734, portrayed his friend Allen in the character of Squire Allworthy in his novel *Tom Jones* (1749). Prior Park has been a Catholic school since 1830, and the park is run by the National Trust. If you go down into the fields of the valley, you will come to two lakes, spanned by a magnificent Palladian bridge (1755), a relic of Bath's Golden Age.

The rise of Bath from a small provincial town to the eminence of Royal Bath, Georgian City, was due not to a king nor to an architect, but to a dandy whose sole expertise lay in the rules of the gambling tables and of the salons. So proficient was he in these that he earned the title 'King of Bath'. His name was Richard 'Beau' Nash. Understandably, Nash was not content with the mere fact that Bath possessed the only hot mineral springs in England, whose waters were naturally diuretic and offered countless other medical benefits to the sick and suffering. People also had to be entertained, but always according to the rules of art and etiquette, the rules of Richard Beau Nash. If a gentleman stepped onto the dance floor in riding boots, he would be asked by Mr Nash if perhaps he had forgotten to bring his horse. Always dressed in a very shabby blue or pink, gold-braided coat and a white three-cornered hat, and armed with a Shakespearian wit,

Beau Nash

Nash became Master of Ceremonies in 1705, presiding over the social life of Bath, which year by year became more and more fashionable. It was Nash more than anyone who transformed the spa into the kingdom's top marriage market and gambling den – or Satan's Headquarters, as the enraged John Wesley called it. Johanna Schopenhauer described him as a 'remarkable man, who knew how to endow the worst triviality with a touch of greatness'. His was 'an existence centred on a shining nothing', and it lived 'only on the favour of the moment, creating a huge, almost immortal monument to this moment, because one of the most beautiful cities in Europe owes her existence to it.' Indeed, without the Nash spirit of good taste, what would all these circuses, crescents and squares be now except elegant fossils of stone? In the Abbey Church (3), his memorial proclaims him *Elegantiae Arbiter*. He spent his last years in the house adjoining the Theatre Royal, now a restaurant called Popjoy's. When he died in 1761, at the age of 87, his mistress Juliana Popjoy

Pulteney Bridge

vowed never to sleep in a bed again, and ended her days collecting herbs and living in a large hollow tree in Wiltshire.

Beau Nash's most popular legacy is the *Pump Room* (4), which he opened a year after he took office (the present building dates from 1786). There people met to stroll around, gossip, and 'take the water in style', with musical accompaniment. Today the Pump Room Trio play while you sip your tea, and Beau Nash himself looks down on you through marble eyes. The large Tompion clock of 1709 is still there, and the unsuspecting tourist can buy a glass of holy water for 45p – those *eaux terribles* of which Sam Weller says in *Pickwick Papers*: 'I thought they'd a wery strong flavour o' warm flat irons.'

About a century before Beau Nash, a traveller from London, also a great pleasure-lover, came to enjoy the good life of Bath. On 12 June 1668, Samuel Pepys wrote in his diary: 'Up at four o' clock, being by appointment called up to the Cross Bath; where we were carried one after one another, myself, and wife ... much company came; very fine ladies; and the manner pretty enough, only methinks it cannot be clean to go so many bodies together in to the same water. Good conversation among them that are acquainted here, and stay together. Strange to see how hot the water is; and in some places, though this is the most temperate bath, the springs so hot as the feet not able to endure. But strange to see, when women and men herein, that live all the season in these waters, that cannot but be parboiled, and look like the creatures of the bath! Carried back, wrapped in a sheet, and in a chair, home; and there one after another thus carried (I staying above two hours in the water), home to bed, sweating for an hour; and by and by, comes musick to play to me, extraordinary good as ever I heard at London almost, or anywhere: 5s. Up, to go to Bristoll, about eleven o' clock.' Thus even for those who were only on the way through, a stylish stop in Bath was *de rigueur*.

At least once every season a star was born. The twelve-year-old Thomas Lawrence dazzled with his portrait-painting; Sarah Siddons triumphed on stage with her Shakespeare and off stage with her beauty; the organist Herschel from Hanover looked out of his garden observatory at No. 19 New King Street in 1781 (6), and discovered a new planet, Uranus. A few streets away and a few years earlier, at No. 17 The Circus, Gainsborough first made his mark as a high society portrait artist. He spent fifteen years in Bath and in the country houses around the city, from 1759 till 1774. At first he charged five guineas for a portrait, but he finished up charging a hundred. In *Holburne Museum* (15) are his portraits of two prominent local doctors. To the coachman Walter Wiltshire, who transported Gainsborough's pictures to London free of charge because he liked them so much, the artist gave one of his most important works of that time, the *Harvest Waggon* (1767, now in Birmingham). In those days Wiltshire's 'Flying Coaches' took two and a half days to get to Bath from London. Today the train does it in 70 minutes from Paddington.

Ever since Chaucer's Wife of Bath, she of the five husbands, went on her pilgrimage to Canterbury, the city has been an inexhaustible source of tales and characters for the literary world. The same society that sat for Gainsborough also recognized with amusement its own image in Sheridan's comedy *The School for Scandal* (1777), the dramatist having spent much of his youth in Bath. In fact he only narrowly survived a duel there, after running off (in a sedan chair) with the beautiful singer Elizabeth Linley, who lived at No. 11 Royal Crescent. 'Oh, who can ever be tired of Bath?' asks Catherine Morland in Jane Austen's *Northanger Abbey* (1818). She lodged in Great Pulteney Street, a splendid row of houses rhythmically punctuated with Corinthian pilasters, started by Thomas Baldwin in 1789. Lady Dalrymple in *Persuasion* (1818) lived in the diamond-shaped Laura Place, and Jane Austen herself lived in Bath for five years, without ever feeling quite at home there. In her novels she portrays the *parvenu* not-so-high society of Regency Bath, for in the meantime Prinny had made Brighton the place for the upper class to be seen in. Even back in those days, Jane Austen complains vehemently about the chaotic traffic, with riders, coaches, carts and Bath chairs all jostling for position. The Bath chair was a three-wheeled, roofed contraption invented by one of the town's own citizens, James Heath, and after 1750 it replaced the sedan chair as a common form of transport which visitors would hire just as they hire taxis today.

'Instead of that peace, tranquillity, and ease, so necessary to those who labour under bad health, weak nerves, and irregular spirits,' we are told in Smollett's *Humphrey Clinker*, 'here we have nothing but noise, tumult and hurry, with the fatigue and slavery of maintaining a ceremonial, more stiff, formal and oppressive, than the etiquette of a German elector. A national hospital it may be; but one would imagine, that none but lunatics are admitted; and truly I will give you leave to call me so, if I stay much longer at Bath.' Not everyone agreed: 'every upstart of fortune, harnessed in the trappings of the mode, presents himself at Bath, as in the very focus of observation.' 'Follow the famous to Bath' was the town postmark's plea. Where else in England could the celebrity-hunters of the 18th and 19th centuries have found so many gods and goddesses, and what better way could there be to study this town than to go from house to house? 'The whole city is an enormous hotel garni,' observed Johanna Schopenhauer in wonderment. In July 1939, shortly before the beginning of World War II, the immigrant Stefan Zweig moved from London to Bath. The landscape reminded him of his native Salzkammergut. 'I retreated to Bath, and precisely to Bath because this city, where many of the best authors of England's glorious literature wrote their works – Fielding above all – presents more faithfully and more impressively than any other town in England a different, more peaceful century, the eighteenth, to the soothed eye.' Stefan Zweig and his wife bought Rosemount, a house on Lyncombe Hill, but even here he was unable to find the peace and quiet he longed for. One year later, their flight from the Nazis took them to South America.

The annual Bath Festival in May and the mild winter climate ensure that Bath still gets its fair share of celebrities. Erica Jong lived here for a while in the late seventies, researching her novel *Fanny*. She confessed to having had more dreams in Bath than anywhere else in the world. Van Morrison has a house in St James Square, where Dickens once stayed. The city is home to the film director Ken Loach, many media people, designers and computer buffs, not to mention thousands of students. Bristol folk used to say that old people never die and young people never live in Bath, but they can't say that today.

Even if Bath no longer revels in its uniqueness as a spa, it has acquired another enviable cachet as the top rugby club in the country. Since the game first introduced national league tables and a cup, Bath has dominated all competitions with a record second to none. Whether they can maintain this astonishing supremacy in the new age of professionalism remains to be seen, but the club has already secured its place in rugby history.

Tourists, buskers, pedlars all make their way to the area around the Pump Room and the *Abbey Church* (3) (col. pl. 30). This church is crammed full with memorials to a degree matched only by Westminster Abbey. It is a kind of communal mausoleum for the famous and not-so-famous people who have been to Bath. But the greatness of this former bishop's seat – where the Anglo-Saxon cathedral stood in which Edgar, the first king of all England, was crowned in 973 – does not rest on these generally mediocre monuments (apart from those designed by Flaxman and Chantrey). Sometimes called 'The Lantern of the West', the Abbey's chief glory is its windows, large and numerous, and its fan vault.

In 1499 Bishop Oliver King, wanting to rebuild the church, claimed to have had a dream in which angels descended to him from heaven on ladders and told him, 'Let an Olive establish the crown and let a King restore the church'. The bishop interpreted this as a divine command to support Henry VII and rebuild Bath Abbey. His rebus – an olive tree surrounded by a crown – is on the west front.

The royal stonemasons Robert and William Vertue promised that they would build the finest vault in England for the bishop, but it is lifeless compared to their work in Henry VII's chapel in Westminster and St George's Chapel in Windsor. On the west front of this Late Perpendicular Church (16th century), above the massive oak portal (1617), there are angels who in all winds and weathers climb up and down stone ladders – just as Bishop King saw in his dream (col. pl. 31). The 600 or so memorials in the Abbey Church led a local doctor to coin the following epigram: 'My lords and my ladies,/ The graves you see here/ Are proof that Bath's waters/ Give no panacea.'

Prior Park and bridge

Let us finish our journey to Bath by returning to its beginnings. These lie more than ten millennia back and ten miles away in the Mendip Hills. Geologists have discovered that a U-shaped band of limestone links the Mendips to Bath. For thousands of years, rainwater has seeped through this gigantic filter down to a depth of 14,110 feet, being heated on the way and enriched with radioactive gases and 43 different minerals, until natural pressure forces it back to the surface into the grateful embrace of the City of Bath. It arrives there after its 10,000-year journey – which after all is considerably quicker than the light from dead stars – and makes its way to the Pump Room, where we may at last drink the rain that once fell upon our Stone Age ancestors.

The legendary discoverer of the springs, the royal swineherd Bladud, was cured of his leprosy here. The rest is history. The natural healing offered by the goddess Sul led to the creation of the luxurious Roman spa of *Aquae Sulis*. Around 54 AD the Romans built a temple to Minerva and a thermal bath for themselves, half open-air with an elaborate system of hot and cold baths, lead piping and hypocaust heating. The emperors Trajan and Hadrian are said to have visited these baths, but when the Romans withdrew, the system disappeared into the marshes. And there the *Roman Baths* remained undisturbed until in 1728 the gilded bronze head of Minerva was discovered, followed in 1790 by parts of the temple. The site of the inner temple of the Roman city has finally been restored, some sixteen feet below the present Georgian Pump Room (col. pls. 27 & 28).

There, the King's Spring continues to provide a ceaseless flow of hot water, 46 degrees Celsius, over a million litres a day. The name of the town is perfectly apt, for a bath it is. But in 1978, a girl died of meningitis after bathing in these waters, and the whole facility was closed down. A new spa centre, designed by Nicholas Grimshaw – a five-storey glass block in the heart of the town that will provide leisure facilities and hydrotherapy, using unpolluted hot springs water – is planned for Easter 2000, and who knows, if another Beau Nash were to come upon the scene, the old glory might yet return.

Present-day Bath is home to 85,000 inhabitants. New buildings have tended to go up on the southern bank of the Avon, but they have never been the high-rise monstrosities of other cities. If you search, however, for modern architecture that is even approximately of the same rank as that of the Woods, you will search in vain. Instead you will find The Podium, supermarket and library all under one roof, a Neo-Georgian monolith beside Pulteney Bridge, built of Bath stone in 1989 but otherwise devoid of all elegance. The shopping centre at Southgate and the Hilton Hotel built in cast stone, with a complete disregard of proportions – these are architectural sins in an architectural Eden.

More than 1000 Georgian houses were demolished here in the 1960's, an act of vandalism which The Bath Preservation Trust fought against and finally put an end to. This trust is one of the oldest in England, has about 1300 members, and is constantly torn between the twin pressures of conservation and commerce, for it is vital that a town with some 5000 listed buildings should not simply turn into a life-less museum: it rehabilitates dilapidated houses, subsidises other restorations, and wages campaigns: for the preservation of traditional shop fronts (successful), against the Batheaston bypass (unsuccessful). This A46 bypass destroyed yet another great chunk of countryside, and served to aggravate Bath's already notorious traffic prob-lems. Relentlessly, the exhaust fumes eat away at the city's buildings, and in the long run perhaps there is only one solution: to return to the old Georgian coaches and Bath chairs.

Badminton in the Entrance Hall

A glorious seaside resort (the 'Hastings of the West') with Regency terraces, Italianate, Tudoresque, even Jacobean villas, a most elegant Victorian pier – *Clevedon* was not yet any of these things when the young Coleridge took No. 55 Church Road in 1795 for his honeymoon with Sara Fricker.

> Low was our pretty cot. Our tallest rose
> Peeped at the chamber window. We could hear
> At silent noon, and eve, and early morn,
> The sea's faint murmur. In the open air
> Our myrtles blossomed; and across the porch
> Thick jasmines twined. The little landscape round
> Was green and woody, and refreshed the eye.
> It was a spot which you might aptly call
> The Valley of Seclusion.

Unfortunately they were not alone in the 'Valley of Seclusion', and so they soon escaped from the gossiping neighbours and returned to Bristol. They were followed in 1850 by another famous poet on his honeymoon: Tennyson. Here he visited a dead man up on the cliffs in St Andrew's. In this dark Norman chapel is a simple memorial plaque to his friend from student days, Alfred Hallam, who had died in 1833, tragically young. It had taken Tennyson seventeen years to fin-ish his great funerary poem, *In Memoriam*, which so moved his contemporaries that they came in their hundreds to pay their respects. Turner had also been to Clevedon, chasing the sun-sets. Love, death and sunsets – this is a place for the romantic soul, and even if Poet's Walk or Lover's Walk cannot inspire you to the lyrical heights of a Coleridge or a Tennyson, at least

Tennyson

107

you will know that you are following in famous poetic footsteps.

Hallam was the nephew of the local squire, Sir Charles Elton, a gifted poet and scholar, who was a friend of Clare, Southey, Lamb and Coleridge. The Eltons still live at *Clevedon Court* (now National Trust), whose charming asymmetry reflects the various Tudor and Jacobean changes it has undergone since around 1320. The present Sir Charles Elton has assembled a fascinating collection of pictures, china and all kinds of souvenirs recording the history of the railways. A former Lady Elton specialized in 19th-century Nailsea glass, in weird and wonderful forms such as hats and pipes and walking sticks – 'charmsticks' to ward off evil spirits. Clevedon Court has a Thackeray room, for the 19th-century high-society satirist often enjoyed a high-society stay in this high-society residence, where he fell in love with the married daughter of the house, Jane Octavia, and immortalized her as Lady Castlewood in *Henry Esmond*. Thackeray sketched the family and wrote parts of *Vanity Fair* here (1847/48).

In the old kitchen, where tea is served in the best National Trust mobcap tradition, there is a display of Elton Ware, the pottery created by Edmund Elton around 1900 and sold as far afield as Tiffany's, New York. The same Sir Edmund used his creative flair to make life safer for all late Victorian cyclists: he invented a clip to help ladies keep their dresses out of the wheels, and the Elton Rim Brake was particularly useful for gentlemen going too fast for their own good.

More great country houses stand where the long green chain of the Cotswolds descends in gently curving, forested hills towards Bristol and the Vale of Berkeley. This is what used to be part of the modern county of Avon, and is locally still called Cuba (County that Used to Be Avon). You built your house in a natural landscape and then you invited Capability Brown to make the landscape look even more natural. In 1764 he worked his natural magic on the Codringtons' estate, with winding paths and a waterfall overlooked by a miniature Gothic castle. This was the setting in which James Wyatt began to reconstruct the Elizabethan Dodington House in 1796. He never finished it. After many diversions caused by the construction of the tower at Fonthill, he died in an accident on the Marlborough Downs in 1813 while on a coach journey with his employer. Wyatt's house, which reflected all the grandeur that could accrue with the eager practice of slavery (his patron, Sir Charles Codrington, was an ardent anti-abolitionist) used to be open but is now terribly private. You can get a distant glimpse from the Cotswold Way. A twinkle indicates the conservatory, or winter garden.

The little church at Doddington had a fireplace in the family pew, which is why Queen Mary always came to church here rather than at *Badminton*, the great country house of the Beauforts, where she lived during the war. It was probably a cold, not to mention windy and rainy day in 1850 when two maiden aunts of the Duke of Beaufort, missing their tennis, stretched a net from one side to the other of the columned, plastered hall at Badminton, and proceeded to toss shuttlecocks to each

Badminton House, by Canaletto

other under the eyes of the baroque putti above the doors. From that day on, the game known to colonial officers in India as 'poona' was christened badminton. The dimensions of the first courts were precisely those of the entrance hall at Badminton House. It was not in fact so unusual for such a space to be used for games, because the long galleries in Elizabethan manor houses were often used for fencing parties and all kinds of sporting activities, especially in bad weather.

The house is never open nowadays, but you will catch a glimpse of it during the world famous three-day horse trials. Inside, the house is filled with pictures of horses and hounds, and riding and hunting scenes. When the 3rd Duke of Beaufort came back from a hunt, he wanted to recapture the beauty of the horse or the thrill of the chase in pictures, so he sent a gifted servant, John Wootton, to study painting in Rome. In 1730 he set Wootton up in a studio at Badminton and completely redesigned the entrance hall in order to accommodate his paintings. As one enters, one is confronted by a lifesize grey Berber, as monumental as any historical scene, painted with all the passion and precision of a man who loved horses as much as he loved art. A generation later George Stubbs was to paint the anatomy of the horse, but Wootton painted its apotheosis. Canaletto also visited Badminton, and was commissioned by the 4th Duke to paint two views of the house (1748-50). One shows the Palladian north façade with its two cupolas, and side pavilions, while the other *veduta*, broad in its scale and minute in its detail, depicts the breathtaking view from the north entrance to William Kent's Worcester Lodge (*c.*1746) three miles away. This is the unbounded space of the English park – as opposed to the rounded symmetry of the French – with grey Cotswold stone and vast green lawns. In the Grand Salon, near the Canalettos, are portraits by Reynolds and Lawrence, though the painter who should be remembered here is Gainsborough. His marriage to a natural daughter of the Duke of Beaufort brought him the dowry that allowed him to set up in business. Somewhere among all these treasures is the wax figure of poor Bébé, King Stanislaus' court dwarf who sometimes gave the royal guests a shock at the dining-table by emerging from a large pie.

Without being invited to dine, you will not see the Grinling Gibbons animal and fruit still lives that adorn the dining room. But there is plenty more of Gibbons' work in the church on the estate, which can be visited. Lord Raglan of the Light Brigade is buried here.

Gibbons was born in Rotterdam, and the connection with Holland in the age of William and Mary is also reflected in nearby *Dyrham Park* (also National Trust). Dyrham was built by William Blathwayt, William of Orange's Secretary of State, who collected Flemish tapestries and leather, wall hangings, Delftware, and the then modern Dutch interiors by Samuel van Hoogstraeten, which were so admired by Blathwayt's friend Samuel Pepys. Nevertheless the front entrance is a classic example of Franco-Italian baroque, a palazzo with rustic and attic storeys designed in 1698 by William Talman, who served under Wren as Comptroller of the Royal Works. Inside, the staircase now contains allegorical ceiling paintingsof *c.* 1754 by the Roman-trained Andrea Casali, which were once at Fonthill.Talman's greenhouse (1701) is one of the first English orangeries to be joined directly to the house, copying that at Versailles.

Bristol

For the youngsters the nineties sound was a Bristol sound – the digital Bristol Blues by a band named Portishead. The older generation may prefer another kind of blue: Bristol Blue, a darkly glowing cobalt-coloured glass. And the whole world is united in its appreciation of Bristol Cream, the sherry produced by Harveys of Bristol. The name of the city is a brand name in itself, and yet Bristol has a bad reputation: the 18th-century slave trade, and the 1980 riots that signalled all the social problems that would lead to the later inner city unrest in Liverpool and Brixton.

Bristol's literary image also follows a certain tradition: in Chapter 38 of *Pickwick Papers*, Mr Winkle visited the city and it 'struck him as being a shade more dirty than any place he had ever seen'. Virginia Woolf saw it in 1935, found its horrors indescribable, and called it 'the most hideous of all towns'.

Until the late eighties, even the city council saw no reason to promote Bristol to tourists. Why visit a port on the Avon when just twelve miles upriver you could go to the World Heritage City of Georgian Bath? Overshadowed by her gorgeous little sister, industrial, working-class Bristol even forgot her own architectural jewels – the Georgian elegance of Clifton, the Victorian warehouses on the docks, and quite apart from the industrial buildings, two churches which are among the finest examples of English Gothic. The city has more than 3500 listed buildings, and no less a judge than Sir John Betjeman proclaimed that Bristol had 'the finest architectural heritage of any city outside London'.

Blue Glass and the Slave Trade: A Trip Round the Port

On the quayside in front of the Arnolfini Gallery sits the bronze figure of a man gazing out to the west. Every schoolchild has heard of John Cabot, and knows that he discovered America – it's a fact as obvious as driving on the left. Bristol's most famous sailor was actually an immigrant from Venice, born Giovanni Caboto. On the orders of Henry VII he set sail on 2 May 1497 from the Narrow Quay, and

Bristol Cathedral, by J. Salmon, engraved by B. Winkles

Bristol
1. Museum of Britain and the World
   (projected)
2. The Exploratory Science Centre
3. St Mary Redcliffe
4. Thomas Chatterton's birthplace
5. Arnolfini Arts Centre
6. Theatre Royal
7. Watershed Media Centre
8. Cathedral
9. Lord Mayor's Chapel
10. Harvey's Wine Museum
11. Georgian House
12. St George's
13. Cabot Tower
14. City Museum and Art Gallery
15. Royal West of England Academy
16. University
17. Red Lodge
18. Christmas Steps
19. Old Council House
20. Corn Exchange
21. John Wesley's New Room
22. Bristol Industrial Museum
23. Maritime Heritage Centre
24. SS Great Britain
25. Clifton Cathedral
26. Clifton Suspension Bridge

went down the Avon and out into the open sea. His ship was the *Matthew*, an 80-foot oak caravel with a crew of barely twenty men. When they sighted land after 54 days, John Cabot recorded it in his logbook and simply named the place New Founde Land. Thus he was the first European to reach the North American mainland, whereas Columbus only got to a few offshore islands. As far as Bristol and the rest of the realm were concerned, this was the discovery of America, and of a new sea and trading route which was a very welcome contribution in the colonial struggle against Spain and Portugal. The importance of this port on the west coast had already been recognized by Edward III in 1373, when he made it one of the very

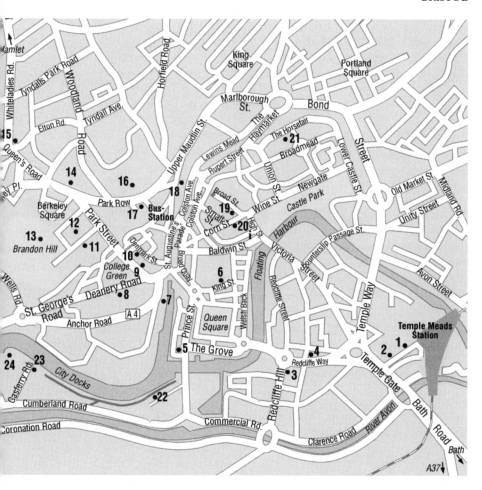

few medieval towns to be granted the status of a county. It retained this status right up until 1974, when the authorities created the ever unpopular county of Avon. Only in the very latest local government reforms of 1996 did Bristol regain its administrative autonomy.

It is said that the leaning tower of Temple Church is built on sacks of wool. Such anecdotes serve to illustrate the fact that the prosperity of this town in the Middle Ages rested on the cloth trade. Bristol exported wool and imported wine: claret from France, port from Portugal. Even the dreadful slave trade of the 18th century was based on a triangular system which Bristol's merchants found to be the most profitable: in West Africa they exchanged cloth and cheap jewellery for slaves, whom they sold in North America and the Caribbean, returning with shiploads of cotton, sugar, tobacco and rum. This appalling commerce remains part of Bristol's hidden history, increasingly discussed, not least by Bristol's vocal black community, redressing years of silence. In St Mary's churchyard at Henbury, in the north-west of the city, the Earl of Suffolk buried his black servant Scipio Africanus. He died in 1720 at the age of 18, and is commemorated by a rhyming couplet: 'I who was born a Pagan and a Slave / Now sweetly sleep a Christian in my grave.' Bristol is a river port, some six miles away from the sea. The early merchant ships used to sail up the river into the centre of the town, and there they would drop anchor right between the houses, 'in the middle of the street, as far as you can see, hundreds of ships, their masts as thick as they can stand by one another ...' This was Alexander Pope's description of a sight that visitors regarded as the embodiment of Bristol's wealth. According to Daniel Defoe, at the beginning of the 18th century there were 3000 ships registered here, and Bristol was second only to London as the most prosperous town in England. *Virtute et Industria* (By virtue and industry) proclaims the city's coat of arms.

At the beginning of its Georgian heyday, Bristol was given a separate harbour area south of the old city, in a horseshoe bend between the rivers Frome and Avon. Its centre was *Queen Square*, which was designed in 1699, and at the time was bigger than all the squares in London except Lincoln's Inn Fields. There the rich Bristol merchant had his house, with a courtyard behind, and at the end of this a warehouse looking out onto the quay or, in the west, onto Prince Street. This was built at the same time (1700-30), and here too merchants had their magnificent homes on one side, and their tall warehouses on Narrow Quay opposite. Of these early storehouses, based on Dutch designs, only two have survived in Prince Street, both of them radically altered. Such buildings were swiftly replaced by bigger ones, mainly for corn, as exemplified by the *Seed Warehouse* on the Welsh Back, at the corner of Little King Street (col. pl. 36). This showpiece (1878) of the Victorian penchant for the Byzantine, or 'round-arch' style is richly decorated with a multi-coloured brick façade, the eponymous round arches, fishtail balustrades and walls ornately pierced for ventilation.

To see a merchant's house as it was in its heyday, go to No. 7 Great George Street on Brandon Hill, built between 1787 and 1791 for the sugar merchant John Pinney. Pinney made his fortune from large plantations on Nevis, and the house, beautifully restored and refurnished, also has an exhibition about the slave trade. Wordsworth and his sister Dorothy were friends of the family and stayed here in 1795 – but did they share their host's enthusiasm for cold water plunge baths?

Incomprehensibly, Queen Square was vandalised in 1935, when the corner houses were torn down, and a four-lane road was built diagonally across the park, with Rysbrack's bronze statue of William III (1732-36) left isolated on a traffic island.

The riot in Queen Square, 1831

Happily, the traffic has now been diverted and the square is being restored as a park. The square was also badly bombed in the Second World War, but the worst damage was inflicted during the 1831 riots protesting against the slow progress of the Reform Act through Parliament. Three days of fighting, looting and arson left 150 people dead and 50 houses burnt; the few original 1702 houses left in the square are of brick while those that had to be rebuilt are of stone. The finest Georgian houses are on the south side (No. 29). Neighbouring King Street has also retained just enough of its old-town atmosphere for the one-legged Long John Silver from Stevenson's *Treasure Island* to head straight for his favourite pub, the 'Spy Glass'. This might have been the 'Llandoger Trow' (1669), a timber-framed inn with a triple gable, picturesque enough to be the setting for many a sailor's yarn. Daniel Defoe is said to have met Alexander Selkirk here, the model for Robinson Crusoe.

On cobbled King Street stands the longest continually running theatre (1766) in England, the *Theatre Royal* (6). Sarah Siddons, Edmund Kean, the Kembles, Ellen Terry and all the great stars down through the ages have trodden the boards of what is still one of the finest provincial theatres in England. Peter O'Toole and Jeremy

Entrance to the Theatre Royal, in 1822

Irons began their careers nearby at the Bristol Old Vic Theatre School, and they no doubt revelled in the Bordeaux-red, blue and gold Georgian interior, intimate and at the same time resplendent, with its boxes and galleries curved round the horseshoe-shaped auditorium. Even the Victorian stage machinery has survived, though it is no longer in use. Nearly a hundred Bristol merchants originally contributed substantial sums – £30 or £50 each – to build this theatre, total cost £5000, equivalent today to about £350,000. In gratitude for this sponsorship, they were given a silver token guaranteeing them and their heirs 'the sight of every performance to be exhibited in this house' – though not necessarily a seat. The almshouses and the old people's homes (there are two of these in King Street alone) are impressive testimony to the social awareness of the rich folk of that time. The 1445 Merchants Venturers' almshouses are still administered by the same society and still house old sailors as originally intended, while the 1656 St Nicholas almshouses now house young disadvantaged people.

Today there are no merchant ships at anchor in the harbour. Instead you will see yachts, floating restaurants, and narrow boats – the bright houseboats of today's leisure captains. Baltic Wharf, where wood imported mainly from Scandinavia used to be unloaded, is now a school for sailing and wind-surfing. If you want the authentic smell of oil and dockyards, you will have to go to the *Industrial Museum*

(22) on Prince's Wharf. There you will find the last five cranes of all those that once lined the docks and quays. Today Bristol's port has gone downstream to the mouth of the Avon. The docks at Avonmouth and Royal Portbury were privatised in 1991, and it is there that all the container and merchant ships are unloaded.

This was a development that could not be halted even by the *Floating Harbour* built in 1809, which had locks at both ends to enable ships to go in and out at low tide. The extreme levels of tides in the Bristol Channel – some 40 feet – scared away the ever-expanding ocean steamers, and even before the turn of the 19th century Liverpool had taken over as the country's main port. The decline of the docks began in the 1960's; Bristol's Floating Harbour was finally closed to commercial shipping, and the inner city docklands were left to disintegrate. The three monumental tobacco warehouses (1906-19) at the entrance – though in fact nowadays put to good use as storage facilities and to house the Bristol Records Office, as well as the city council's environment centre – stand there like abandoned fortresses. Once they held enough tobacco, apparently, to keep England's smokers happy for two years. Imperial Tobacco used to employ 3000 people, but now the number is down to 100. The Wills family, the original tobacco kings of Bristol, left other marks on the city, including the bombastic *Wills Memorial Tower* (16) in Queen's Road (1925), the neo-gothic centre of the university which they so richly endowed.

When Bristol lost its ships and its heavy industry, and then stopped producing railway engines and motor cycles, the seafarers turned their attention to the skies. In the entrance hall of the City Museum hangs one of the bi-planes used by those Magnificent Men in their Flying Machines. The 'crates' were built in Bristol, and later so were Harrier jets and Tornado bombers and Concorde. In the mid 1980's British Aerospace and Rolls Royce in Filton employed some 21,000 people; today this has dwindled to about half that number.

'From John Cabot to Concorde': thus does the 'City of Adventure and Innovation' seek to attract new enterprises to its friendly embrace. Media and computer firms have indeed moved in – Wallace and Gromit were born here – and, next to London Bristol is also the biggest insurance centre in the country. Furthermore, it is the world's champion producer of hot-air balloons. Fry's chocolate was established here in 1728 – the playwright Christopher Fry stems from this Quaker family – but the company has now been taken over by Cadbury's. Courage beer comes from here, as does Harvey's Bristol Cream. In Denmark Street, down in the 13th-century cellars where John Harvey's uncle Thomas Urch first began his wine business in 1796, there is now a gourmet restaurant with a selection of 350 wines and a superb *Wine Museum* (10). Harvey's have recently started bottling their sherry as Bristol sherry should be bottled – in 'Bristol Blue', the blue glass that was so fashionable around 1800, and is still made here (though not only in Bristol any more). It took its name from the fact that a Bristol merchant had the import monopoly on the cobalt oxide from Saxony which gave the glass its special colour.

119

You can go to see the glass being blown at the site of the *SS Great Britain*.

Just around the corner from Harveys is the Bristol Hippodrome theatre. Designed by Frank Matcham, it is Edwardian and has the largest provincial stage in the country. A certain Archibald Leech (b. Bristol, 1904) was callboy at the theatre before he went to Hollywood and became Cary Grant.

Not far from here lies another Bristol. It begins just behind the Broadmead shopping centre, in *St Paul's* and *Easton*. This is the poor, inner city and it stretches out into the desolate fringes of *Hartcliffe* and *Knowle West*. About 40% of the people here are unemployed, and over half of the younger generation are without a job. The quality of housing is well below the national average, and the infant mortality well above. Recession, depression, drugs, unemployment – the mixture is potentially explosive. In April 1980, it did explode. It happened in St Paul's, and the nation was stunned. Later the same thing happened in other deprived areas of England: there was fighting in the streets, looting, cars and houses set on fire. St Paul's is the red light district of Bristol, where half the population is black. From their ranks came the first black mayor of Bristol, Jim Williams – originally from Jamaica – who was elected in 1990. But the riots that took place in St Paul's were caused by problems of class, not race, and it was the same in the working-class area of Hartcliffe in 1992. Two years later, the Tory government in London – which had brusquely turned down a plea for aid from the Labour-run City Council – finally agreed to finance a programme to improve living conditions in Hartcliffe.

'The politics of despair' was how a professor from Middlesex University described these riots. It was the same message that had been delivered over and over again, loud if not always clear, by Tricky, the rapper from Knowle East. 'Nobody loves me', 'All for nothing' sang Beth Gibbons, who comes from the coastal suburb of Portishead. It was she more than anyone, with the digital soul-duo of her eponymous band Portishead, who made the icy, melancholic Bristol Sound into an international hit.

When I first visited Bristol in the early 1970's, the docks were a wasteland in the centre of the city. Today they are a unique leisure centre, the attraction for locals and tourists alike. And yet the town planners in their wisdom had actually planned to fill them in. This act of sheer folly was prevented by the Bristol Civic Society, which is far more than an ordinary conservation group. Thanks to their efforts, restoration began on Bristol's historic port in the mid 1980's, and the docks are at the very heart of a whole programme to revitalise the city centre.

The former warehouses became offices and flats, and in moved art galleries and businesses, restaurants, bars and boutiques. Where wine was once stored at St Augustine's Reach, the *Watershed Media Centre* (7) now presents films, videos and photo exhibitions. Diagonally opposite stands the *Arnolfini Gallery* (5), Bristol's home of the avant-garde. In the best downtown manner of the true artist, it moved there in 1975, when the whole area was still a mess. The building, at the end of the

Narrow Quay, had once been used to store tea. With its mixed media programme, the Arnolfini soon became one of the finest contemporary art galleries in England. The café-bar was designed by the painter Bruce McLean, and if the new heart of the city is beating anywhere, this is the place.

The most prominent corner of the port, the tip of *Canon's Marsh*, is occupied by Lloyd's Bank in two flat-topped, round buildings – a poor piece of town-planning and a mediocre piece of architecture (Arup Associates 1990). Once occupied by the Augustinians, situated behind the Cathedral, Canon's Marsh is the meatiest section of the harbourside development, and by the new millennium this industrial waste-land is due to be transformed, with new homes, new jobs, a science museum, centre for the performing arts and virtual reality zoo. This is one of the largest Millennium projects in the country outside London, and has garnered £42 million from the Lottery Fund.

Let's go on a trip in one of the yellow water taxis, the *Emily* or the *Independence* – old launches which have now started a new ferry service around the docks, from Temple Meads Station in the east to the lock at the western end of the Floating Harbour two and a half miles away. It's a nice leisurely way of following the bends in the harbour and the history of the city, going past old warehouses and new settle-ments, from Redcliffe Backs to Baltic Wharf, and no matter where we step ashore, there will always be something to see: an industrial museum (22), a maritime museum (23), and right at the end a real ship (24), Brunel's finest: the *S.S. Great Britain* (see p. 130) And at every stop, the dockers' favourite place: the 'Mardyke', or the 'Pumphouse', or the 'Nova Scotia'. From one of these harbour pubs, the 'Ostrich' at Bathurst Basin, a street of pastel-coloured Georgian houses leads to St Mary Redcliffe.

The Church on the Red Cliffs of the Avon

The tower of *St Mary Redcliffe* (3; col. pl. 40) soars high into the sky above the east-ern docks, and you might at first think that this is Bristol's cathedral. With its magnificent and almost oriental north porch, and more than 1100 golden bosses in its roof, it is an everlasting monument to the wealth of its builders. These were the merchants who had their homes, their docks and their warehouses in this suburb outside the medieval city walls. Originally (1115) recorded as *Blessed Mary of Radclive* and later known as *Our Lady of Recliffe*, this parish church was named after the red sandstone cliffs on the southern bank of the Avon, and was praised by Elizabeth I in 1574 as 'the fairest, goodliest, and most famous parish church in England'. Now the good queen herself stands as a painted 16th-century wooden statue below the tower, globe and sceptre in her hands, the figurehead both of a ship and of an empire. Not far from her, preserved like a holy relic, is the rib of a whale,

North porch, St Mary Redcliffe

said to be a souvenir from John Cabot's voyage to America. In this church Handel played the organ and Hogarth painted three large canvases for the High Altar now in the Tourist Information Centre at St Nicholas. Merchants and mayors, admirals and ship-owners lie buried here in pomp, and outside the southern transept a simple stone commemorates 'The Church Cat, 1912-27'. Apparently she was very musical, and her favourite place was the lap of the organist.

The architectural history of St Mary Redcliffe is still visible, ranging from the sublime Early English of the crocket capitals of the north tower to the Neo-Gothic spire of 1872. The nave received its stone vault (very rare in a parish church) in *c.* 1400, which was the time of Bristol's first golden age of commerce. Between lofty arcades and broad clerestory windows are slender vertical shafts in clusters, rising uninterrupted by capitals from floor to ceiling, where they open out into a lierne vault with a profusion of bosses: Perpendicular at its richest and most original. The knobbly star-shaped tomb recesses in the south aisle (early 14th century), the intricate ogee arches of the north porch (*c.* 1300) – these are unmistakeable trademarks of Bristol's stonemasons. Their masterpiece is the hexagonal interior of the north porch, with its mosque-like doorway covered with stone foliage in which animals, humans and angels meet as in a Garden of Eden. This was the suitably poetic frame

122

for the Romantic Double Wedding of the Year in 1795, when two poet-friends, Samuel Coleridge and Robert Southey (who was the son of a Wine Street merchant) married the sisters Sara and Edith Fricker.

A quarter of a century earlier, the church archives housed above the north porch had been the source of youthful inspiration and youthful suffering for another poet. Thomas Chatterton, imbued with the Gothic spirit, wrote poems which he passed off as the work of a 15th-century monk, pretending that he had found them in St Mary Redcliffe. His ingenious deception, however – unlike the successful Ossian fraud by his contemporary James Macpherson – was very soon discovered. Chatterton went to London, ambitious but poor and disillusioned. He was barely eighteen when he ended his life in 1770 by taking arsenic (col. pl 37). English Romantics worshipped the boy poet as a martyr: 'the marvellous boy,/The sleepless soul that perish'd in its pride' (Wordsworth). He once stood on a pedestal outside the church, dressed in the long gown of Colston scholars. Opposite, beyond the queueing cars, is the house where he was born. There can be few other churches in England so utterly throttled by traffic as St Mary Redcliffe. Bristol's planners after 1945 were obsessed with the motor car, but at least a start is now being made on undoing the damage in certain historical nerve centres of the city. The first step was to close the road to the Cathedral, and to join the latter up again with its green. Next, the road through Queen Square is to be removed, and so perhaps after that they will turn their attention to the 'most famous parish church in England'.

Wesley Preaches and Bristol Sins: The Old City

Bristol's old city centre was badly bombed in the war, and badly rebuilt in the peace. There are a few interesting buildings, but even if you add them together, you still come up with nothing you can call character. The empty green of *Castle Park* with the ruins of St Peter's are a reminder of what was once here – the very heart of the medieval city. Right up until Cromwell's time a mighty fortress stood here to defend the bridge over the Avon; then it became Bristol's main shopping area. Behind it lay *Broadmead,* an old quarter full of workshops and businesses. It all came crashing down in November 1940 under the weight of German bombs. Broadmead was then rebuilt in the monotonous style of the fifties, and a shopping complex – 'The Galleries' (1991) – between the bleak pedestrian zone and Castle Park, is just one more lowlight of Bristol's modern commercial architecture.

In front of the elder John Wood's *Corn Exchange* (1740-43) in Corn Street are four bronze pillars, called 'nails'; here people used quite literally to 'pay on the nail' before the Corn Exchange was built. In the same street Sir Robert Smirke, architect of the British Museum, built the neoclassical *Old Council House* (19; 1822-27), which was the model for the temple-like Victorian banks all around. Near the

Corn Exchange is the indoor market, and behind that, just before Bristol Bridge, stands the church of *St Nicholas*. Once the church of the seafarers, with a fine Gothic crypt, it is now the Tourist Information Centre. In the midst of all the brochures and the handbills and the showcases, the chancel now houses Hogarth's monumental Resurrection Triptych (1755-56, originally in St Mary Redcliffe, see p. 122). This must certainly be the most unusual information centre in Britain.

If you like jigsaw puzzles, you can put together the fragments of the old city and get something like a picture, from the proud Perpendicular tower of St Stephen's Church to Edward Everard's art nouveau façade in *Broad Street* (1901). Everard was a printer, and the fact that on his brightly glazed tiles he paid homage to the inventor of his art with a misprint would certainly have amused 'Gutenburg' (*né* Gutenberg). Broad Street leads out through *St John's Gate*, the only city gate remaining, and one of the few anywhere with a church atop it, to the river Frome, but along Quay Street nothing flows except the traffic, and the river has long since disappeared beneath the road. (There are tentative plans to open it up again and make it decorative; but as much of the river's flow has been diverted, they may be obliged to be content with marking its bed with fountains suplied from the mains: an allegory of a river.) Over on the other bank are the picturesque Christmas Steps (18), which climb up to Park Row. There *Red Lodge* (17; *c.* 1590), the oak-panelled town house of Sir John Young, gives a good idea of how Bristol's merchants lived in Elizabethan times.

Two towering 18th-century characters left their mark on the city: the statesman and philosopher Edmund Burke, and the preacher John Wesley. Burke sought in vain to prevent the loss of the American colonies, and with brilliant speeches and writings fought the pernicious ideas of the French Revolution. A Whig with a classical education, he represented Bristol in Parliament from 1774 till 1780. His statue is one of four to lighten up the dull and faceless city centre, the others being Edward Colston, slave-trader and alms-giver, Neptune, and I. K. Brunel, unrecognisable as a Chaplinesque clown. John Wesley also has a statue, on horseback, for he rode thousands of miles all over the country with Bible in his saddlebag and fire in his heart. It was a fire that inflamed many. Bristol's sins, he would thunder, were idleness and love of money. This was an ideal place for him to build the first Methodist chapel in the world (1739). *Wesley's New Room* (21) lies between Horsefair and Broadmead. The room, originally rectangular, is pale green, with four Tuscan columns bearing an octagonal lantern, and dominating the end wall is a two-storeyed pulpit. Right next to this house of puritanical prayer and preaching, *The Arcade* leads us back into the glittering world of the shopper. It was built in 1825 'for the better use of foot passengers'. Even the pedestrian zone is an old idea.

Flying Ribs and Stars: The Cathedral

If the simplicity of Wesley's Chapel marks one end of the scale, the fantastic forms of Bristol's Anglican *Cathedral* (8) certainly mark the other. Its chancel was a landmark in European architecture, bold in design, perfect in 'spatial imagination' (Pevsner) and decorative wealth. It was begun in 1140 as an Augustinian abbey, and achieved cathedral status only in 1542 through Henry VIII. Its monastic beginnings partly explain the fundamental principles behind its construction: there is no spatial development from the aisles rising to a dominant nave; instead the interior maintains a consistent height throughout. It is a hall church, not a basilica. The precedents were the churches of the mendicant orders and the Cistercians, and also the retrochoirs of English cathedrals such as Salisbury and Winchester. But the Bristol master who began to create the chancel in 1298 – no doubt competing with the recently begun chapter house in Wells – had his own very personal spatial vision, which can catch the breath even today. Instead of there being a triforium and a clerestory, the arcades rise all the way up to the vaulting, giving a clear view to all sides. In the chancel, the compound piers lead straight into the roof, where they link up with liernes to form a stellar vault, which leaps almost playfully over the blind arches in the bays. Here the decorations have become an end in themselves, independent of their structural function. And where the supporting structure is actually exposed – as in the free-flying tie-rib buttresses of the choir aisles – architectural necessity is turned into aesthetic virtue. Between these bridges are pairs of little ribbed vaults, like bat's wings. The inward facing buttresses of the choir aisles are imaginatively matched by the flying ribs in the ante-chapel (or sacristy) of the *Berkeley Chapel* (c. 1305-10), which for once quite literally fly, freely through the air, unconnected by stone cells under a flat ceiling – a motif that may well have inspired Peter Parler for his Central European masterpiece fifty-three years later, Prague Cathedral.

In the Lady Chapel are bizarre, star-shaped monumental recesses for the abbots of Bristol, similar to the tombs in St Mary Redcliffe, and candlesticks given in thanks for the safe return of two ships in 1712, *The Duke* and *The Duchess*, which brought back one unexpected passenger: Alexander Selkirk, the original of Robinson Crusoe. 'Those who went down to the Sea in Ships to be Harbingers of Empire' were chronicled by the first historian of England's destiny, the travel-writing collector, Richard Hakluyt who is commemorated here (he is buried in Westminster Abbey). For more architectural excitement we must go out to the cloister and into the *Chapter House* (c. 1150-70). Here we have the full range of Late Norman virtuosity: blind arcades with intersecting arches, and diagonal trellis work leading to zig-zag patterns in the lunettes – exuberant experiments in geometry. The Cathedral's central tower was built in the 15th century, when the nave was also begun, but it took over 300 years for the nave and west front to be completed.

This task fell to the neo-gothic architect George Edmund Street (1866-88).

Every weekday at 5.15 p.m. a few choristers and even fewer worshippers join for sung Evensong. Like the ritual of the stones, this is a matter of praising God, and it doesn't matter whether people are there or not. At such moments, music and architecture come together in a combined force that with wondrous ease can simply sweep away all the centuries of doubt. But the future is knocking at the door. In March 1994 the Bishop of Bristol ordained 32 deaconesses as priests in this cathedral. It was the first time women had been ordained in Britain – a dramatic counter to protests against 'transvestites in priests' clothing'.

There are two small churches near the Cathedral which are well worth a visit. On College Green, opposite the Council House (1935-56) with its golden unicorns on the roof, stands the *Lord Mayor's Chapel* (St Mark's) (9), which has been the official place of worship for the city fathers since 1722. It was originally the Chapel of the Hospital of the Gaunts, and is the only English church to be owned by a council. Also unique are its windows – fragments of French and Flemish stained glass from Fonthill Abbey, collected by William Beckford and bought by the city when he auctioned them off. Halfway up Park Street is Great George Street, which leads to *Brandon Hill*, where the Cabot Tower (13; 1897) offers the finest view over the city and its port. In this Georgian area Robert Smirke, England's foremost Greek Revivalist, built a Doric temple in 1823. *St George's* (12) was threatened with closure and inevitable ruin in the 1970's, but this little gem was saved by a group of enthusiasts and was made into a recording studio (Radio 3 listeners will know it well). It is occasionally open for concerts: jazz could have no nobler venue.

If, after all these ancient churches, you hanker for something more modern, you will find it in Clifton: the Catholic Cathedral of *St Peter and St Paul* (1973), crowned with a hexagonal pyramid roof that has an expressive concrete top. It was designed by Percy Thomas Partnership, a local firm whose modernity is sufficiently mature for Prince Charles to have commissioned them to build his model town of Poundbury (see p. 58).

Wandering Round the Village: The Terraces of Clifton

On the north bank of the Avon, Hotwell Road leads to Clifton. In the 17th century, the warm springs that gave *Hotwells* its name made the place into a spa that was fashionable enough to attract even London society. The Duchesses of Kent and Marlborough came to stay here, as did writers such as Pope, Fanny Burney and Maria Edgeworth. This was the start of a building boom around 1790 similar to that in Bath, but suddenly the rich clients disappeared, and even before the 18th century came to an end, everything went up if not in smoke, then in hot steam.

Clifton, though virtually bankrupted by its efforts to become a second Bath, is

Bristol from Clifton Wood, by W. J. Muller, 1835

nevertheless the best address to have in Bristol. Here the Mayor has his headquarters at the Mansion House, overlooking the Clifton Downs. This great stretch of unspoilt green high above the Avon is the same for Bristolians as Hampstead Heath is for Londoners. It is the city's lungs, playground, picnic area, where dog, master and jogger can run as free as the wind. And anyone who can afford it will live close by in Sneyd Park, Clifton's most exclusive residential quarter. Media and fashion folk, lawyers, professors and hundreds of students are here, and so too is Bristol Zoo (1836), the fifth oldest zoo in the world, and famous for its scientific research and conservation work. Opposite the zoo stands Clifton College, a famous public school built in 1862. One day it will become a magnet for worldwide pilgrimage – not perhaps to see the room where Bradley planned the D-Day landings, nor the playing field where Newbolt wrote 'Play up, play up, and play the game!', but the very spot where John Cleese, imitating his teachers as he paced the boundary, first became a Minister for Silly Walks.

It is not only the situation, on the western outskirts of the city, that makes Clifton so attractive. It did not become part of Bristol until 1835, and it has managed to retain its character even today, as a large village free from the normal horrors of suburbia. It has small shops, houses, elegant business quarters, all next to one another in relaxed village style. This mixture provides part of the charm, but the biggest attraction is the architecture.

In a series of serpentine terraces, the crescents of Clifton wind their way down the steep hill, one below the other, looking out over the Avon Gorge and the city itself. Their situation makes them even more spectacular than the crescents of Bath. Indeed, the latter provided the model which Clifton was to transcend. Bath stone was used here too, but there was no John Wood. However, what *Royal York Crescent* (1791-1820) lacks in architectural finesse, it makes up for with sheer magnitude: it has an enormous façade of 1290 feet, the longest Georgian crescent in the world. Altogether there are 46 brick houses here, with three storeys plus basement and attic, and with Regency balconies on the first floor. The façade unfolds the whole range of pastel shades so beloved of the Georgians, and in front of the houses is a broad terrace for promenaders.

Below Royal York Crescent is the slightly shorter *Cornwallis Crescent* (1791-1830), and west of that the solemn *Windsor Terrace* (1790-1810), with its monumental Corinthian pilasters. Here the Bristol-born writer Hannah More spent the last years of her life, admired by Dr Johnson, whose only regret was that, as the archetypal literary bluestocking, she had not married her fellow-Bristolian Chatterton, 'that posterity might have seen a propagation of poets.'

Between the crescents, as if in an urban terraced garden, are beautiful old beeches, chestnut trees and cedars. There is nothing more invigorating than a wander up and down the hilly streets of Clifton. Go from the *Paragon* (1809-14) (col. pl. 34), with its convex side facing the Gorge, past Bellevue with its striped awnings, across to *Prince's Buildings* (*c.* 1796), behind which is what used to be an old stone quarry but is now a huge wild garden plunging down towards the gorge. Then go up again to *Caledonia Place* (1788) and to the long and narrow *West Mall* (*c.* 1840) with a park in the middle. On this mall are Clifton's most exclusive shops – not to mention tea-rooms for those weary of hills.

After that, you can climb a little further to admire the absolute highlight of high-lights: *Clifton Suspension Bridge* (26, 1831-64). It's hard to know whether to look first at the gorge or at the bridge, since both are equally breathtaking. The bridge stretches 245 feet above the Avon, and spans 702 feet between its two mighty pylons. It is not the first, but it is certainly the most beautiful suspension bridge in England, and was designed by a genius named Isambard Kingdom Brunel (1806-59), using secondhand materials from the Hungerford Bridge in London. The cables that hold it weigh some 1500 tons, but from down below they seem as slender as bamboo. The bridge is administered by a trust, and is financed by a toll taken from the 8000 cars that go across it every day. Sadly, its beauty is a magnet for would-be suicides, and there is at least one tragedy here every month.

The Engineer of Imperial Dreams: Isambard Kingdom Brunel

The Clifton Bridge is a symbol of Bristol, and Bristol is synonymous with Brunel. 'The great engineer was small in stature and gigantic in nerve. / A manic early riser. Fifty cigars a day.' This was Hans Magnus Enzenberger's portrait of him in one of his *Ballads from the History of Progress*. Isambard Kingdom Brunel, engineer, inventor and entrepreneur, designed bridges and canals, ships and railways, stations and docks. In 1833, at the age of 26, he became chief engineer for the Great Western Railway. When the 118-mile London-Bristol route was opened in 1841, it cut the 24-hour coach journey to a 4-hour trip by rail. GWR, 'God's Wonderful Railway', now takes under 90 minutes from Paddington to Bristol (and from there you can go on to Penzance). Its most expressive monument is the stark neoclassical entrance to Box Tunnel in Wiltshire. Bare though it is, it gives little indication of the problems caused by the two miles of darkness. More than 100 navvies lost their lives building

Isambard Kingdom Brunel,
by Robert Howlett, 1857

this tunnel.

On the eastern edge of Bristol, at Temple Meads – a field that once belonged to the Knights Templar, and where they built a little church for pilgrims to the Holy Land – Brunel built a Great Western Railway Station. *Temple Meads Station* (1840) welcomes you with turrets and battlements, but behind the conventional Tudor Gothic façade lies a fascinating feat of engineering: a three-aisled shed with a hammerbeam roof with a 72 foot span – broader even than Westminster Hall. Forty cast iron arches support this, the roof of the oldest railway station in the world to survive in something like its original condition. It soon had to be extended, but when the last train left there on 6 September 1966, this cathedral of the railway age – in typical Bristol fashion – became a car park.

The Empire and Commonwealth Museum Trust began restoration of Brunel's station in 1981, and it has cost millions. It was to be the first museum of Empire in England, documenting the history of discovery and conquest, the slave trade, and migration. This mighty theme extends far beyond Bristol's own role, and is surely capable of touching the very nerve ends of the new multi-cultural, devolved nation. In order that it should be politically correct, the word 'Empire' does not occur in its name, which is to be rather innocuously 'Museum of Britain and the World'. It is privately financed, with not a penny from nervous government sources, and may yet never open. Meanwhile a highly successful science museum has been established in Brunel's old station building – the *Exploratory*, full of hands-on experiments that children can perform. For parents who find it hard to keep up, there are special evening classes.

Brunel, the engineer of imperial dreams, did not regard Bristol's station as a destination in itself. For him it was an intermediate stop on the route from London to America. The long journey west was to continue by ship, on his *S.S. Great Western*. This was the biggest paddle-steamer of the age, was launched in Bristol in 1837, and was the first liner to cross the Atlantic, which it did in the record time of fifteen days. In St George's Road stands the once magnificent Royal Western Hotel (1837-39), which Brunel had planned to accommodate his transatlantic passengers, but which has long since turned into an office block. Brunel's finest memorial, however, is the *S.S. Great Britain* (col. pl. 39).

On 5 July 1970, Bristolians stood in their thousands on the banks of the Avon, and many of them had tears in their eyes. On this day, a Sunday, the hull of the *S. S. Great Britain* was towed back in triumph to its home port, into the very same dry dock where it had been built 127 years before and launched by Prince Albert. This was the first-ever iron screw-steamer. It had six masts, the tallest of them nearly 100 feet high; the mainmast had to be removed during restoration and now lies on the quayside beside the ship. At first a passenger ship, it then carried freight, and later still troops whom it transported to the Crimea and to India, until in 1886 on its way to San Francisco it suffered heavy storm damage and had to put in at the Falkland

Islands for repairs. These would have been so expensive that the ship was abandoned. The hulk was used initially as a store for wool and coal, and finally beached as a wreck in Stanley Cove. In 1970, it was rescued, and has now been restored as a museum – the jewel of England's maritime heritage.

Once more, with his third and last ship, Brunel beat his own record. The 'Great Eastern' was more than 693 feet long, designed to carry 2996 passengers, and driven by a screw propellor, two giant paddle-wheels, *and* sails – a monster of progressive technology and fantasy. Only a few days after its first trial run, in September 1859, Brunel died. His 'Great Ship', as people called it, proved to be a technical and financial disaster. However, his successes far outweighed his failures, and among them is the bridge at Saltash, opened during the year he died, but still carrying us safe and sound across the Tamar.

Blaise Hamlet: Fertilising the Soul

Contrary to its reputation as an industrial city, Bristol has more greenery per head of the population than any other town in England. If you can only take one trip out into the country, then go to *Henbury*. This village is in the north of Bristol, and here John Nash, Pope of the Picturesque, was commissioned in 1811 by a Quaker banker to design a settlement for retired farm workers. The result, *Blaise Hamlet*, conforms as much to our modern taste for the rustic as it did then to the fashion for the picturesque. There are ten cottages with tall chimneys, stone, pantiles, and thatch, grouped idyllically round a village green, a work of art to fertilise the soul. These houses (col. pl. 38) became the prototype for the *cottage orné*, the rustic style of country house in which even the tea is served from a cottage-shaped teapot.

Nearby, in keeping with this sentimental architecture, is the pseudo-medieval *Blaise Castle* (1766). This is a showpiece, a natural stage set framed by Humphry Repton's country park. It was the picturesque, illusory world of Blaise Castle that Jane Austen had in mind when she wrote *Northanger Abbey* (1818), satirising the Gothic fashion of her time. The new *Blaise Castle House* (1796), now a branch of the city museum, was the country home of the same Bristol banker who built Blaise Hamlet.

The park and forest of Blaise Castle extend south-west as far as the park of another country house: *Kings Weston House* (1710-25). This was designed by Sir John Vanbrugh, the architect of Blenheim Palace. Kings Weston was one of his smallest mansions, typical English Baroque, not overloaded with decoration, but monumental in its simplicity. Vanbrugh created this effect through dense rows of tall chimneys which he linked with arches to form a strange sort of roof arcade. The practical use of this eccentric-seeming design was instantly recognized by a German colleague of Vanbrugh's, for it provided stability and protection against storms.

Karl Friedrich Schinkel was on a visit to Bristol, and on 27 July 1826 he made a trip to Kingsweston. 'Many people come here to enjoy the view,' he wrote. But since those days the view has been blocked by man and nature.

Where Are We Going? Round in Circles with Richard Long

Richard Long walks. He walks straight across Exmoor. He walks in circles on Dartmoor. He walks through the labyrinth of country lanes around Bristol, and on Midsummer's Day he sets out from Stonehenge at sunrise and gets to Glastonbury at sunset. He walks across, through, round, over, from and to Scotland, North America, the Himalayas, the Sahara, and the Arctic. His luggage consists of camera, cards and compass, tent and notebook. And a piece of string with which to make circles. Richard Long is an artist.

For over thirty years he has been setting out from his hometown of Bristol on these long, strange journeys. His is an art marathon which has taken him from the Avon to the Andes, from his local Arnolfini Gallery to the spirals of the Guggenheim Museum. If there is any kind of avant-garde festival on, Richard Long will be there, a living legend: the man of the stone circles.

It all began in a very simple, very English way: a line in the grass. By walking up and down a field, Richard Long created a dead straight line in 1967, and he photographed this track before it disappeared. He called it *A Line Made by Walking*. And that was the start of a lifetime's walk in lines, circles and wanderings all over the world.

Long was born in Bristol in 1945, and studied at art school both there and at St Martin's School of Art in London. His teacher, the sculptor Sir Anthony Caro, was himself thoroughly avant-garde, and Long never touched the traditional tools of the sculptor. While he was still a student, in 1968, he held his first one-man exhibition in Düsseldorf, at the Konrad Fischer gallery. The exhibits consisted of pieces of wood which he had collected on the banks of the Avon, and which he laid out in parallel lines along the floor of the gallery. During the avant-garde time of the Woodstock generation, and long before the New Age Travellers, he began his odyssey between Land Art and conceptual art, natural mysticism and minimalist aesthetics.

In that same year of 1968 he went on a ten-mile walk straight across Exmoor, and he presented this work as a line drawn absolutely to scale on the official map. 'In the early days, when I used to make straight walks across Dartmoor, one of the things I used to like about walking in a straight line was that, apart from the intellectual beauty of a straight line, it is the most practical way to cross a moor.' In 1981 he walked for one day in a circle over Dartmoor, and listed every river, stream and rivulet in a word circle (*Circle of Crossing Places*). This water walk was followed by

33. City gate, Bristol

35. Parade in front of the Town Hall, Bristol

36. Seed Warehouse, Bristol

34. The Paragon, Bristol, built 1809-14

37. Thomas Chatterton, by Henry Wallis, 1870

38. Cottage, Blaise Hamlet

39. Brunel's SS Great Britain

40. St Mary Redcliffe, Bristol, dawn, 1802, by John Sell Cotman

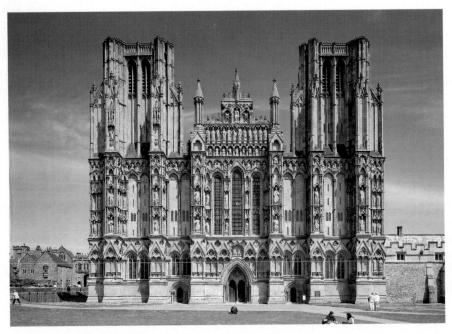

41. The West Front, Wells Cathedral

42. Interior, Wells Cathedral

43. All Saints Church, Selworthy

44. Castle Drogo

45. The painter John Virtue in his studio

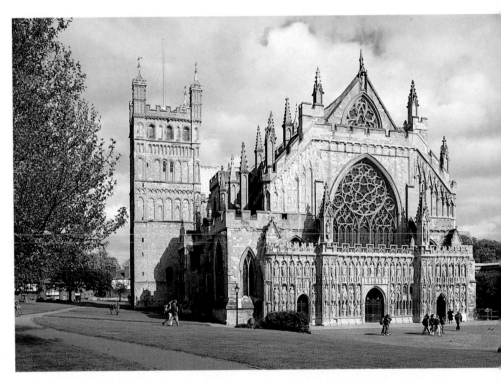

46. West Front, Exeter Cathedral

47. Kings on the West Front, Exeter Cathedral

48. *Henry Moore sculpture in the park at Dartington Hall*

49. *High Cross House, Dartington*

50. The fishing village of Clovelly

wind experiences in the West Country, captured by linear or circular pictograms made out of arrows denoting the wind direction – graphic abstractions, highly realistic, familiar to any hiker. *Sound Circle* is the title of another of his Dartmoor works: 'Larks/ Brooks/ Wind/ Grasshoppers/ Aeroplane/ Rolling Stone/ Kicking a sheep's skull' These were the sounds he had heard on his way, and they are printed as a word circle on a card of Dartmoor – a written picture of precision poetry.

As he walks, this artist absorbs the countryside with his body and with all his senses, and in concise sequences of words he records his routes, with place names, times and distances. *From Tree to Tree*, a walk through Avon, names all the trees seen en route, in what is half list and half evocation. On another occasion he noted down everything red that he saw between Bristol and Dawlish on the Devon coast: holly berries, a plastic shoe, letter box, thimble, sunset. This was called *Red Walk*. No one has rediscovered the art of the landscape more simply yet more richly and imaginatively than Richard Long. His studio is Nature, his material whatever he finds on the way: branches, driftwood, peat, clay, stones. Out of these natural materials he makes sculptures on the spot, creating elementary geometrical forms such as lines, circles, spirals, rectangles and crosses. This is an art that derives straight from nature and symbolically returns to it, an echo of prehistoric rites, and at the same time a Utopian restoration of man's lost harmony with Nature.

At the core of Long's art are his open-air works, recorded only on cards and in photos and texts. Unlike American land artists, he does not interfere with Nature, or if he does, it is only quite literally in passing. His water drawings, and footprint circles in sand or snow, are the fleeting traces of the wanderer. Transience is part of the essence of this art, but so too is the wish for permanence. His favourite material is stone, and museums are a second home to him, as the resting-places of nomadic art. 'A walk expresses space and freedom and the knowledge of it can live in the imagination of anyone, and that in another space too.'

Beckett's Molloy always had sixteen pebbles in his pocket to play with, and Richard Long too remains in close contact with his stones. Sometimes he sets them up in lines or circles, sometimes he carries them, or he throws them through the countryside following the specific rules of a game, a ritual, age-old and wonderful. Time for him is an accumulation of steps, and stones are like grains of sand in the space of the landscape. In the museum his rows of stones build up a strange, paradoxical aura of their own – relics and evocations of the countryside from which they come and through which he has walked.

'I use stones because I like stones or because they are easy to find, without being anything special, so common that you can find them anywhere.' Working on them in order to change them into conventional sculpture, into representative art, does not interest him. 'I'm not interested in representational art – that's art history. It's enough to use stones as stones, for what they are. I'm a realist.'

His style is succinct and direct, as impersonal as it is unmistakeable, a universal

Home Circle, by Richard Long, 1989

language of signs, magical and reflective. This art is an archetype of modernity. It touches on general and deep layers of experience and on actual needs and fears in relation to the raw material of Nature.

From his West Country home, Richard Long wanders out to the moors and deserts of the world. Whether he is on Dartmoor or in the tundra he is always searching for isolated, unspoilt landscapes. He is an art adventurer who combines the explorer's drive of a Livingstone with the Nature-loving mysticism of a Wordsworth. For him, biographical circumstances are more important than the tradition of English landscape-painting in which people like to place him. What he regards as far greater influences are his childhood on Dartmoor, where he was brought up by his grandparents, and the River Avon in Bristol, where he still lives. Water, mud, stones, the rhythm and relics of the seasons, these were early experiences of fundamental modes of expression that he systematically developed. Again and again he goes back to these original inspirations, with pictures made in mud from the River Avon, and monumental white water circles of Cornish kaolin.

'I think I get my energy from being out on the road, having the world going past me. That's the time when I'm conscious of the energy in the world and in me.'

Simply being on the move is a vital precondition for this experience. The only person who is occasionally allowed to break into the loneliness of the long-distance artist is his friend Hamish Fulton, likewise an artist for whom walking is the basis of his art.

In a catalogue, Fulton says 'Old Muddy' his friend is a 'walking sculpture', and he reflects on the common root of their artistic method: 'Why make walks? To clear the mind, thoughts drifting effortless to the surface like tea leaves. Why walk? To make sculpture. Why walk in nature? To attempt a balance of influences. (Quantities of time). Why walk? Partly to live in "real time".' What every walker feels during his best moments is an enhanced sensation of self and the world. Artists like Richard Long put such existential experiences into exemplary forms.

Devon

England was invaded through Kent and Sussex, but from Devon England invaded the world. This is the county which 400 years ago saw the triumphant beginnings of what unexpectedly became the British Empire. Without the men of Devon, Elizabeth I's England would have been much the same as Elizabeth II's – a loveable island of middling international importance. From Devon's ports they sailed away, and back they came, stained with the smoke of tobacco and cannon fire, privateers lording it with the riches of the New World, heroes of the history books. From Devon Francis Drake beat back the Spanish Armada, and from Devon Captain Cook set off on the *Resolution* to circumnavigate the globe. Two great Devonians, Walter Raleigh and his step-brother Humphrey Gilbert, established the first English colonies, in Newfoundland and Virginia, the latter named by the gallant Sir Walter in honour of his Virgin Queen. These authorized pirates, or merchant adventurers as they preferred to be known, lived in an age which Egon Friedell has called 'the adolescent years of capitalism'.

St Boniface of Crediton, who converted the heathen tribes of Germany, was killed in Friesland, and is buried in Fulda – he too came from Devon, from a village near Exeter. A few miles further south, in the seaside resort of Torquay, was born the most successful detective story writer of our time, Agatha Christie. And one of the two living sculptures Gilbert & George comes from Devon: the conceptual artist George Passmore, who has joined forces with the South Tyrolean Gilbert Proesch in an eccentric duo of English avant-garde – melancholic missionaries of a new art for all.

As diverse as Devon's people are its landscapes: two coasts and two moors, Dartmoor and part of Exmoor. The north coast around Lynton, with its grey granite rocks, is the 'English Switzerland'; the south coast has red sandstone cliffs, subtropical vegetation and deep estuaries. Devon is the biggest county in southern England, covering 2595 square miles, and yet has barely a million people, scarcely enough to fill one big city.

Devon's climate is milder than that of Somerset, very damp but on the coast

Tarka, by Charles Tunnicliffe

almost frost-free, providing ideal conditions for all sorts of trees and shrubs which could not be grown elsewhere. This was what the gardener Russell Page discovered, though the vast range of botanical rarities seemed to him to turn into a 'Latin exercise'. The myrtles and agaves of Overbecks' terraced garden on Salcombe Bay, the camellias and magnolias of Marwood Hill – everywhere in Devon, and not just in the famous Bicton Park Gardens, the traveller will come across the most wonderful surprises, right through to the evergreen pack of hounds in the topiary at Knightshayes Court.

The Stone Kings of Exeter

Literary history owes a great deal to vicarages, as we can see yet again when we cross the Dorset border on our way to Exeter. *Ottery St Mary* is a village named partly after the little river Otter, and partly after its church. Here, in 1772, Samuel Taylor Coleridge was born, thirteenth child of the local vicar and schoolmaster John Coleridge. The last of the baker's dozen was to become a famous poet. We who live in the Age of the Pill, and find nothing unusual about families with just one child, may well gasp at the plethora of children. After his father's death, the nine-year-old boy was sent by his mother to Christ's Hospital School in London, so that he might be brought up there among other 'poor children', as the widow wrote in a petition, a copy of which is to be seen in the church. Thus Charles Lamb acquired a schoolfriend in the 'inspired charity-boy'. Throughout his life, just like his father, Coleridge was short of money, but his poetry and his theoretical writings were a decisive influence on English Romanticism. Coleridge's birthplace, the village school next to the church, was replaced by a Victorian vicarage, but on the wall of the churchyard is a relief based on the albatross from the *Rime of the Ancient Mariner*.

For me the thing that evoked Coleridge's childhood most vividly was not a sight but a continuous sound: the ticking of St Mary's clock, on whose painted wooden casing the sun, moon and stars revolve ptolemaically round the earth. This astronomical clock, which is as old as those in Wells and Exeter, still shows the time as it was before Galileo. Like the cock on the steeple, reputed to be the oldest weather vane in England, the clock dates from the first half of the 14th century, when Bishop Grandison of Exeter founded a seminary in Ottery, and extended St Mary's from Early English to Decorated, from village church to village cathedral. The real highlights of this building are only visible through a telescope: the figured bosses on the vaults of the choir and the Lady Chapel. In the Perpendicular side aisle (*c.* 1520) there is an elephant's head on the capital of one of the columns. The rood screen, chiselled in wood (*c.* 1350), is one of the oldest in Devon, where there are almost 200 churches with such screens. John Haydon is buried here, but of much greater

Ottery St Mary

interest than his tomb is this London lawyer's country house: Cadhay Manor, a Tudor house north-west of the village.

In *Bicton*, between the seaside resorts of Sidmouth and Exmouth, the gardens are far more attractive than the house, which is now an agricultural and horticultural college. The Italian Garden is said to have been laid out from designs left by Le Nôtre, Louis XIV's master of geometrical gardens, dead and out of fashion in France half a generation previously. The Palm House with its glass dome (1815-30) was more up to date: it is one of the oldest in the country, and then there are the trees: Chilean araucaria, Mexican juniper, Tasmanian cedar, Himalayan deodar – even if Britain is no longer a world power, at least its international connections are still flourishing in Bicton. This would scarcely be an English garden if we could not view it from the narrow-gauge Bicton Woodland Railway, which carries us in royal blue carriages on bright red wheels across a splendid pine grove.

Two miles south-west of Bicton Park Gardens is the thatched country house where Sir Walter Raleigh was born in around 1554: *Hayes Barton*. Raleigh gave Europe the potato and tobacco, was a favourite of Elizabeth I, and a sonnet-writing friend of Spenser. He was a soldier, sailor, poet and scholar, and one of the great winners and losers in the Golden Age of Good Queen Bess. During his year's imprisonment in the Tower, he wrote a *History of the World* (1614), with those famous final lines addressed to Death: 'Thou hast drawne together all the farre stretched greatnesse, all the pride, crueltie, and ambition of man, and covered it all over with these two narrow words, *Hic iacet.*' When Raleigh failed to find the promised Eldorado on the Orinoco, James I had him beheaded in 1618, for the sake of peace with Spain. The Raleigh family coat-of-arms can still be seen on one of the richly carved benches in the church at *East Budleigh*. Only St Mary's at *High Bickington*, south of Barnstaple, has a collection of bench ends from Devon's village Renaissance comparable in number and quality.

A royal welcome in *Exeter*: beneath the stone canopies on the west front of the cathedral, are four statues with crossed legs and crinkly beards. Nobody knows for sure who they are, but they have been sitting there for more than 500 years, in the company of prophets, angels and apostles, sometimes hit but never destroyed during attacks by the English Reformation, the German Luftwaffe, salty winds from the west, and pollution from all over the place. The finest of these grey and pale-gold sandstone figures are not those that have been smoothly restored, but those whose faces are scarred and worn. They are the victims of time so vividly described by Henry James: '... when the long June twilight turns at last to a deeper grey and the quiet of the close to a deeper stillness, they begin to peer sidewise out of their narrow recesses and to converse in some strange form of early English, as rigid, yet as candid, as their features and postures, moaning, like a company of ancient paupers round a hospital fire, over their aches and infirmities and losses, and the sadness of being so terribly old.' When the last of the statues on the west front were completed around 1350, this great wall of images shone with polished gold, red, green and white, like a huge page from a medieval illuminated manuscript. The 'natural' hue of the stone which we admire today is as beautiful but as false as the 'pure' marble of ancient temples.

Exeter survived the bombing raids of May 1942, but a great deal of the medieval city was lost. The bombs exposed mosaic surfaces from *Isca Dumnoniorum*, the Roman town to the west. Part of the old walls can be seen in Southernhay, an elegant Georgian street, and in the park next to the main railway station. There, on the 'red mountain' of *Rougemont Gardens* (6), mentioned in *Richard III*, stands the ruined Norman castle with Aethelstan's Tower. The nearby *Royal Albert Memorial Museum* (8) has some good English watercolours, but nothing by Nicholas Hilliard, who was born *c.* 1547 in Exeter, the son of a goldsmith, and himself became a goldsmith as well as the creator of many delightful miniatures; he rose to be the first great English painter at the court of Elizabeth I and her successor James I.

St Winfrid's School is named after the Saxon Wynfrith, known as Boniface, who was born ten miles away in Crediton and was probably educated at the monastery school in Exeter. One corner of the old city still survives, on *Stepcote Hill* (12) near the Exe Bridge, and from there Fore Street (with its many antique shops) leads to the High Street and the medieval *Guildhall* (2).

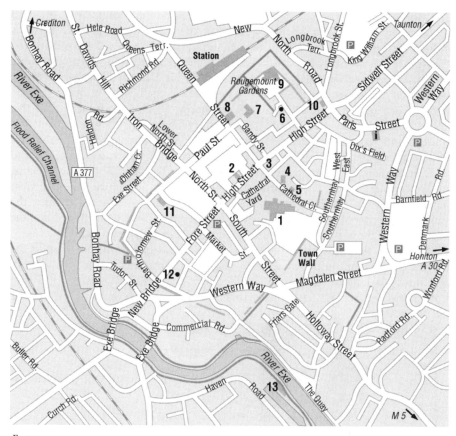

Exeter
1. *Cathedral*   2. *Guildhall*   3. *Ship Inn*   4. *St Martin*   5. *Mol's Coffee House*   6. *Rougemont Gardens*   7. *Exeter and Devon Arts Centre*   8. *Royal Albert Memorial Museum*   9. *Rougemont Castle*   10. *Underground Passages*   11. *St Nicolas Priory*   12 *Stepcote Hill*   13. *Maritime Museum*

With its timber-framed and red sandstone houses, Cathedral Close is the nearest we can ever come to the former character of this county capital. The lions of *Mol's Coffee House* (5), built directly onto the little church of *St Martin* (4), proudly display the figure 1596 in the coat-of-arms nestling amid the bays and windows of the façade. The curved gable, however, is a Victorian addition, and furthermore you can't get any coffee here now. Instead, though, you can walk a few yards further on, and down a pint of ale at the *Ship Inn* (3), whose shiver-my-timbers atmosphere was advertised in 1587 by no less an expert than Sir Francis Drake: 'Next to mine own shippe I do most love that old Shippe in Exon.'

Absorbed in his Bible, surrounded by students and city dignitaries, Richard Hooker, the 'most accomplished advocate that Anglicanism has ever had', as well as one of the finest writers of English, sits calmly on his pedestal in front of the *Cathedral* (1). Hooker, born at nearby Heavitree, gave strength to reasonable Protestantism against fundamentalist Puritanism; his *Laws of Ecclesiastical Polity* insisted on the primacy of natural law, whose 'seat is the bosom of God, her voice the harmony of the world'. Behind him, the bosom of God in visible form is this great Cathedral, begun in 1270 and, like Salisbury Cathedral (whose west front was finished only five years earlier), is a unified whole, pure Gothic, with the exception of its massive twin towers which were left over from its Norman predecessor and were incorporated into the transepts (A) of the new building. With sixteen shafts, the cluster piers spread out to form an avenue of stone, and above them like great palm leaves extend the thirty fans of the vault. Where they meet, at the vertex of the vault, a dense row of bosses draws the eye away from the west door (B) and into the depths of the choir; there is no interruption here from the crossing, and in its earliest days only the stone choir screen (F; 1320) would have broken a view of the longest Gothic vault in the world. This magnificent instinct for space and rhythm was clearly lacking in the Baroque builders who stuck a monumental organ over both view and screen. Otherwise forms and styles mix harmoniously: the

King on west front of Exeter Cathedral

Exeter Cathedral, plan
A Nave with Norman
towers
B West Front
C Choir
D Lady Chapel
E Chapter House
F Screen

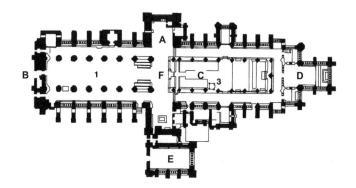

Perpendicular west window counters the rosette of the Lady Chapel window; 14th-century tracery is answered by 20th-century glass. On one console an acrobat stands on his head to the musical accompaniment of an angel, and the Virgin Mary sits on the console opposite. This Cathedral is alive, right down to its last bosses, on which Samson kills the lion and a knight kills Thomas à Becket. The hugeness of this interior is in no way oppressive, and it does not overwhelm the individual details. The Victorian choir stalls have incorporated the oldest misericords in England (*c.* 1230-70): an elephant with cow's hooves, a scene from the story of Lohengrin, and a king sitting in a boiling pot. In the choir, held together only by dowels and tenons, is the mighty bishop's throne, carved out of oak and towering to a height of 60 feet; it is covered with exquisite human and animal heads, and is the oldest (completed in 1312) and finest of its kind in England. The bishops themselves are buried beneath canopy and marble mitre.

There are other relics, too: the flag from the sledge used by Scott of the Antarctic, who was born near Devonport; a Canadian Indian on Flaxman's tomb of General Simcoe, the first Governor of Canada; Chantrey's lifesize statue of the painter James Northcote, son of a Plymouth watchmaker, complete with brush and palette. The famous 'rondels' – the tapestry cushions which cover the stone seats running along both sides of the nave – were not finished until 1989 and contain some 14 million stitches. But the Library has perhaps the greatest treasure of all. Almost all the secular Old English poetry apart from *Beowulf* that has survived is contained in the Exeter Book (copied *c.* 975), which was given to the Library in 1072 by Bishop Leofric, and catalogued as 'one big English book about every sort of thing, wrought in song-wise'. *The Wanderer* and *The Seafarer* have all the grandeur and melancholy of this far-off heroic civilization; *The Ruin* may well be a description of Bath: 'Well-wrought this wall,' it begins in Michael Alexander's translation, 'Wierds broke it./ The stronghold burst.../ Snapped rooftrees, towers fallen, the work of the Giant, the stonesmiths/ Mouldereth...'

Keats & Co: Last Days in Torquay

The estuary of the Exe forms a long bay on which lies a park where deer run free and falcons are bred; in the park stands *Powderham Castle*, which since the 14th century has been the family home of the Courtenays, whose French ancestors came to England with Eleanor of Aquitaine, Henry II's wife. This idyllic country castle was the scene of one of the great homosexual scandals. William Beckford came here in 1779 – a hundred years before Oscar Wilde – and met the eleven-year-old William Courtenay; their relationship was to end in personal and social disaster for them both (see p. 25 ff.) No Courtenay was ever more advanced in culture and taste than William. To him we owe the domed music room, designed by James Wyatt, the gold-painted Regency furniture of William Marsh and Thomas Tatham, and the signature rosewood and brass inlay furniture of John Channon. The portrait of Powderham Castle's own Dorian Gray, painted in 1792 by the Devonian Richard Cosway – England's last great miniaturist – shows an elegantly dressed young man, already a little on the corpulent side.

Teignmouth, situated naturally enough on the mouth of the Teign, is a coastal town with Regency houses, a really delightful little family resort; the pier was Pier of the Year in 1997. It is a pleasure simply to take a boat upriver, bathe in the sea, or wander along the red sandstone cliffs which, because of their strange shapes, have been christened the Parson Rock and the Clerk Rock. In a letter to his friend the painter Benjamin Haydon, John Keats wrote, 'I have enjoyed the most delightful walks these three four days beautiful enough to make me content here all summer long could I stay.' 1818 was to be Keats' 'living year' because he was so happy and achieved so much. He came here from London in the spring and autumn of 1818,

John Keats

and enjoyed the sea air. He wrote a rustic poem *Where be you going you Devon Maid?*, praised the beautiful hills and the delicious cream, and began his epic *Isabella*, which was so admired by the Pre-Raphaelites. At the time he was 23, had just abandoned the idea of a career in medicine, and wanted to be nothing but a poet. The condition of his sick brother Tom worsened, and evidently so too did the weather, for Keats now set to cursing Devon in no uncertain terms: 'It is a splashy, rainy, misty, snowy, foggy, haily, floody, muddy, slipslop county.' That same year his brother died of tuberculosis, and not long afterwards Keats himself, the Romantic poet of eternal beauty, began to cough blood. He died in Rome at the age of 25. The year of his Teignmouth stay, 1818, saw the publication of *Endymion*, which begins: 'A thing of beauty is a joy for ever:/ Its loveliness increases; it will never/ Pass into nothingness…' A memorial in Teignmouth (Northumberland Place) commemorates his short and tragic life. Just before his death, he wrote: 'I have loved the principle of beauty in all things.' In a Grecian urn as in the song of a nightingale.

Teignmouth was also home to an important maritime painter, Thomas Luny. You can often see his work on show at the town museum in French Street. Luny House in Teign Street is now a hotel and welcomes the painter's admirers.

There are shining red cliffs and beautiful beaches in Tor Bay, and palm trees and tropical plants, and hotels called Riviera, San Remo or Palm Court. If there is really such a thing as an English Riviera, this is it. *Torquay*, at the northern end of the bay, is the elegant resort, Paignton is the folksy one, and Brixham at the southern end is still more or less what it used to be: a fishing port. This region has always been a magnet for writers and statesmen, and sailors of course fully appreciate the touch of the Mediterranean in the Channel, while the sick and the elderly seek the protection of the hills in the winter, perhaps venturing forth for the odd game of golf. Torquay is a popular centre for learning English, which is best done while floating in the sea. Thanks to Napoleon's continental blockade, the town developed into a Regency resort for rich English people deprived of sunnier climes.

Torquay is built on seven hills. It is a natural garden city, and was so a good hundred years before Ebenezer Howard pioneered the concept. Its architectural charms are most evident in the villas of Babbacombe and the terraces of Meadfoot, while its landscapes are at their most impressive seen from Babbacombe Down or Anstey's Cove. But the concrete boxes on the cliffs show how things have been developing since the sixties, culminating in a monstrous shopping centre right in the middle of the old town.

The Irish playwright Sean O'Casey lived in Torquay for thirty-eight years, following the example of Edward Bulwer-Lytton, the prolific author of *Last Days of Pompeii*. For those who like detective stories, Ashfield is the all-important house in Torquay. There the Queen of Crime or, as she preferred to call herself, the Duchess of Death was born in 1890. Agatha Christie was made a Dame in 1971, having murdered scores if not hundreds of Her Majesty's loyal subjects. English country houses were the most favoured settings, and there the comic Continental Hercule Poirot, and later the staunchly British Miss Marple would solve even the most fiendishly difficult crimes. These detective novels, cleverly crafted and gently seasoned, have sold more copies than Shakespeare or Dickens. More than 400 million at the latest count. When she died, on 12 January 1976, her play *The Mousetrap* was entertaining its audience at the Ambassadors' Theatre, London, for the 9611th time, having run uninterrupted for 24 years. Despite transferring to St Martin's, it was still going strong twenty years later.

Overlooking town and bay is the church of St John the Evangelist, built with multi-coloured Devon marble and Neo-Norman zig-zag patterns by the Victorian architect George Edmund Street (1861-71). One of Street's first assistants was William Morris, whose firm made the great west and east windows, designed by

145

Edward Burne-Jones: the west window (a copy of Burne-Jones' window in Jesus College, Cambridge) is deep red and blue, with the nine orders of angels, and the east is white and aubergine with Christ, angels and saints – a rather morbid and melancholy gathering. Burne-Jones also painted the original frescoes on the north and south walls of the choir, the Magi and the Jew and Gentile being led by two angels into the light out of the forest. The originals were sold to Andrew Lloyd-Webber, who sold them on to America, and what you see today in the church are replicas commissioned from Barrington Bramley. If the high-minded, high Church melancholy that even the copies convey gets to you, check the crucifix outside for spelling.

In 1688, William of Orange landed in the bay at Torquay. England's parliamentary Opposition had appealed for his help against the policies of his father-in-law James II, and so together with his wife Mary he took power and led the European Coalition against Louis XIV in the War of the Spanish Succession. Among Britain's gains from the war was the island of Gibraltar. In the port at *Brixham*, between two cannons, stands a monument to this Protestant king, who ended the reign of the Stuarts.

If you walk from the port to Berry Head, you will follow the route taken by all the good people of Brixham in July 1815, when they assembled to witness the end of another, much further-reaching rule: that of Napoleon. After his defeat at Waterloo, he arrived with six coaches and 45 horses on board the *Bellerophon*, hoping for a nice easy exile in England. It was not to be. To the disappointment of himself and all those who had been looking forward to the show, he was made to change boats in mid-sea, climb aboard the *Northampton*, and set sail for St Helena.

The English Rhine: From Dartmouth to Totnes

If you want to go from Brixham to *Dartmouth* without going through Totnes, take the ferry from Kingswear. There, on the cliffs you will see the square-shaped tower of the castle (now a holiday home), while opposite on the west bank is Dartmouth Castle (1481-1509), dominated by the tower of St Petrox Church. This estuary offers as romantic a picture as you will get on any river. One can easily imagine the heroic scenes of yesteryear: the crusaders sailed from here in 1147 with a fleet of 164 ships, and they repeated the exercise in 1190; 480 Allied warships set sail in 1944, to wait for D-Day in Warfleet Creek. If invaders tried to return the compliment, a huge iron chain was raised to close off this natural harbour. But most of the time Dartmouth has been an idyllic little coastal town. In the Middle Ages its main interest was its wine trade with Bordeaux. Today it is the tourists that bring in the trade. Dominating the northern side of the town is Aston Webb's monumental Royal Naval College (1899-1905, opened in 1902), the English navy's equivalent to

Eton, which counts among its more illustrious cadets the Duke of Edinburgh. Royalty still occasionally attend the Port of Dartmouth Royal Regatta, a stirring sight on the last weekend of August.

Butterwalk is a magnificent 17th-century building, with a granite colonnade supporting beautifully carved half-timbering (1635-40). It is now the Dartmouth Museum, and is open on weekdays. On the quay stands the Royal Castle Hotel, an old coaching inn with a galleon bar built from the beams of wrecked Spanish Armada ships. 1588 was indeed the year in which a whole armada of smoke-blackened English pubs sprang up along the Channel coast.

Up the hill from the port is Higher Street. Here and in the narrow side streets are houses with overhanging storeys, some of the finest timber-framed buildings in Dartmouth. On Ridge Hill is Newcomen Lodge, built from parts of a house in Lower Street, and it was here that a famous son of the town had his home. Thomas Newcomen was a blacksmith who invented the atmospheric steam engine in 1712. There is a model on display in the Tourist Information Centre in Royal Avenue Gardens. The machine was of little practical use until James Watt, while repairing a model, realized that the steam could be saved in a condenser.

The first showpiece of *St Saviour's* is its massive oak door in the south porch, decorated with wrought iron: two leopards guarding the Tree of Life. The church goes back to 1286, but the door is a 14th-century masterpiece, restored in 1631. The second treasure is made of stone – a richly sculptured, octagonal pulpit (*c.* 1500); and the third is made of wood – a choir screen (1480) with the remains of old paintings, filigree tracery, and a frieze of foliage in which birds are picking grapes or being devoured by monsters. A monumental brass of 1408 shows the Mayor of Dartmouth, John Hawley, standing between his two wives, dressed in helmet and armour, ready for the final battle.

If you have just spent the night in Queen Victoria's four-poster bed at the Royal Castle, you will feel doubly majestic as you sail up-river from Dartmouth to *Totnes*. Queen Victoria called the Dart the 'English Rhine', and on your two-hour trip you will pass forested hills and the Anchor Stone, where Sir Walter Raleigh sat in midstream smoking his pipe and enjoying the view. The little town of Totnes actually consists of nothing more than a single long street, which becomes increasingly steep, narrow, and picturesque. Totnes also boasts a national legend. The *Brutus Stone* in Fore Street may not be anywhere near as impressive as the splendid stone screen of *St Mary's* (*c.* 1460), but nevertheless it has a mighty tale to tell. Brutus, grandson of Aeneas, is said to have landed here in 1170 BC and, as the first king, to have given 'Britain' its name. This at any rate is the claim made by the Norman bishop and chronicler Geoffrey of Monmouth in his *Historia Regum Britanniæ* (1136), which even if it is more story than history, has nevertheless had immense influence on the island's literature. The chronicles have been the source material for all the books and plays and poems written about such legendary figures as King

Lear, King Arthur and Merlin his magician. From the Brutus Stone, the very foundation stone of the realm, the town fathers of Totnes still inform their citizens whenever a new monarch mounts the throne of England.

Art and Apples: Dartington Hall

The scent of azaleas wafts through the park of *Dartington Hall*, two miles northwest of Totnes. In the terraced gardens lies one of Henry Moore's typical reclining ladies (1947), looking down with beautiful eyes at the line of Twelve Apostles cut out of 300-year old yew trees (col. pl. 48). The inner court of this medieval country house on the Dart, shaded by a deciduous cypress tree, looks like the idyllic place to lie down like her, and have a good read; but Dartington is also a hive of activity, as one of the liveliest art centres in south-west England.

The story of this inspirational place began in 1925 when Leonard Elmhirst, son of a Yorkshire clergyman, married Dorothy Whitney, who happened to be one of the richest American women of her day. It was a strange match as far as background was concerned, but they both shared a missionary zeal for education. When they married they bought Dartington Hall, then a decaying, 14th-century mansion, which they restored and turned into a school which, next to A. S. Neill's Summerhill, was the most progressive in England.

'For us it is vital that education be conceived of as life, and not merely as a preparation for life,' wrote the Elmhirsts in their first prospectus (1926). Dartington was to be the exact opposite of the conventional public school: anti-authoritarian, with no social or sexual barriers, quite simply a community of boys and girls, children and adults. Far more important than rules and timetables was the principle of enjoyment. This included practical training in as many fields as possible, 'learning by doing'. The Elmhirsts set up a model farm, a construction company, a sawmill, a cider press, a pottery and a weaving mill. Everything had its place, its own discipline, and above all the common aim of exploring the vast worlds of art and life in order to establish and enjoy an art of living. For all its egalitarian principles, Dartington was nevertheless an upper-class school, and for all its pacifism and nudism, it was not radical enough for a left-winger like George Orwell, who was scathing about the snobbishness of this alternative society and its new pedagogics: 'all that dreary tribe of high-minded women and sandal-wearers and bearded fruit-juice drinkers who come flocking towards the smell of "progress" like bluebottles to a dead cat.' Parents included Bertrand Russell, Julian Huxley, Barbara Hepworth, Ben Nicholson, Jacob Epstein, Victor Gollancz and the Freuds, fleeing from Vienna; teachers included the potter Bernard Leach and the composer Imogen

Dartmouth: Brass to John Hawley and his two wives, 1408, St Saviour's

Holst, and Jewish artists, such as the Dutchman Kurt Jooss, who were fleeing from the Nazis and found refuge with the Elmhirsts.

Dartington was a centre for the international, cultural élite, imbued with the spirit of European and transatlantic liberalism. It closed in 1995, after financial problems and a pornography scandal, but its spirit lives on in *High Cross House* (col. pl. 49). Situated on a hill below Dartington Hall, and built in glowing white and blue cubes, High Cross is refreshingly modern and urbane in the midst of the antiquities of the countryside. Here William Curry, the first headmaster, lived. It was thought that the children who were growing up in the spirit of modern times, with modern dance and modern theatre, should also experience modern architecture. The Elmhirsts decided to change the original style on their estate from Arts and Crafts to New International Modernist; their architect, William Lescaze, had just finished one of the first international-style skyscrapers in Philadelphia. By 1936, Lescaze had designed a whole series of new buildings for Dartington, including the Warren, now the Centre for Social Policy. High Cross House, however, was his masterpiece.

The house exudes geometrical Bauhaus clarity, which never ossifies into rigidity, but remains alive and generous – an of the educational liberalism characteristic of Dartington. Interior and exterior are blended into each other, with a series of terraces opening the house up to the landscape, and abundant light penetrating through the vertical bars of the windows. This model 1930's house has been open to the public since 1995, with changing exhibitions from the Elmhirsts' art collection: ceramics by Bernard Leach and Shoji Hamada, Lucie Rie and Hans Coper, paintings and drawings by Ben Nicholson, John Nash, David Jones, Cecil Collins, Frances Hodgkins, Winifred Nicholson and others.

Nowadays, Dartington is run by a trust, whose declared aims are 'to promote patterns of living which draw strength from a rural environment, are economically viable, meet the emerging needs of society and offer the individual a fulfilling and well-balanced life.' A wide range of activities, from organic farming to seminars at Schumacher College on economic and intellectual problems are on offer; there is also an alternative training centre for social and ecological work. The Dartington College of Arts (a separate institution on the site) offers courses in theatre, dance and music.

Visitors to Dartington can enjoy a wide range of pleasures. In the medieval Great Hall itself, there are about 120 concerts a year staged publicly as part of the International Summer School. The Elmhirsts' cider press is a major tourist attraction, and has a turnover of millions, selling natural and synthetic products, including apple juice, organic foods, Dartington glass, and the ever popular ceramics, designed since 1984 by Janice Tchalenko. There is also a huge gallery displaying the work of dozens of local potters and other craftsmen. Dartington still has a name for craftwork of the highest quality.

Off the coast between Dartmouth and Plymouth is another modern building well worth going to see: *Burgh Island* is probably the only art deco island hotel in the world. It was designed in 1929 by Matthew Dawson, and is built of shining white cubes with flat turquoise window frames of iron and a copper green tower. This was the guesthouse run by the entrepreneur Archibald Nettlefold (who owned the Comedy Theatre in London where several of Agatha Christie's plays were put on) and his friends. There they would charleston and tango with the stars and starlets of London's theatre world. The Prince of Wales and Wallis Simpson stayed there, as did Noel Coward and Agatha Christie. The latter's *Ten Little Niggers* and *Evil Under the Sun* were written there, and Burgh Island was the model for the hotel where Hercule Poirot took his holidays. In the mid sixties, John Boorman made his first film there, *Catch Us If You Can*. But by then the hotel was already in sharp decline.

It was rescued by two London fashion experts, Beatrice and Tony Porter. In 1986 they bought the island in Bigbury Bay and began to restore the hotel: the Palm Court, with its peacock-coloured lead glass dome, the glass mosaics of the cocktail bar, the salmon-pink mirrors, the sin-black glass panelling on the stairs that lead from the foyer into the ballroom. To the few remaining items of furniture they added their own art deco collection, acquired from purchases at auctions: lamps from the London Savoy, doorhandles from the Odeon, film posters and advertisements from the thirties. Today Burgh Island is art deco pure and simple, with furnishings of aluminium, chrome and wicker, curtains of moiré, and of course a bakelite radio. With waitresses dressed in black and white sailor's suits, and the host in a cream smoking jacket, the guests can hardly allow themselves to be outdone. They dine nostalgically in their tulle and red chiffon and paste jewels, to the sounds of Ginger Rogers and Bing Crosby and 'Puttin' on the Ritz'. This art deco hotel is literally an island in an everyday sea, and you can reach it on foot at low tide, or by a strange sort of aquatic tractor when the tide is in. But hurry – the news is that it is on the market.

On the main road into Plymouth stands the first supermarket I ever liked. This vast Sainsbury's Superstore (opened August 1994) is a simple brick complex, sunk four metres into the earth, with a really spectacular front: arcades spanned by a series of transparent sections that shine at night rather like a fleet of ghost ships. This is maritime supermarket architecture, designed in 1993 by Jeremy Dixon and Edward Jones.

Plymouth: Pirates, Pilgrims and a Dwarf in Aspic

Plymouth is Devon's largest town and England's most heroic port. It is built on rock and history, and stands some 165 feet above the sea, like its own monument, mourning the greatness it has lost. It was here, in the 16th century, that England began its rise from medieval mediocrity to world power. As witnesses to the former greatness of Plymouth, there are many towns in the former British Empire that still bear its name. It was the Golden Age of the admirals, the royal pirates and explorers, the slave traders, and the Pilgrim Fathers; but there is not much to see after the march of progress and the bombings of the Luftwaffe. A few statues, street names, businesses like Mayflower Antiques, Mayflower Cakes, Pilgrim Taxis. Above all there is the 1950's Armada Way (10), which runs majestically from the city centre straight to the south, past a bronze version of Drake's Drum, broadening out like a green carpet as far as the sea. *The Hoe* (which means 'high place') is the name of this park overlooking the port, and there is no finer view of England's history. Nor can there be a more English legend than that of the Admirals Drake and Howard, with

Plymouth
1. *Plymouth Dome*   2. *Smeaton's Lighthouse*   3. *Statue of Drake*   4. *Civic Centre*   5. *St Andrew's*
6. *Prysten House*   7. *Merchant's House*   8. *Charles King and Martyr*   9. *City Museum*
10. *Armada Way*   11. *Mayflower Steps*   12. *Citadel*

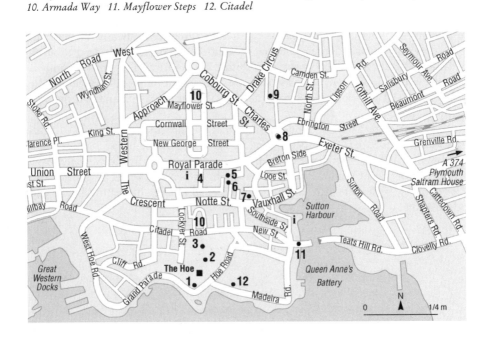

their captains Frobisher and Hawkins, insisting on finishing their game of bowls while the 130 ships and 50,000 men of the Spanish fleet sailed into view on 31 July 1588. England's staunchest ally that day was the weather, or to be more precise the north-west wind, but even that is part of the legend, for did it not show that God was on the side of freedom and the Protestants? As cool as bronze, with stance imperious and imperial, left hand on hip, right hand dividing the globe – which he was the first Englishman to circumnavigate – Sir Francis Drake stands for ever upon his pedestal (3). It was Elizabeth I who sent him secretly on his epic voyage, not for scientific so much as economic and political purposes, in order to show Philip II of Spain that Britannia ruled the waves and the trading routes. Elizabeth II used Drake's sword when she knighted Francis Chichester at Greenwich, who in 1966 – at the age of 65 – sailed from Plymouth in *Gipsy Moth IV* on a solo voyage round the world, which he accomplished in 107 days. Lovers of historical continuity did not miss the fact that Sir Francis had emulated Sir Francis. Drake's voyage took

nearly three years, and when in September 1580 he returned to Plymouth in the *Golden Hind*, loaded with Inca gold plundered from the Spanish, a service of thanksgiving was held in the magnificent church of St Andrew's (5; 15th century). Perhaps it was one of his fans who scratched the Drake crest of ship and globe by the first window west of the south porch. All this, of course, was long, long before the German bombers got to

Drake's circumnavigation, graffito, St Andrew's

work and smashed Plymouth to pieces in 1941. The church was rebuilt, however, in 1957, and now boasts six brightly coloured windows by John Piper – contemporary English stained glass of rare quality. It was in this church that the Pilgrim Fathers supposedly said their final prayers before leaving their homes after long years of persecution under James I. These pioneers, who founded the Massachusetts Bay Colony, actually consisted of only 35 non-conformists ('saints') and almost twice as many adventurers ('strangers'). Plymouth gave the intrepid group a big send-off and their descendants come back in droves to see where they spent their last night in England, Island House on the Barbican, where there is a full passenger manifest waiting to be photographed. The two memorial stones on the Barbican stand for two different worlds: where the *Mayflower* set sail in 1620, and where the American seaplane NC 4 landed in 1919, after making the first transatlantic flight.

Plymouth has always been the site of historic arrivals and departures. The Black Prince sailed to France in 1355 to fight the Hundred Years War; Catherine of Aragon, Henry VIII's first wife, arrived in 1501; Sir Walter Raleigh returned from his disastrous Orinoco expedition in 1618; and the body of Robert Blake came back after his victory over the Spanish in 1657. When James Cook and the *Endeavour* set sail in 1768 to discover *Terra Australis Incognita*, he would have seen Smeaton's new, epoch-making lighthouse flashing from Eddystone off the shores of Plymouth. By the time Ernest Shackleton weighed anchor for his last Antarctic expedition in 1921, the Eddystone Lighthouse had long since been put into mainland retirement, and is still a much-loved observation tower on the Hoe. Nearby stands the *Citadel* (12), built in 1666 by Charles II, more to frighten his own subjects than to scare off the enemy. The Baroque gatehouse leads to the old city on the original port of Sutton Pool. A few Tudor houses survive, two of which are open to the public: Prysten (Priests') House (6) near St Andrew's, and 32 New Street.

In the midst of the traffic in Exeter Street is a Second World War ruin, *Charles Church* (8), originally a memorial to the King, and now a reminder that Plymouth was one of the most heavily bombed of all English towns. The Drake spirit had not been lost however. At No. 3 Elliott Terrace you can see the former home of Lord and Lady Astor. Waldorf Astor was MP for Plymouth from 1910-19 and on his father's death, when he inherited the title, his wife took the seat – the first woman in history to take a seat in Parliament. She represented Plymouth for 25 more years and in her sixties, during the Blitz, she led dancing on Plymouth Hoe to show public defiance of the bombing.

There are two painters also associated with Plymouth: Beryl Cook (now living in Bristol) is a naïve artist, the Grandma Moses of the West Country, and Robert O. Lenkiewicz is the man who literally paints the town red. Beryl Cook is self-taught. Her figures are fat, vulgar and good-humoured, and her pictures are bright and satirical – a mixture of Botero and dirty seaside postcards. She found her models and subjects in the working class, demi-monde world of Plymouth – the pubs, gay bars and bingo-halls. One of her paintings has even made its way onto a Royal Mail postage stamp.

Robert O. Lenkiewicz paints house-sized pictures of Plymouth's history – fancy-dress parties with Elizabeth I, Raleigh, Drake, and all the other notables. In the old quarter of the Barbican you can see two of his wall-pictures, a Last Judgement in Southside Street and the famous 'Elizabethan' group near the Tourist Information Centre. Lenkiewicz has at least seventeen children, and thousands of pictures that make up a vast record of Plymouth's darker side: prostitutes, drunkards, lunatics, suicides. For a while he lived with homeless people, and painted their portraits. One of them is still with him, albeit as a corpse embalmed in synthetic resin: this is his friend Diogenes, a dwarf. 'He's like a large paperweight.'

Saltram and Buckland: Reynolds Paints and Drake Fiddles

The peninsula of Stonehouse, with its Georgian houses, links Plymouth to *Devonport*. It was from this naval base, founded in 1691 by William III, that the British Fleet set sail for the Falklands war. Joshua Reynolds had a studio here for four years, before he achieved fame and a knighthood as the first President of the Royal Academy. Sir Joshua grew up in *Plympton*, the son of a clergyman and schoolmaster. The house where he was born no longer exists, but the City Museum in Plymouth has the first edition of his *Discourses* on art (1778), his palette, his mahlstick, a self-portrait, and portraits of his family.

Ten much finer paintings are displayed in the great house of *Saltram*. This stands on the eastern bank of the Plym, and long before the Plymouth bypass cut through its park, the lord of the manor was leaning casually on a gate, in silk shirt and velvet coat, his hunting rifle over his arm. Thus did Reynolds portray his friend and patron John Parker 200 years ago, and he also painted the Parker family in the dark shades of a Rembrandt and with the elegance of a van Dyck. Landowners and rich Londoners loved to find themselves ennobled a second time by such portraits, and Reynolds was their favourite artist. In his theoretical writings, he gave precedence to history painting, but in total he painted some 2,000 portraits. In one year, 1759, he did no less than 150. Today any self-respecting English country house has a Reynolds, though not always without the help of one of his pupils, and not always of top quality. When the owner of Saltram was collecting old masters for his gallery, Reynolds acted as his adviser and also introduced him to many contemporary artists. In the Library at Saltram, there are nine portraits by the American Gilbert Stuart, who learned his trade in London before going on to paint the portrait of the first American President. But John Parker – or Joshua Reynolds – had an even higher regard for Angelica Kauffmann, who worked in London from 1766 till 1781, and is represented at Saltram by eleven history and mythological paintings. On the staircase, looking down on us in gentle contemplation, is Reynolds himself, portrayed by Angelica (col. pl. 57). She loved his art, but rejected his proposal of marriage. The Italian Antonio Zucchi was certainly a lesser painter, but evidently he had other qualities which attracted Angelica more. In the Saloon (col. pl. 56) are ceiling medallions and lunettes by him, and there are mythological landscapes in the Dining Room, painted only as decorative fillings for the magnificent plasterwork of Robert Adam (1768 ff.).

Adam, the father of English neoclassicism, gave this house a richness which one would never suspect from its simple early Georgian façade – a contrast which was particularly popular at that time. His style of quiet elegance fitted in perfectly with a society whose taste was both cultured and refined. The large Axminster carpet, echoing the design of the ceiling, the furniture, mirrors and mantelpieces, wine-coolers in the shape of antique urns, and even the keyhole covers were all designed by Adam. The gracefulness of his work reaches into every nook and cranny. Robert Adam was the designer of designers. To have a true connoisseur's delight, book ahead for the National Trust's candlelit evenings. Only by the flickering light of the candelabra and the glass chandeliers do these rooms (still not wired for electricity) shine forth in their true glory, as Adam meant them to do. There are more feasts for the knowing eye: all the Chippendale furniture, the Boulle writing desk in the velvet drawing room, the kitchen of 1779 with its 600 copper pots and pans, and the splendid collection of china (Worcester, Wedgwood, Derby, Dresden) in the Mirror Room. The pictures are the biggest surprise: look at them and they look straight back at you. The colourful Chinese scenes are not an avant-garde questioning of the rôle of the viewer, but 18th-century Chinese mirror paintings in black lacquered or gilded wooden frames with Chippendale Rococo ornamentation. The chinoiseries of Saltram House are outstanding early examples of a fashion that persisted right through to the Regency. Surrounded by hand-painted Chinese silk wallpaper from the early 18th century there is a mahogany four-poster bed (Chippendale again), next to which is a porcelain Chinese chamber pot, with painted lotus blossoms and a gold lion-knob on the lid. Almost worth getting out of bed for.

You will not find any such delicacies at *Buckland Abbey*, Drake's country house near Plymouth. Go towards Tavistock along the A386, for apparently that is where Drake is still riding in his black coach, pulled by four headless horses. Why? Because Crowndale Farm, the house south of Tavistock where he was born, and where he would certainly have liked to make the occasional appearance, has been

Sir Francis Drake

pulled down. Winding paths lead us to the Cistercian abbey (founded 1273 by Amicia), which only survived the attentions of Henry VIII because a neighbouring landowner bought the estate. His grandson, Sir Richard Grenville, made the church into a comfortable country house. After this renovation it was bought from him anonymously and deviously by his arch rival at court and at sea, Sir Francis Drake, who wished to invest the booty he had brought back from his voyage in some good solid real estate. From the doorway of the oak-panelled drawing room, Drake himself looks down on us somewhat mockingly in a portrait that was probably painted by his contemporary Marcus Gheeraerts the Younger. He was of somewhat small stature, but powerful, a *nouveau riche* who enjoyed living the high life at Buckland, and was married to the rich and beautiful Elizabeth Sydenham. This was his second marriage, and like the first it was childless. He died, as befits a sailor, far from his Buckland bed, off the coast of Panama in 1596, a victim of dysentery.

Faithful models of the *Revenge*, the *Golden Hind* and other famous ships are displayed on the first floor of the old abbey, where the history of navigation is charted from sailing ships to steamships. Drake's Drum, perched like a crown jewel on a velvet cushion, is probably a posthumous product. But what patriotic heart can remain unstirred by the sight of this national emblem, which according to legend sounds the alarm whenever England is in danger.

Dartmoor: On the Back of a Dinosaur

Generations of soaked Dartmoor hikers will assert that it rains here most days and when it doesn't rain, it mists. Of course it doesn't rain here any more than over the rest of Devon – which *can* be very wet – but I wouldn't advise you to go without your sou'wester. Dartmoor in the sudden sun is as uplifting an upland experience as you can find, and rich, creamy sunlight there is plenty of, enough to dispel any foggy phantoms or ghostly dogs.

Rain or snow, *Dartmoor* is a place for enthusiasts, be they archaeological, biological, metereological or even ichthyological (the brown trout and salmon are delicious). The moor is full of ferns, heather and lichen, crooked birch and stunted pine. What used to be called the 'forest' was royal hunting ground and not necessarily wooded. Water dances down the slopes of this 'mother of rivers', for they spring from the green marshes and flow to the coastal towns of Devon to which they give their names: the Teign, the Plym, the Dart. If you lose your way, just follow the right river. This place is dripping wet, and yet stone dry, for the mighty reservoir is also England's biggest repository of granite.

Two hundred square miles of it, to be precise, at an average height of 1500 feet. On the highest hills (Yes Tor, High Willhays), and at the most prolific river source (Cranmere), the Royal Marines do their training. The grey granite tors reach up into

Standing stone near Merrivale, Dartmoor

the grey sky, taking their name from the Celtic word for 'tower'. These strangely shaped blocks of stone were formed by erosion, and there are ten particularly steep ones which find themselves being energetically climbed once a year in the Ten Tors Race. London Bridge, Nelson's Column and many buildings in London are made of Dartmoor granite, much of it quarried in *Haytor*.

The early settlers did not find Dartmoor at all inhospitable. There was plenty of water, not much forest, stone for their houses, and hills for their protection. Ideal conditions by prehistoric standards. They lived in 'pounds', in round, thatched huts surrounded by stone walls. *Grimspound* near Manaton is one of the best preserved Bronze Age settlements, with the foundations of 22 such huts. One can even still see the various demarcations. Nearby, at *Hound Tor*, the remains of a medieval village have been discovered – a beautiful, isolated spot which was inhabited right up until the end of the 13th century. There are very few places in England which give such a clear picture of early medieval farmhouses, or at least of their groundplans, as here on Dartmoor. Yeo and Yardworthy, near Chagford, are prime examples. There are also faithfully reconstructed 17th- and 18th-century farmhouses around *Widecombe in the Moor*.

Three Boys, Nine Maidens: not pubs, but Bronze Age graves near Shovel Down (2¹/₂ miles south-west of Chagford). There are hens cackling around Spinster's Rock, a Neolithic megalith one mile west of Drewsteignton. But most of these prehistoric stones stand in mysterious silence on the moor, forming magic circles or ritualistic double rows, or simply on their own like forlorn sentinels. In much-visited Merrivale (2¹/₂ miles north-west of Princetown on the B3357) there are circles, rows and menhirs all together. Colin Wilson, the Outsider, who lives in Cornwall, compares being on Dartmoor to being on the back of a dinosaur. The Beaker People, who came to Dartmoor around 1900 BC, left no Stonehenge behind, but they did leave impressive sites, and just as enigmatic: the stone circle at Hound Tor, one mile west of Throwleigh, the stones at Merrivale, the lines of stones at Watern Down (1¹/₂ miles north-east of Warren House Inn, B3212), and Green Hill Row, whose 700 stones constitute the longest of these avenues (Stall Moor, 5 miles northwest of South Brent).

The Celts built some hill forts on Dartmoor, but the Romans gave the area a wide berth. For centuries, nothing happened, and then suddenly all hell broke loose: the Dartmoor Tin Rush. From the middle of the 12th century onwards, tin was hauled out of the richest mines in Europe. New settlers arrived, and the Dartmoor ponies which now carry tourists were used then to transport the all-important metal. Their first route across the moor, from north-east to south-west, is now the B3212. The date of the first clapper bridges, made of huge slabs of stone, is uncertain, but they are probably Iron Age. The romantic clapper bridge at *Postbridge*, however, which crosses the East Dart, is a prime specimen built in the 13th century to take the tin-mine packhorses. The Black Death, however, put an end to this first boom in 1349. The second began in the late 15th century, but by then the mines in Cornwall had proved to be even richer. In the 19th century, Dartmoor produced not only tin, but also copper, lead, silver, iron and even arsenic (col. pl. 51). The last tin mine, the Golden Dagger, near the remote Warren House Inn, closed in 1930. Industrial archaeologists have found traces of medieval tin-mining there, and on a boss in the nave at St Michael's, *Ilsington*, there are three rabbits with three conjoined ears – an alchemical symbol adopted by the guild of tinners as their emblem. The main relics, however, of the tinners' prosperity are the 'Cathedral of Dartmoor' in Widecombe (where Old Uncle Tom Cobleigh and all went to the famous fair), and the ruined castle at *Lydford*. This was the centre of jurisdiction for the four Stannary towns, as set up by Edward I – Tavistock, Plympton, Ashburton and Chagstock. Lydford Castle (1195) and not Princetown was the first prison on Dartmoor, notorious for its rough-and-ready justice: 'First hang and draw, and then hear the cause, is Lydford Law.'

Dwarf oaks and Old Man's Beard grow in *Wistman's Wood*, a nature reserve on the West Dart, near the Two Bridges Hotel. The Wist Man is another name for the Devil, and on nights of the full moon, the Prince of Darkness, with his red-eyed, flame-spitting Wist Hounds, comes riding out of the forest and across the moor. This leads to strange accidents on the B3212 where, it is said, two hairy hands have been known to seize the steering wheel. It was stories like that of the Wist Hounds that inspired Arthur Conan Doyle to write his Sherlock Holmes mystery, *The Hound of the Baskervilles* (1902). He wrote some chapters in the Duchy Hotel, which is now the excellent Visitors' Centre in *Princetown*, where you will find out all you need to know about the moor.

The prison capital of Dartmoor was named after the Prince Regent, later George IV. The present Prince of Wales, as Duke of Cornwall, still owns a third of Dartmoor, including the prison and the Two Bridges Hotel. Napoleonic prisoners-of-war built this wasteland jail in 1805-9 to Thomas Tyrwhite's design, and they were its first occupants. It also housed American prisoners captured in the 1812 war, 9000 of them in buildings designed for only 5000. Virtually empty from 1818-50, it became a civilian prison in 1852. Today there are 600 inmates behind the granite walls, but no longer any lifers, only Category B offenders. Ironically, this macabre attraction lies right in the middle of the leisure centre which is Dartmoor National Park. It is the last great wilderness of southern England, and in the high season it is overrun. Nature-lovers, climbers, mountain bikers, school classes, hikers and coach parties pour off the few roads and out into Mother Nature, covering the bare, grey, olive-green, dark brown slopes like multi-coloured beetles.

Dartmoor is not the place for castles, and yet it is the setting for the last castle to be built in England: *Castle Drogo* (1910-30; col. pl. 44). It stands almost 1000 feet above the forested gorge of the River Teign, a granite building on a granite rock. It was built by the tea millionaire and businessman Julius Drew, founder of the Home and Colonial Stores, who traced his family tree right back to Drogo, a Norman knight who came to England with William the Conqueror. He simply had to have a castle, and so Sir Edwin Lutyens designed a Tudor one for him, in the International Style of the thirties, with Roman and Norman elements in the interior – a modern medieval castle with Piranesian moments. Lutyens built it to an asymmetrical groundplan, using layers of smooth stone in cubes, like a monumental sculpture whose surface is devoid of decoration and variation. Lutyens also designed some of the furniture. Originally the castle was meant to be even bigger, but the money ran out.

Would anyone want to live in Drogo? Personally, I much prefer Gidleigh Park, in nearby *Chagford*. Nearby – well, the path winds endlessly along the Teign, and just as you think you're never going to find it, there it is: a late-1920's country house, absolute peace and quiet, and food for the gods. The chef is Michael Caines, not star of the screen, but star of the palate, brilliant pupil of Raymond Blanc. If you like good food, this is your journey's end.

Richard Long: A Sixty Minute Circle Walk on Dartmoor (1984)

JUMP · SHADOW · GRASS · ICE · SCUFF · SQUELCH · SOFT · BLUE · BREATHE · HOLLOW · BANK · RED · POOL · REEDS · GURGLE · SWISH · REFLECTION · SKYLINE · BELCH · TOR · WIND · DOWNHILL · LOPING · SUNLIGHT · ROCK · CRUNCHING · TUSSOCKS · HEATHER · TWIST · SQUELCH · BUBBLING · FLOODLINE · SNIFF · SLANT · SQUINT · SHEEP · KICK · CLITTER · SLOPE · GURGLING · WATCHED · SPLASH · WARM · MOTH · HAZE · LARK · MOSS · BROWNISH · SKULL · CAW · STUB · CAWING · SLABS · ALIGNED · SPIDER · SCRUNCH · DROPPINGS · SLITHER · PANTING · YELLOWISH

ONE HOUR

A SIXTY MINUTE CIRCLE WALK ON DARTMOOR 1984

When I eventually managed to tear myself away, I went to a village on the northern edge of Dartmoor to meet the painter John Virtue (col. pl. 45). Since 1988 he has been working in *South Tawton*, with a view over the green vales and bare heights of Cawsand Beacon. His studio is a barn owned by Barry the milkman, and his subject-matter is Nature – Nature in the abstract, for he is the most radical landscape artist since John Constable, whose opinion he shares, that 'painting is but another word for feeling.'

Virtue is a man of explosive temperament, a former pupil of Frank Auerbach. For years he has been painting only in black and white, using layers of charcoal, ink, acrylic and shellac. A constant theme is light and dark, and nowhere is this more dramatically to hand than on Dartmoor. Every day in all seasons he explores with drawings and paintings the immediate surroundings of South Tawton. He does not use an easel, and even out in the open he spreads his giant canvases flat on the ground. 'I like being in the landscape and in the painting,' he says. His art lives from this direct physical identification and tension. With vehement yet subtle strokes he lays on the paint, using spatulas, syringes and sprays, sticks and calligraphic brushes, hands and feet. Earth, grass, raindrops, sheep's tracks – they all belong to the elemental nature of this art. 'It all has to do with the light and the weather, and with the steam rising from a field, the glitter on the leaves, wind crossing the land.' John Virtue's pictures erupt. The countryside (and its destruction) become more tangible, more immediate than in traditional landscape painting, even if South Tawton only appears in topographical fragments: the church tower, the roofs, the curves of streets and hills. This is Nature not as we see it, but as we experience it.

What Makes Clovelly So Beautiful?

Inland the hills curve gently, but the cliffs drop sheer to the sea. Streams meander softly through the countryside, then suddenly hurl themselves in waterfalls down the steep rocks into the ocean below. A place for beachcombers, or it used to be, for while the sheep grazed safely in the green fields beyond, the ships came crashing to their doom. 'From Padstow Point to Lundy Light / 'Tis a watery grave by day or night.' Hartland Point, the north-west tip of Devon, falls 300 feet or more down to the sea. The next land to the west across the Atlantic is America. From the clifftop hotel Hartland Quay you can see *Lundy*, the granite island that runs for some three miles along the entrance to the Bristol Channel. With its strangely shaped, strangely named rocks, like the 'Devil's Slide', what else could it have been over the centuries other than a pirates' lair? Today it is a sanctuary for seabirds like puffins, guillemots and gannets, and indeed its very name is derived from the old Norse word for 'puffin'. Birdwatchers with plenty of time to spare can spot around 400 species here. The island is now owned by the National Trust and administered by the Landmark

Norman font, Hartland

Trust. It has twenty inhabitants, three lighthouses, two churches and an hotel. And it's a good place for lobster.

For miles around you can see Hartland's Perpendicular church tower, which at almost 40 metres is the tallest in Devon. The church, dedicated to the Welsh missionary St Nectan, is in the little village of *Stoke*, where the great Allen Lane, inventor of the paperback as we know it, is buried. It has two treasures: a choir screen with 15th-century tracery, and a Norman font (1169) from the four corners of which the heads of the baptised look down on the unbaptised at the bottom.

Christian or heathen, everyone wants to go to *Clovelly*. This little fishing village nestling on the rocks of North Devon is unique (col. pl. 50). What makes it so beautiful? Good press, above all. Victorian novelists drew the world's attention to Clovelly. Charles Kingsley, who went to school here, described it as 'his dear old paradise' in *Westward Ho!* (1855) – a title so evocative that a once-remote little bathing resort was actually named after it, complete with exclamation mark.

Dickens and Wilkie Collins, in their story *A Message from the Sea*, called it Steepway, and that indeed is the trademark of Clovelly – the long, steep, cobbled street that no vehicle can enter. It is a stone waterfall of steps and doorsteps and whitewashed houses, from the old New Inn to the even older Royal Inn down by the pier below.

A brilliant advertisement for paternalism, Clovelly has belonged to the Rous family since 1738 and John Rous today has firm ideas on what England should be like. It could be a model village – but real tenants live here, and the picturesque fishermen catch real fish. Go to Clovelly for a briny smell of crab and lobster and herring. 3000,000 other people do.

The bridge at *Bideford* (1460) has 24 arches, and across them runs the road to Barnstaple, the market town on the estuary of the River Taw. *Barnstaple* contributed five ships to the fleet that defeated the Armada – or were they Bideford ships sailing via Barnstaple? Local feelings still run high. Barnstaple also gave a dramatist to European literature: John Gay. He was born in 1685 at the corner of High Street and Joy Street, and he went to school in St Anne's Chapel, (no longer the local museum but open by appointment). After that he was apprenticed to a silk merchant in London. But he preferred writing poems, fables, satires like *Trivia, or, The Art of Walking the Streets of London*, and the ballad-based *Beggar's Opera*, whose success was to be made even more sensational 200 years later by Bertolt Brecht as the *Threepenny Opera* (1928). Peacham and Macheath were the criminal citizens, or citizen criminals at the socio-critical heart of Gay's entertainment, and this satire on contemporary Italian opera made him rich and famous.

In 1992, at Barnstaple's old railway station, Prince Charles opened a truly royal footpath: the Tarka Trail. With detours round cycle tracks and railway lines, it runs for 175 miles through North Devon all the way to Exmoor, along the steep coastline, through dunes and valleys, more or less faithfully following the route that Tarka took. Tarka – the name means 'little water wanderer' – was an otter. He was the hero of a novel published in 1927 that is unique in its total engagement with the life of a wild creature. 'What the critics say about its being too tightly packed is right,' Williamson wrote later, after he had recovered from the exhaustion of writing *Tarka*. 'Yet I enjoyed it all. I knew the prose was straight, keen and true. It is all here in Devon, if you just happen to see and hear or smell it.' Williamson had helped dig out an orphaned otter cub, and brought it into his house, where it lived with him until it was caught one day in a rabbit gin. He managed to release it, but the otter slipped out of his grasp and disappeared, never to return. Williamson spent onths tracking his otter, with its maimed paw, up and down the Torridge and the Taw, learning to see the country from an otter's eye level, understanding their life in the quick waters.

Otters were not protected by law until 1970. They are shy creatures, very rarely to be seen on the Taw or the Torridge, and totally absent from the Tarka Trail. This

52 Stone Cross, Dartmoor

53. Path on Dartmoor

54. Dartmoor

55. Cotehele

56. Saltram

57. *Sir Joshua Reynolds, by Angelica Kauffmann, 1767*

58. Tin mines at Botallack

59. Minack Cliff Theatre, near Porthcurno

60. Egyptian House, Penzance

61. Polperro, by Oscar Kokoschka

62. Fishing boats at Newlyn

63. On the Sands by Walter Sickert, 1883

64. Barbara Hepworth's studio

65. Barbara Hepworth Museum Garden

66. St Ives, Cornwall, by Ben Nicholson, 1943-45

67. St Ives

68. St Michael's Mount, by J. M. W. Turner

ends where it begins, on the Taw estuary in Barnstaple, where Tarka fled from his pursuers to the open sea and death. Henry Williamson is buried in *Georgeham*, a nearby village, where he had gone to live at the age of 25, having turned his back on London. No great lover of civilization, he was sympathetic towards Hitler during the 1930's.

You can botanize at Braunton, play a round of golf in Saunton, and go bathing on the long beach of Woolacombe. Devon offers excellent 'capabilities', as Lancelot Brown used to tell his clients. But if the weather is bad, go to the church of St Brannock, the Celtic saint, in *Braunton*, for there you will find the finest 16th-century pews in Devon. Carved in chestnut, the saint himself is to be seen riding a ox, and all around him are richly decorated initials and instruments of passion on about fifty other bench-ends. There are also carved pigs galore, including a sow with a litter of seven. The church on the hill above the present site was twice destroyed: after the second time the vicar had a dream in which he was told to build the new church wherever he found a sow with her litter, and this is just what he did.

The coast of North Devon, from the Victorian resort of Ilfracombe to Lynmouth on the edge of Exmoor, is picturebook country. Halfway between them, in the old silver-mining town of *Combe Martin*, is the strangest inn you will ever see. 'Pack o' Cards' was apparently built after its owner had had a big win in 1690. There are four floors, each with 13 doors, and there were once 52 windows altogether (though several of these were boarded up to save on window tax). This hand was well planned, and its trump card was certainly a vivid imagination.

An Epitaph in memory of Thicksaid
Thomas Fleming Gent...

Cornwall

After Plymouth, you cross the Tamar, leaving Devon, and leaving England. The other side of the river is Saltash and Cornwall. Brunel's Royal Albert Bridge (1859) is the right spot to lift the spirits of Englishmen about to tour Cornwall, and Cornishmen intending to leave England. *Kernow*, it says in proud, official letters – for Cornish, though not exactly a living language, is far from a dead one.

As in Wales, language is the defining factor in national feelings. It is Cornish – still recognizable in place and family names – that sets Cornwall apart rather than the landscape, since initially this is simply a continuation of the Devon coast. It may not be quite so mild and green, but it is full of similar branching, fjord-like estuaries. On the other side of the Tamar, the names are predominantly Celtic in origin, and not Anglo-Saxon. Sir Walter Scott summed up the typical prefixes: 'By Tre-, Pol- and Pen-/ You shall know all true Cornishmen.' Trerice, Polperro and Penzance: the roots of this language are more closely akin to Welsh and Breton than to Scots Gaelic. Yet already in Scott's time the last fully native speaker of Cornish had died. Does anyone still speak *Kernewek*? A few hundred, thinks Professor Charles Thomas of Exeter University, who specializes in linguistic archaeology. Around 2600, think the Cornish Language Board in Saltash. There is even a publishing firm in Helston; Helston and Liskeard each have a shop that sell books in Cornish and act as language 'infocentres'; in addition the Cornish Gorsedd organizes classes and competitions in Cornish. Even if no independence movement is more peaceful than *Mebyon Kernow* (Free Cornwall), it is far from slumbering. Cornish has been recognised as a living language by the EU, and the Commission for Racial Equality has recognised the separate identity of the Cornish people.

The Romans never really got a foothold here, the Saxons were resisted by Cornish warlords – perhaps including a certain Arthur – and the Normans took two years to conquer Cornwall. The Devil didn't even try. It is said that Old Nick never came across the Tamar because he knew that Cornish women put whatever they can lay their hands on into their pasties. The typical Cornish pasty is a pastry case containing potatoes, turnips, meat and onions. It was the traditional dish of the tin miners, and is a great way to fill a man's stomach.

Slate monument in Madron, near Penzance, to Thomas Cock, Thomas Fleming, their wives and children: 'just like playing cards' (Pevsner)

Evidence of Arthur? A sixth-century slate plaque with the name Artognov, recently discovered at Tintagel Castle

Edward III knew what this remote and inhospitable tip of his island had to offer: natural resources and ultimately loyal subjects, provided they were properly treated. He gave Cornwall precedence over all the other counties by making it a duchy in 1337, the Duke being his eldest son the Black Prince. Since then the land and the title have always been inherited by the heir to the throne. Prince Charles is the twenty-fourth Duke of Cornwall, and his duchy in fact extends way beyond the borders. He owns some 130,000 acres of land across 23 counties, though more than half of this is on the somewhat uneconomic Dartmoor. Infinitely more profitable are his 35 or so acres of London. The Isles of Scilly belong to the duchy, along with 155 miles of coastal waters, and the freight of any wrecked ships. The Duke has 285 farms, half a dozen pubs, and such legendary holy sites as the Oval and Dartmoor Prison. As Prince of Wales, Charles only controls 700 Welsh acres, but as Duke of Cornwall his possessions include the forests around Lostwithiel, the ruined castles of Restormel and Tintagel, the mouth of the River Camel, the Padstow ferry, and extensive mineral rights. This is all worth a bit more than the fifteen bezants – as the crusaders called the gold coins they brought from the Holy Land via Byzantium – which are part of the Duke of Cornwall's coat-of-arms, along with two red-beaked, red-legged Cornish choughs.

The centuries-old link between Cornwall and the Crown was particularly useful to Charles I during the Civil War. There was no more royalist county than Cornwall. A copy of his thank-you letter of 1643 can still be seen hanging in many a village church between Launceston and Land's End. True royalists are often also true Christians, and the pioneering work in this field was done by missionaries from Ireland and Wales during the 5th and 6th centuries. St Enodoc, St Neot, St Teath,

St Mabyn and St Mawgan have all left their mark on Cornish place names, even if most of them have failed to get themselves into the official Roman catalogue of saints. One of them, St Piran, became patron saint of the tin miners. Their flag is a white cross on a black background – white for tin, black for rock, and these are the colours that Cornish patriots raise beside the Union Jack. But they are not separatists. For real freedom fighters, you need to go back to 1549, when Cranmer's Book of Common Prayer was introduced. That was too much for the Cornish, who rose up against King Edward VI in a kind of Counter Reformation: the Western Rising was a declaration of cultural independence, but the bloody rebellion was all for nothing.

Anyone not born within the sound of *Sancreed's* bells used to be called an 'emmet' (an ant) and the fact is that modern Cornwall does indeed swarm like an antheap with folk from outside the county. In the churchyard at Sancreed there are two age-old crosses that stand like lost signposts in the wasteland of West Penwith. Indeed there are prehistoric dolmens, Celtic crosses and holy wells all over the place. Life is harder here than elsewhere, and the mists are thicker, so the gods are more urgently needed in order to keep the evil spirits at bay. The Methodist John Wesley had his greatest successes in Cornwall, where he began his work in 1743, out in the open, preaching to thousands in Gwennap Pit. This great hollow near Redruth, made into an amphitheatre, is still the meeting-place for Methodists from all over the world who congregate here on Spring Bank Holiday.

At some point in history, the Devil must have conquered his fear of Cornish pasties, since he has a frying pan and a pair of bellows on the Cornish coast. These are just some of his rocks, and in March 1967 the supertanker *Torrey Canyon* ran into one of them and became an early symbol of the plague of oil pollution. Between the Lizard and Land's End, England reaches out into the sea like a pair of pincers, and this is the coast that for centuries has seized the ships of nations. It was always the cape of no hope, and the kingdom of pirates and smugglers. Today, though, we can peacefully wander along the clifftop paths of the National Trust, protected by the sign of the yellow acorn. These paths make up a scenic route beyond compare – 270 miles, from Saltash in the south, along the Channel coast, around Land's End, right up to Morwenstow on the Atlantic. There is only one golden rule for you to remember: in Cornwall it rains once a day, and twice on Sunday. As for the population, there were just 470,000 people at the last count. You could fit them all into Bristol.

'My word – what a country!' Virginia Woolf wrote to Vita Sackville-West. She was staying at St Ives in 1936. 'Why do we ever spend any part of our short lives in Sussex, Kent or London?' It all made her feel 'so incredibly and incurably romantic' and she was not alone. In 1870, in Vallency Valley near St Juliot, surrounded by trees and bellflowers, a young architect named Thomas Hardy first went on a picnic with Emma Gifford. She became his wife, he became a novelist, and their romance became a Cornish tale called *A Pair of Blue Eyes* (1873). Village churches, which at that time Hardy was busily restoring, were a lifelong love of John Betjeman's, and when his time came, the Poet Laureate had himself buried next to St Enodoc's, on the mouth of the River Camel. 'Those golden and unpeopled bays, / The shadowy cliffs and sheepworn ways.' Betjeman's remote church is now right in the middle of a golf course.

Cornwall is Pilcher Country. With novels like *The Shell Seekers* and sales of millions, Rosamunde Pilcher has made her county famous all over the world. The name she gives to St Ives in her Cornish novels is 'Porthkerris'. She was born nearby in Lelant, and one of her favourite subjects is the romantic one of 'Coming Home' to Cornwall. But Cornwall is not pure romance. It is the county with the lowest average income, and its unemployment rate is far above the national average. Pilcherland has as much to do with Cornish reality as best-sellers have to do with literature.

The Inn on Bodmin Moor

If you take the ferry from Devonport to Cornwall, you will enjoy a breathtaking sight on your arrival. *Antony* was built by an unknown architect in 1711-21 – a Queen Anne house whose proportions are simply perfect. The windows, set in rhythmic groups of three, are pure reflections of good sense and modesty; the regulated splendour of the oak-panelled rooms is in contrast to the extravagant irrationality and picturesque exuberance of the park – probably by Repton, since a Red Book for it survives, but in any case in his spirit. All this was not quite enough for the pompous Victorians. They had to stick a colonnaded entrance on the front, just to show that it *was* the front.

Upriver, high above the Tamar near Calstock – where like a tightrope walker the railway crosses the valley over a twelve-arched viaduct – stands a medieval contrast to Antony, *Cotehele*: a proliferation of granite, full of angles, the Tudor manor house (1485-1539) of the Edgcumbe family, who lived here until 1947. The Great Hall is filled with weapons, banners and trophies just as it might have been in the 15th century, and the rooms are hung with Flemish and Mortlake tapestries. Down on the river is the little chapel that commemorates the escape of Richard Edgcumbe from his enemy Sir Henry Trenowth – he jumped 70 foot into the river, right here, in 1483.

Further up the same river in *Launceston*, more or less contemporary with Cotehele, is the most spectacular church west of Exeter: *St Mary Magdalene* (1511-24). All round, the granite blocks are carved like reliefs into ornamental patterns, with row upon row of Gothic quatrefoils, heraldic roses, lilies and Cornish fern.

The Great Hall, Cotehele

Mary Magdalene herself reclines inside a niche in the east wall, flanked by angels and musicians playing medieval instruments. The decoration of the interior reaches its peak in the filigree carving of the pulpit, which has been restored to its original colours and is one of the few wooden pulpits to have survived from the Reformation. Such a magnificent forum would have been superfluous to the requirements of the itinerant preacher George Fox, founder of the Society of Friends, or 'Quakers'. However, for his missionary activities in Launceston he spent six months of 1656 in the Norman dungeons of Castle Terrible.

Not until the 19th century did the more centrally situated *Bodmin* replace the hill town of Launceston as the county capital (though it in turn has now been supplanted by Truro). The road 'into Bodmin and out of the world', as the locals say, leads across *Bodmin Moor*, which is approximately half as big and half as wild as Dartmoor. Before it became a favourite haunt of the hiker, this too was an eerie place, with strange knocking sounds from abandoned mineshafts, and ghostly carriages driven by maniacal skeletons. On the main road of *Bolventor*, right in the middle of the moor, is an inn where for centuries travellers would rest and smugglers would smuggle. Then Daphne du Maurier arrived, had a drink, had a look round, and wrote *the* Cornish novel of the 1930's: *Jamaica Inn*. It soon became a film set, and a meeting-place for all friends of literature and pub-life. Today it houses the Museum of Curiosity, the life's work of the Victorian taxidermist Walter

Font at St Petroc's, Bodmin

Potter. He stuffed the animals, dressed them up, and organized them into tableaux: cats' wedding, rabbits' school, and so on. Whether this puts the animals on a par with us, or us on a par with the animals is a moot point.

The importance and splendour of Bodmin in the Middle Ages is summed up by a single stone: the font in *St Petroc's*. There are four angels' heads at the corners, and in the midst of wild animals is the Tree of Life, which branches out into endless forms of decoration. This is one of the finest Norman fonts of the hundred or so still to be found in Cornwall (at Altarnun, for example, and at Roche, Launceston and St Austell).

Lanhydrock, south of Bodmin, belonged to the Augustinians of St Petroc until the dissolution of the monasteries. Then a Truro dealer in tin and wool seized the opportunity to buy the land, and built himself one of those houses that we all dream about. It stands on a hill overlooking the River Fowey, is surrounded by forest and parkland, has a gatehouse just as medieval castles had, and a formal garden where the yew trees stand in solemn readiness like evergreen butlers. A fire in 1881 virtually gutted the house, but the Victorian restoration did nothing to destroy the Jacobean symmetry of 1642. Only the north wing survived the fire intact, and that contains the longest and brightest room, the Gallery, with a superbly decorated plaster ceiling. The chrysanthemums on William Morris's wallpaper could have bloomed in the bronze amphorae of the garden, and they are typical of the natural harmony between the interior and exterior of Lanhydrock.

If you want to see a really strange house, go to the end of a dead-end road between Mount and Warleggan, in a remote valley on the southern edge of Bodmin Moor. There you will be confronted with turrets, pyramid roofs, coloured tiles, walls of rubble masonry decorated with slate, marble and pink granite intarsia, and geometrical and symbolic ornamentations spreading over long, narrow windows like dragon's wings. The interior too glows with the dark colours and textures of another world: Minton tiles, carpets and wallpaper by Morris and Pugin, wrought-iron railings and Gothic doors taken from redundant churches. This is *Barley Splatt*, an architectural collage in the style of postmodern Gothic Revival. Since 1973 Graham Ovenden has been at work on this house, and if you ask him when it's going to be finished, he will echo Antoni Gaudí, one of his heroes: 'The client is in no rush.'

Graham Ovenden and his wife Annie, painter and graphic artist respectively, were born at least a hundred years too late. Together with Peter Blake, a painter friend and a sort of secular Pre-Raphaelite like themselves, they founded the Brotherhood of Ruralists in 1975. Originally there were seven members of this community. They celebrate Nature and her mysteries in very detailed and ecstatic landscapes, still lives and portraits. They want to play their part in the preservation of the countryside by painting, drawing, holding rural festivals, and reviving arts and crafts in all areas of everyday life. It is a very romantic, very English movement. William Morris and

Samuel Palmer are among its godfathers, and Alice in Wonderland and various countrified Lolitas among its favourite themes.

Like many families, however, the brotherhood has had its problems. Friendships have cooled, Peter Blake has long since returned to London, and David Inshaw to Wales. Only Barley Splatt remains unperturbed, and incomplete, in its damp dark valley on Bodmin Moor. There the Ovendens live with their cat Ogden, their dog Birdie, and a chicken. And if he hasn't yet gone under the grill, Gilbert the Trout is still swimming in his pond.

From Fowey to Manderley: The Coast of The Birds

Along the coastal route from Looe to Fowey, I saw *Polperro* again. I first saw this old fishing village in the Tate Gallery, painted by Oskar Kokoschka (col. pl. 61). In the foreground is a seagull which, like the painter himself, has a bird's eye view of the bay, the illuminated water, and the houses on the cliff. And what I saw was as elemental as Kokoschka's panorama. What has, however, very wisely been left out of the picture is the flood of visitors that collects in this narrow spot during the summer, like eels in a trap – much to the commercial advantage of the former fishermen and smugglers of Polperro. Born in Austria, Kokoschka had fled to England in 1938, and the following year he moved into a log cabin on the clifftop, because it was cheaper, London was overcrowded, and he liked to breathe the fresh sea air. He was not allowed, however, to paint outside because of military security; so he did crayon sketches on the beach, including some for *The Crab*, a monster waiting on the shore for the shipwrecked – an allegory on his own situation as an exile.

The River Fowey has its mouth in the harbour town of the same name, and its source is on Brown Willy, the highest hill on Bodmin Moor. Like a fjord, this estuary reaches far into the land, and it is a favourite bay for sailing. In the Middle Ages *Fowey* was a thriving port. Cornish sailors used to leave from here to raid the coasts of Normandy, even long after Edward IV had made peace with France in 1475. Place, the mansion of the Treffrey family near the church, is a rich reminder of Fowey's prosperous past, but almost totally rebuilt in the 19th century. Pevsner was puzzled here. 'Delightful', he says, and 'overwhelming', before coming out with 'It is of an ambitious, somewhat elephantine Walter Scott romanticism.'

A ferry links Fowey to *Bodinnick* on the other side of the bay. In 1926 a young authoress moved here from London, after her parents had bought Ferryside as a holiday home. Daphne du Maurier was to spend the rest of her life on this coast, her Cornish novels as popular as those of Rosamunde Pilcher a generation later.

'Last night I dreamt I went to Manderley again.' Thus begins *Rebecca* (1938), which Hitchcock filmed as a psychological thriller. *The Birds* too was based on a du Maurier story. Manderley was Menabilly, du Maurier's country house, which she rented in 1943 on an isolated peninsula west of Fowey. There she was able to fulfil her childhood dream: 'Here was the freedom I desired, long-sought-for, not yet known. Freedom to write, to walk, to wander; freedom to climb hills, to pull a boat, to be alone.' It was the freedom, in Cornwall almost a magic compulsion, to join King Arthur and his Round Table and his questing knights. Does the Menabilly obelisk with its Latin inscription refer to the death of Tristan? Were the earthworks of Castle Dore, north of Fowey, perhaps the ancient Lancien, the golden castle of King Mark? Daphne du Maurier's literary archaeology led her to Malpas, near Truro.

Daphne du Maurier

There, on the banks of the Fal, she found nothing but the memory of her own honeymoon, which she had spent here on a yacht, called the *Ygdrasil*, after the great Earth-Tree of Norse mythology, a strange name for a boat if ever there was. That was in the summer of 1932, when she had sailed west along the coast with her husband, behind Falmouth and into the River Helford. They stopped in Frenchman's Creek, which duly became the title of another novel (1941). Thus did Daphne du Maurier transform the landscapes, smuggler's tales and myths into the great Cornish saga of her life. Fiction replaced the reality that she feared so much. In the end there were seventeen novels, five biographies, one autobiography, fourteen volumes of short stories, and the title Dame of the British Empire. In 1969 she moved with her family from Menabilly to neighbouring Kilmarth, where she died in 1989. Her ashes were thrown into the sea at Gribbin Head.

Behind Fowey, near *St Austell*, is an extraordinary landscape. 'This strange white world of pyramid and pool,' wrote Daphne du Maurier. Miniature Alps in the middle of Cornwall, pyramids of icing sugar, with dark green pits between them. It was the Quaker apothecary William Cookworthy who discovered china clay here in the mid 18th century, the first to be found in England, and he set up a factory in Plymouth in 1768. Cornish kaolin was ideal for the manufacture of fine white porcelain, and factories in Derby, Minton and Worcester soon leapt onto the bandwagon. Ever since, kaolin and petuntse (or chinastone) have been extracted from around St Austell, and this is now Cornwall's biggest industry following the closure of the tin and copper mines. You might ask – does Cornwall make all the world's dinner plates? You need to add electrical wiring, paint, plastics, cosmetics, agricultural products, pharmaceutical rubber appliances, whatever horrors that might include, and most of all, paper. Every glossy page in this book is glossy with clay coating. All of this uses tons of kaolin; and for every ton extracted nine tons of spoil are left, and this is what makes up the strange white pyramids. With 1.6 million tons of kaolin being produced every year, it is scarcely surprising that the landscape is growing ever more peculiar. The best view of it is from the specially constructed viewpoint within the Wheal Martyn China Clay Heritage Centre.

St Michael's Mount: Pilgrims, Monks and Mimosa

You can see the whole range and the fascinating forms of Cornish minerals at the museum in *Truro*. This provincial museum is in fact full of interesting discoveries: the geological and industrial archaeology of the region, Cookworthy's first china-ware, still imperfect, pictures by John Opie (1761-1807), Cornwall's first important painter, and mementoes of the county's beloved sport of wrestling. At the bottom of the stairs, in the main gallery, is the 'Cornish Giant', Anthony Payne, with halberd and burning fuse. Charles II had him painted lifesize by Sir Godfrey Kneller, his court painter from Germany, because wherever Payne took his 7-foot bulk during the Civil War, the Roundheads would have second thoughts about the wisdom of fighting the Cavaliers.

Truro Cathedral (1880-1910) rises majestically out of the flock of houses gathered around it. After St Germans (1050) had ceased to be a bishopric, it was not until 1876 that Cornwall regained that status, and Truro became the bishop's seat. J. L. Pearson's cathedral is an ambitious and far from unsuccessful attempt to link up with the great traditions of the Middle Ages. It is an heroic anachronism created at the turn of the century, and the pointed arches and galleries, the rectangular east end with its lancet windows, the double transepts, Early English elements all, create space that might have been interesting. But the overall effect is hollow, for the arts and crafts of the time have left nothing memorable in this cathedral. The pointed spires of the crossing tower and the French twin-tower façade are unusual for Cornwall. Originally they were all meant to glow in Cornish-green, like the copper-covered side tower of the transept.

If you go downriver from Truro to the sea, you'll come to a harbour which the fishermen of *Falmouth* simply took over from Nature. Merchant ships and then seaside trippers came virtually of their own accord. Henry VIII rated the bay worthy of two fortresses as part of his coastal defences: *Pendennis Castle* (1546), at the highest point of the foothills, and *St Mawes Castle* (1543) directly opposite. The overall effect is to create one of those scenes in which history and Nature intertwine in such a manner that the landscape is unimaginable without its castles or at least their ruins.

There are subtropical gardens at *Penjerrick* and *Glendurgan*, and exquisite fish at the Riverside in *Helford* (I recommend the oysters), and after you've gorged yourself there, why not take a walk around the *Lizard*? Along the clifftop path you will see blackberries, sloes, gorse, fern and heather. 'The sea wind sang/Shrill, chill, with flakes of foam' was how Tennyson saw the Cornish sea, as he followed the tracks of King Arthur. Between the fishing village of Cadgwith and the rocky sculptures of Kynance Cove, there is the soft, dark green stone known as serpentine, which is so often polished up for use as ashtrays or souvenirs. The Lizard is more southerly than Land's End, and closer to the Equator than Prague, but that doesn't make it any warmer. The cold winds have their uses, however: the great dishes on the bare heights of Goonhilly Downs have been joined by giant propellers to provide an alternative source of energy. There are many such wind farms in Cornwall, though not everyone welcomes them. *Poldhu*, near the picturesque bay of Mullion, saw the introduction of another form of power at the turn of the century, and it is commemorated by an obelisk. Here Marconi invented the wireless. From the telegraph station (which no longer exists) the Italian physicist succeeded in sending the first radio message across the Atlantic to St Johns in Newfoundland. The message was *pip-pip-pip*, the letter S.

There is no silhouette in Cornwall more beautiful than that of *Mount's Bay* near Penzance and *St Michael's Mount*, its offshore island (col. pl. 68). In such a romantic setting, most people would have heard the songs of the Sirens or seen an alluring Lorelei, but in the year 495 some Cornish fishermen sailing through the mist found themselves confronted by St Michael. As 'captain of the heavenly host', he was always a pugnacious saint, and so from the very start the island had two faces: a place of quiet reflection and raging battles, monastery and fortress, pilgrims and pirates. The monks made the music, but the warriors set the tone. It was from here that in 1588 the first beacons blazed to announce the approach of the Spanish Armada. The strategic importance of St Michael's Mount – in the Hundred Years War, the Wars of the Roses, and the Civil War – always outweighed its religious side. After the Norman Conquest, it was made a dependency of the Benedictine Mont St Michel in Normandy. However reasonable such a link may have seemed in terms of church politics and nomenclature, the few monks who built their church here never had much influence.

At low tide you can walk across a narrow granite causeway from Marazion to the island. The fishermen's cottages cluster round the mole at the foot of the mount. Perhaps this is the island of Ictis described by ancient historians as the port from which Cornish tin used to be exported to the Mediterranean countries. Such islands abound with legends. 'Pilgrims,' says the guide, as he leads us up the steep and stony path, 'this is the spot where the bold Cornishman Jack killed the giant Cormoran. And Cormoran's stone heart is still beating. If you put your right foot on this stone and your right hand on your own heart, you'll hear the beat!' At the top of this 230-foot high mount, the granite of the rock turns into the granite of the castle. The aesthetic unity of the place owes not a little to this natural transition, despite the different functions and phases of its construction. In the 17th century the monastery-cum-fortress became the summer residence of the St Aubyn family. But who would want to live permanently in a place so exposed to the sea, the storms, and the pirates? Only a generation brought up on Romanticism could have cherished the charms of a house on the ocean wave. Piers St Aubyn transformed St Michael's Mount into a permanent house in 1875, without altering the age-old silhouette. The Chevy Chase Room, formerly the monks' refectory, is decorated with a plaster frieze containing scenes of bear and deer hunting and hare coursing (1641). What used to be the Lady Chapel is now the Blue Drawing Room and boudoir, with white decorations on the ceiling, ogee arches, and Chippendale furniture, all in elegant Rococo-Gothic style even before Strawberry Hill (1740-50). The Cornish artist John Opie, a friend of the owner, painted the highly effective *Mount by Moonlight*, but the star turn was created by the butler Henry Lee: he used the large quantity of discarded champagne corks to build a model of the granite rocks and castle. This is a real work of art, constructed out of the leftovers of his job. Truly this servant was a master.

The Victorian south-east wing rises like a sea-eagle's eyrie over the pounding waves. It was there that I met John St Aubyn, 4th Lord St Levan. He was wearing a Burgundy-red waistcoat beneath a brown tweed jacket with a badly worn left sleeve. His Lordship is a humble tenant of the National Trust, though his lease runs for 999 years. He still had the power to prevent the construction of a new entrance for visitors: 'My father wanted to preserve the beauty and the charm of the island, without any new commercial buildings for tourism. That was why he gave St Michael's Mount to the National Trust in 1954.' Since then, it has been farewell to the island's splendid isolation: almost 200,000 visitors a year come here. 'I don't think you can live in such a remarkable place and not share it with others,' says Lord St Levan. 'Stately homes are just like theatre, and they're also a factor in the economy.' He attaches particular importance to maintaining the religious tradition of this former monastery. 'Catholics, Protestants, Anglicans, Quakers, Methodists, they all come here. We can have any form of service we like. Since the Middle Ages we've been entirely independent. We're not subject to the jurisdiction of the bishop.' There is still, however, an official chaplain, and there are still the six 14th-century bells in the chapel, which Lord and Lady St Levan themselves ring on New Year's Eve.

Above the fortress flutter the Cornish flag and the Union Jack side by side. When I asked His Lordship what had been his most significant contribution to the family home, he replied: 'The ten tons of manure I had brought to the island.' For what he loves most here is his garden. There are subtropical plants in abundance, including yuccas, and in spring mimosa blooms between the rocks, and delicate tamarisk and wild narcissus. Even in winter there are fuchsias and hydrangeas. This is a maritime terraced garden, begun in the 18th century, twenty acres in all, wrung from the reluctant soil, exposed to the Atlantic storms and the salty spray – a unique garden with plants from China, Tibet, Australia and South Africa, some of them very rare, some that in Britain can normally only be grown in hothouses. In the old days, pilgrims used to flock to the shrine of St Michael, and today they come from all over the world to admire his garden.

By now the tide has come in. An amphibious craft takes us back to the mainland, and we find ourselves in *Penzance*, the harbour town on Mount's Bay. *Pen Sans*, the 'holy headland', has a population of just 20,000, a pub with a pirate on the roof, and a folly called the *Egyptian House* (col. pl. 60). Quite unexpectedly you come to it in the midst of all the typically English houses of Chapel Street. The doorway is flanked by clustered papyrus columns, above which are two caryatids with palm-leaf capitals, crowned in turn by the royal lion and unicorn, and a spread eagle under the roof. The front has trapezoidal windows – strangely reminiscent of art deco – and is green, brown and ochre. This exotic piece of street theatre was produced around 1836 by John Foulston, the Plymouth city architect. In 1823 he had already built an Egyptian-style library in Devonport, and before that in 1812 the prototype of this new fashion had been built in Piccadilly: P. F. Robinson's Egyptian Hall. The Egyptian Revival between 1800 and 1840, which had its origins far back in the 18th century, was given new impetus by Napoleon's Egyptian campaign. Everyone was fascinated by the colossal pyramids and the mysteries associated with the cult of the dead. The result was entrances to graveyards, freemasons' lodges, lawcourts and prisons, all in Ancient Egyptian style. Just like the fashion for chinoiserie slightly earlier, it was simply a playful exercise in the exotic – a folly, as was the Egyptian House in Penzance.

Penzance's greatest son was Sir Humphry Davy (1778-1829), the Miners' Friend 'Instructed in the rudiments of science by a saddler,' as the DNB says, he became the leading scientist of his day, and among other achievements he discovered that a filter of wire gauze would prevent gas from exploding. The Davy lamp which resulted saved the lives of countless miners. His achievements in chemistry also had a notable spin-off: a flash of inspiration in the school laboratory made E. C. Bentley write of Davy (who detested gravy) 'He lived in the odium/ Of having discovered sodium', and thus at a stroke to invent the clerihew. There is a statue of Davy outside the Market Hall.

In nearby *Newlyn* there is a smell of fish. At the quayside are the red, green and blue deep-sea trawlers, nets are being patched, buoys and lobster baskets are being loaded on board (col. pl. 62). Newlyn is at present England's biggest fishing port – one of the last ports in Cornwall with a fleet of any consequence. Its market (opened in 1988 by Diana, Duchess of Cornwall) sells £20m worth of fish a year. Over 200 trawlers are based here, each with a crew of five men. The decline of the Cornish fishing industry goes back to the 1930's, when the shoals of sardines disappeared and hundreds of fishermen left their villages. Today there are only about 1200 fisherfolk left in the county, and the number dwindles every year. The sea around the coasts has been fished out, foreign competitors are better equipped, and European fishing quotas mean that the end is nigh. The desperate plight of the Cornish fishing industry was graphically illustrated in 1994, with the 'Tuna War' against Spain. The everyday life of these people will soon be nothing but an exhibit in a museum, though it may not find itself housed in the old museum in New Road which now shows (very) contemporary art. If you want to see the Newlyn school

179

you have to go all the way to Penzance: Stanhope Forbes, Norman Garstin and their fellows were all packed off there, to the Penlee House Gallery.

The End of England: Land's End Ltd

The sheltered bay of Penzance, like the beaches around Torquay, is a Riviera – according to the guidebooks. But with one gust of Cornish wind, this coast can blow away all its French and Italian make-up and reveal the rugged British beauty we know and love so well. As for the deep-sunk, hedge-guarded, leafy lanes of England, they can lead you to some surprising places. For instance, we set out for Mousehole, and suddenly found ourselves in the Perpendicular church of St Buryan. We then decided to go to St Levan instead of Mousehole, and found ourselves promptly in Mousehole. There are strange forces at work in Cornwall. *Mousehole* is a fishing village with granite-grey, slate-roofed houses, and it was here that Dolly Pentreath (1685-1777) lived and died, supposedly the last person to speak only Cornish and no English. In summer 1937 Dylan Thomas married Caitlin in Penzance, and they spent their honeymoon in the 'Lobster Pot' in Mousehole, with no money, no prospect of money, far from friends and family, and completely happy. The great Welsh poet may well have looked out and seen a Flying Dutchman in full sail going from St Levan across coast and land towards *Porthcurno*. There, close to the wind, is an open-air theatre in the rocks high above the sea. *The Minack Cliff Theatre* (col. pl. 59) is an English Epidauros, much younger and much smaller, but no less beautifully situated than its ancient Greek counterpart. The stone seats rise in steep rows, and on some are engraved the titles of plays and the year of their first performance in Minack. The theatre opened in 1932, fittingly with a production of Shakespeare's *The Tempest* by a village drama group. It all came about because of a local lady's passion for the theatre. Virtually single-handed, Rowena Cade spent decades cementing her stage and her seats, and now thousands of people come every year to her theatre, which today is run by a trust. They stage the classics, avant-garde plays, musicals, put on by amateurs and professionals, heroically performed and heroically watched, no matter what the weather. 'Only the English have mastered the art of being truly uncomfortable while facing up to culture,' wrote the theatre critic of the *Times*.

When the summer comes to an end, the peninsula of Penwith takes on a special, almost desolate beauty. The rocks are greyish-black, the faded ferns are rust-brown, the fields have turned dark green. It is Cornwall's winter coat. To this wilderness the hero of John Le Carré's novel *The Night Manager* withdraws, into the rocky nest of *Porthgwarra*. Le Carré himself lives a few miles away in St Buryan.

From the moors at West Penwith you can see the sea on both sides. The fields are stony and bare, and it is said that there are not enough trees here to make a coffin.

The land becomes narrower and narrower, and finally you come to *Land's End*, England's most westerly point. The Romans called it the seat of storms, and the Anglo-Saxons 'Headland of Blood'. People come rushing here like lemmings, and yet there is nothing to see except a few cliffs, neither steeper nor more beautiful than elsewhere. But for the English, Land's End is World's End, for here beginneth the Atlantic, or Europe, or infinity – who knows? This is a proud symbol of England's splendid isolation, a political myth acted out by the forces of Nature – the main roles being played by 'The Diamond Horse', 'The Armed Knight', 'Dr Syntax', 'Dr Johnson's Head' and 'The Irish Lady', England's most famous cliffs after the white ones of Dover. Here the cameras click overtime, and visitors strain their eyes through their binoculars, because in places like this you are desperate to see more than there actually is to see. Not just the Scilly Isles, 25 miles away, but also the Lost Land of Lyonesse, which legend and more recently archaeologists, too, suppose to be buried somewhere between Land's End and the Scilly Isles. Perhaps the lost people of Lyonesse are listening in to the telephone conversations of nations as they make their way through the great Atlantic cables which come ashore here. Land's End is a place of silly souvenirs, beautiful views, dark symbols, and endings. 'Funeral. Land's End and Life's End,' Lord Tennyson moaned to his diary. Wilkie Collins wrote that this was the sort of country where one would find the last Englishman when the world ended. I don't think so. I think you'll find him a little further inland, inside England's First and Last Pub.

When I visited Land's End during the seventies, there was a simple hotel, as plain and unspoilt as the region itself, and nothing else. Today the place is a nightmare. Perhaps the National Trust could have done something to save it. They wanted to buy it in 1982, but were outbid by a London businessman. Not long afterwards, Peter de Savary bought the 120 acres, as well as John O'Groats at the other end of the British Isles – two names with unique publicity value. 'Cornwall is a goldmine,' he declared, built a holiday village in Falmouth, planned a Cornish Port Grimaud in the Hayle estuary, and made Land's End into a theme park. In 1994 his firm went bankrupt, and today the tourist trap is baited by Kevin Leech, a former funeral director from Manchester. Car parks framed with anchor chains, a giant hotel and amusements complex with Doric Temple entrance, helicopter, fishing cutter, and other glorious attractions. Land's End has hit rock bottom.

Wild Times in Zennor: Frieda in Love, Patrick in the Garden

'I like Cornwall very much. It is not England,' wrote D. H. Lawrence. In the bare, dark, elemental nature of this county, the author of *Lady Chatterley's Lover* sought the simple life, 'Rananim', the ideal society at peace and remote from the world. In order to escape from the war hysteria, he and his wife, Frieda von Richthofen (a cousin of the German air ace Baron von Richthofen), moved in March 1916 to the little village of *Higher Tregerthen*, near Zennor in West Penwith. There he wrote parts of *Women in Love*, but if the Lawrences were in love, it did not always show. 'Lawry used to beat the stuffing out of Frieda,' recalled one of their neighbours. For a few weeks Katherine Mansfield and her husband also lived in one of the cottages, and once again there were wild scenes. What really got up the neighbours' noses, though, was the fact that Lawry and Frieda would keep singing German folksongs – and this in the middle of the Great War. In any case the locals didn't trust the bearded stranger. He didn't do anything except write, and drink in the 'Tinner's Arms', and besides he had a German wife. They were accused of spying, and at the end of 1917 were sent packing. D. H. Lawrence described this episode in his semi-autobiographical novel *Kangaroo* (1923).

High above the sea at *Higher Tregerthen* there is a grey granite house on a ledge of rock: *Eagle's Nest*. It's an extraordinary place, exposed on all sides to the elements – the storms from the Atlantic, the mists that roll silently down from the moorland hills, and then the sun shining from a broad sky spreading far across the sea to the knife-sharp horizon behind which lies America. The painter Patrick Heron lived in Eagle's Nest from 1955 until his death in 1999. When I met him, on a calm and windless spring day, he was wearing a pink shirt, a 'violent violet cobalt' pullover, and turquoise socks. A man of many colours.

Patrick Heron (see inside front cover) was born in 1920, son of a textile manufacturer from Leeds. His striped paintings and 'wobbly hard-edge' made him one of the key figures of English abstract art. Space, colour and light were for him the only true subjects of painting, 'the reality of the eye'. It is an art that derives from art, from Braque, Matisse, Bonnard, his great models. His paintings were also evocations of the visible, 'crystallizations' of his surroundings: the sharp coastlines, the rocks made round by the storms, the Bronze Age fields between his house and the cliffs, punctuated by their drystone walls. 'The fact is actually that you see my shapes in the landscape because you've seen them in my paintings first,' says Patrick Heron, wary of offering simplistic explanations. But then he adds: 'I'm certain that I would never paint as I have painted if I hadn't lived exactly where I do them. This place gives me enormous energy.' It was a feeling shared by Virginia Woolf in 1920, when she wrote of Eagle's Nest that she wished it belonged to her.

Behind its hedges lies something quite unexpected: a very unusual garden. It was laid out in 1921 by William Arnold-Forster, the previous owner of the house. He planted trees and shrubs from Australia and New Zealand, some of them making their first appearance north of the Equator; there were plants from other islands and mountainous regions which he knew would flourish in the damp, mild climate of the Cornish coast, in spite of the high winds, the salt spray, and the exposed position of his house. What this horticultural pioneer began, Patrick Heron continued, with the expert eye of the painter.

The garden lies on three sides of the house, and each section is subdivided into a series of smaller gardens, each with its own character. You can see *Libertia*, a white grass from New Zealand, snowgum from Tasmania, and a Chinese lantern tree with red pendant blossoms. In August the white flowers of the Chilean *Eucryphia* tree send their honey-sweet scent wafting into your nostrils, and at Christmas the *Gloire de Nantes* comes into flower, a pink camellia. In Patrick's garden there are 55 different sorts of camellia, and some 70 different azaleas and rhododendrons, many of them rare. Here the brilliant colourist found subtle inspiration for his pictures, just as Monet used to do in his garden. Eagle's Nest was Patrick Heron's Giverny.

Like a thick fur coat, lichens have enfolded the branches of trees and shrubs. 'They show the air is clean and unpolluted,' said Patrick. Since the mid-1950's he waged ceaseless campaigns for the preservation of the moors and coasts of West Penwith – fighting against proposed military training areas and the destruction of prehistoric fields and ancient markers. What did he fear most? That the narrow, winding coastal road from St Ives to St Just would be widened, and thus lose its 'magical beauty'. 'If we're not careful, this peninsula will be turned into a gigantic theme park.' Land's End all over again.

The patina of Cornwall is greatly enhanced by the ancient monuments that lie between Penzance, Land's End and St Ives, and around Penwith. Excavations at *Chysauster* north of Gulval have revealed what a Celtic village looked like. It was inhabited by miners right up to and through Roman times, and there were nine 'courtyard houses' altogether – huts consisting of three or four roofed rooms arranged round an oval-shaped inner courtyard with terraced gardens (400 BC-3rd century AD). Ritual stone circles and dolmens, standing in the fields like giant abandoned milking stools, are so abundant here that even a Cornwall aficionado like the German writer Wolfgang Hildesheimer had to admit that he'd had enough. 'A piece of degenerate mythology to frighten the children,' was his verdict. He may be right. When nine little girls went dancing on a sacred English Sunday, they were turned into stone. And the Nine Maidens have been petrified ever since.

Cornwall's Industry: Fish, Tin and Copper!

Between Land's End and St Ives, the countryside is dotted with the thin stacks of the *jinjies*, the remains of the old tin and copper mines. *Botallack*, with its dark grey, granite houses, is a bleak, run-down area north of St Just. From the 18th century onwards it used to be one of Cornwall's biggest mining centres. Everywhere you can see the stumps of the chimneys and the crumbling walls poking out of the grass and debris (col. pl. 58). In between, the sheep and the horses graze peacefully. These are the fields of the industrial archaeologists.

The silhouettes of the *jinjies* are as unmistakeable as those of the oast houses of

183

Kent. From a distance they look like romantic chapels: rectangular houses with narrow, often round-arched windows and doorways, the chimney stack built onto the side just like a bell-tower. Somehow industrial and religious ruins come to resemble one another. It is no coincidence that the 18th-century romantic yen for ruined castles and churches has developed into the industrial romanticism of our own time. We seem to enjoy our technological monuments, the relics of our dead industries. The paradoxical beauty of these defunct mines is strangely moving; they seem sadly abandoned in the midst of the bare landscape, and there is a poetic wildness about them too, perched as they are on the clifftops high above the Atlantic, beneath whose waves there were once men digging in tunnels. Now the shafts are full of water, and the wind whistles through the empty pump houses. No more hustling, bustling men going to work, no more smoke rising from the chimneys, no more movement, no more noise – the still and silent ruins fulfil the secret death wish of those who always wanted the polluted industrial landscape to return to Nature. And here, in the good clean air of Cornwall, let us pay tribute to these ruined icons of progress and to the pioneers of the Industrial Revolution who once worked here. Bare, or overgrown with ivy, the carcasses of the mines now lie strewn over the countryside, monuments to a lost age, melancholy outsiders now in their last stage of production: the fabrication of dreams.

'Fish, tin and copper!' is a typical Cornish toast. Way back in the Bronze Age, the settlers were using the tin and copper to forge their weapons. In the 12th century Richard I gave the Cornish tin industry a charter underlining its importance: Helston, Liskeard, Lostwithiel and Truro became *Stannary towns* with their own jurisdiction and their own parliament. Until 1752 the tinners met regularly at Lostwithiel in order to use their right of veto against Westminster on all matters concerning tin. Even as late as 1838, they were still not paying their taxes to the Crown; their 'coinage' went directly to the Duchy of Cornwall. Tin-mining was difficult, dangerous, and hard work for a doubtful reward. Moreover, the Cornish miner undertook it without a fixed wage; he was a free man, and as such took both the risk and the profit. With the industrial revolution tin-mining moved from being mainly a surface operation to proper shaft-mining, undertaken in atrocious conditions. Unsurprisingly, progress tended to enrich the owners and not the miners. Cornish engineers played a big part in this, for they replaced water-driven pumps with steam engines; Newcomen's engine, improved by Watt, was greatly improved by the Cornishman Richard Trevithick, whose use of high pressure steam led to the design of the beam engine. One of these is preserved by the National Trust at *Pool*, between Camborne and Redruth. has preserved a perfect working model of one such engine: the East Pool Whim of 1887.

The great tin boom began early in the 19th century, when 'tins' were first used for the conservation of food. Around 1850 Cornwall was also the world's greatest producer of copper. There were some 650 mines in the county, and over 50,000 miners.

Abandoned tin mine near Botallack; the shafts run out under the ocean

Many of them met an early death. Toxic gases and arsenic fumes were a major cause of the fact that the average life expectancy of a Cornish miner was forty. After 1860, copper was discovered at Lake Victoria, and tin in Malaysia, as well as in Bolivia and Australia, and prices fell catastrophically. It was the beginning of a mass migration, and by the end of the 19th century, a third of Cornwall's miners had left the county. They were all specialists in the field, and as such were in great demand. It was a commonplace that 'at the bottom of any hole anywhere in the world, you are sure to find a Cornishman.'

The old Cornish coat-of-arms shows a tin miner on one side, and a fisherman on the other, with a Cornish chough above them – all endangered species, if not extinct already (the chough died out in 1960). In the 1920's there were just two dozen mines still in operation. In 1985, there were six, with 1500 miners. In March 1998, the last miner emerged from the last shift at the last tin mine in Cornwall – or so it seemed. Shortly after the closure of South Crofty appeared to have brought an end to a whole way of life, a rescue package was organized and the mine reopened, to carry two thousand years of history into the next millennium.

Despite this small piece of cheer, unemployment in Cornwall far above the

Redruth tin stamp

national average (20% in West Penwith). Another is the Camborne School of Mines, which has acquired an international reputation. The rest is Cornish Heritage – mining museums with such delectable souvenirs as earrings in the shape of Cornish pasties, made from South Crofty tin. There is one relic, though, that has acquired a real fan-club all over England: Ross Poldark, an impoverished 18th-century mine-owner, gambler and adventurer. He is the hero of a family saga by Winston Graham in several volumes that became a television series, and is certainly the most colourful figure in the history of Cornish tin-mining. Whoever said that truth is stranger than fiction?

Artists, Surfers and Pilchards: St Ives

No director in Britain has a better placed office than the Director of the Tate Gallery in *St Ives*. He can look out of his window straight down onto the white sands of Porthmeor Beach, and watch the surfers flexing their kneecaps. The bay flashes turquoise in the sun, and further out it deepens into ultramarine. You sometimes see dolphins leaping over the water, which is all very well, says the Director, 'but it takes three days for a letter to come from London to St Ives.'

The old fishing port of St Ives (col. pl. 67)lies on the outermost tip of England, where the Cornish peninsula stretches its granite finger far out into the Atlantic. It is sheltered by the hills of Penwith, and is just a few miles away from Land's End. The town and the church are named after St Ia, a 5th-century Celtic missionary. Surf white or mussel grey, the houses nestle against the slope, their slate roofs shimmering with a yellow-green patina of moss and lichen. Many of these houses have stone steps outside that lead up to the first floor: at ground level are what were once cellars for the fish, though now they have been made into holiday flats. 'Downalong' is the name of the fishing area down at the port, by Smeaton's ancient pier. Above is 'Upalong', where the miners had their cottages, the captains and fish merchants their large houses, and the Victorians built their new-town terraces. Linking everything together is a dense network of narrow lanes.

For centuries the trawlers put out to sea in the early summer, when the pilchards came. There were vast shoals of them, and the smell of fish in those days was so strong that it is said the church clock would stop. But when the 19th century changed to the 20th, the pilchards stopped coming, and instead different shoals began to arrive, transported from London by the Great Western Railway.

St Ives became a holiday resort. For Virginia Woolf, her stay was 'the most important of all my memories'. Her first recollection was of colour: the red and purple of her mother's flowered dress as she sat on her lap during the long train journey to the end of England, and to the house overlooking the bay. There, 'to hear the waves breaking that first night behind the yellow blind; to sail in the lugger; to dig in the sands; to scramble over the rocks and see the anemones flourishing their antennae in the pools.' Happy childhood days in Cornwall, where the Stephen family spent their summer holidays between 1892 and 1894 in Talland House, with a view of Godrevy Lighthouse. 'The Lighthouse was then a silvery, misty-looking tower with a yellow eye that opened suddenly and softly in the evening.' Talland House has now been divided up into five holiday flats, and most of the garden has been concreted over to make a car park. Sir Leslie Stephen, Virginia's father, must have guessed what was coming, for when the Porthminster Hotel was stuck in front of his nose, he sold Talland House.

In her novel *To the Lighthouse* (1927), Virginia Woolf's lighthouse is on a Hebridean island. One of the characters is a woman artist, Lily Briscoe, who sets up her easel out in the open. 'In those days St Ives, save for a few painters, had no visitors.' One of the very first was J. M. W. Turner, who drew a panorama of the bay in 1811. At first it was Newlyn that attracted the artists. As Cornwall's biggest fishing port it became a centre for landscape and seascape painting. But when it began to get overcrowded, the artists moved across to the other side of the peninsula. After James Whistler and his pupil, Walter Sickert, spent the winter of 1883 in St Ives ('to paint ships and seas and skies') (col. pl. 63), more and more painters made their way to this remote village: the Swedish Impressionist Anders Zorn, artists from Holland, France, America and Australia. In 1890 a Japanese painter put up his easel on the harbour's edge, and was pelted with stones by local children – not because he was Japanese, but because he was working on a Sunday.

St Ives became England's Barbizon. From 1895 onwards, the artists opened their studios to the public once a year, and this Show Day became so popular that the Great Western Railway laid on special trains. Posters advertised 'Britain's Art Colony by the Sea'. Every year, the railway carried 300 paintings from St Ives to the Royal Academy Summer Exhibition in London. Laura Knight, later made a Dame, wrote that Cornwall was 'an easy part of the country for an artist to go to sleep in,' and all one needed was a rainproof coat and a good pair of shoes. Much of what the artists were looking for was at hand all around St Ives: the majesty of Nature, a mild climate, picturesque subject-matter, cheap lodgings, and an archaic, back-to-the-roots lifestyle. Cornwall was the land of myths, a stretch of Celtic coast with Ægean light.

Light is perhaps the greatest and truest of St Ives' myths: it glows invincibly, even on the greyest of days. It is a fact that ultra-violet radiation is higher here than anywhere else in the country, reflected on three sides by the mirror of the sea. When Patrick Heron, the English forerunner of American colourfield-painting, was preparing a lecture he was due to give at the Museum of Modern Art in New York, he made slides of his paintings in the street outside his studio in St Ives. 'Great pictures, Pat,' said his artist friend Barnett Newman after the lecture. 'Great idea, photographing them in the street!' Heron replied that he had only done so because of the light, but Barney should try it himself. 'Well, I can't do that, Pat, my studio's in Wall Street.'

Patrick Heron's studio was in Back Road West, right next to the beach – one of the thirteen Porthmeor studios. Fishermen still keep their nets in the cellars, and it is in the storerooms above – where they used to dry their sails – that the painters stretch their canvases. When the wind blows, the old wooden buildings shake and groan like boats on the high seas. The studios have been in use for over a hundred years. They belong to a trust, and the Director of the Tate Gallery in London is always a member of the board, as is the Curator of the Tate St Ives. These heroic shacks are museum pieces in themselves and must surely be the most romantic, not to say the most rheumatic studios in England.

What Patrick Heron showed me first were not his own pictures, but the relics of his famous predecessor, Ben Nicholson: messages on the door ('Back at 2 p.m.'), faded flecks of paint on the floor, and a little cardboard box containing the Master's pencil stubs ('his famous 6B'), a piece of marble on which he used to sharpen the pencils, a few pink drawing-pins and a broken pair of compasses. 'Ben was horrible, he was naughty – and wonderful! Without him I would never have got this room with this fantastic light. It changed my life.'

When Ben Nicholson gave Patrick Heron his studio in 1958 and moved to 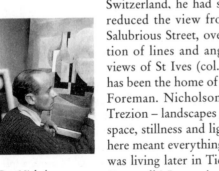 Switzerland, he had spent nearly twenty years in St Ives. He reduced the view from the terrace of his house Trezion, in Salubrious Street, over the roofs, port and bay to a composition of lines and angles that has become one of the classic views of St Ives (col. pl. 66). Since the mid 1980's, his house has been the home of the London artist and illustrator Michael Foreman. Nicholson painted some of his finest pictures in Trezion – landscapes and still lifes, geometrical meditations on space, stillness and light. 'There's no doubt that this landscape here meant everything to him,' said Patrick Heron. 'When Ben was living later in Ticino, he asked me to send him photos of

Ben Nicholson Cornwall.' It was in St Ives that Nicholson painted *Aug '56 (Val d'Orcia)*, for which he was awarded the Guggenheim Prize. When General Eisenhower handed over the cheque, he asked what the picture represented. 'Oh, it's an Italian landscape,' replied the artist. In fact it was a still life of jugs and carafes, arranged on his kitchen table in St Ives – a prime example of his ability to create a poetic combination of the visual and the abstract, the figurative and the cubist.

Nicholson, his wife – the sculptress Barbara Hepworth – and their triplets had moved to St Ives in August 1939, before the first bombs fell on London. Shortly after the beginning of the war, the Russian Constructivist and former Bauhaus teacher Naum Gabo also sought refuge in St Ives. Together with the Nicholsons, who had been his neighbours in Hampstead, he had spread the gospel of abstract art in England. They almost succeeded in persuading another of their immigrant friends to move to Cornwall, but Piet Mondrian, so it is said, tossed a coin and went to New York instead. Gabo followed him there in 1946, but before he did so, he developed his transparent shapes of perspex and stone in a tiny bungalow on Carbis Bay (Faerystones). Gabo was a particular inspiration to some of the younger artists of the time, like Peter Lanyon and Wilhelmina Barns-Graham. The former died in 1964 but Wilhelmina is still painting in her Porthmeor studio.

The avant-garde of St Ives, however, were only following in the footsteps of another pioneer, who shone as brightly in St Ives history as Godrevy Lighthouse. Bernard Leach, the guru of modern pottery, was born in Hong Kong, and after studying for eleven years in Japan, came to St Ives in 1920 with the potter Shoji Hamada. Here he founded a studio which he ran for almost 60 years. Bernard Leach made some 25,000 pots and bowls, and became a legend. But before the arrival of all the London artists, he often felt lonely and cut off in St Ives. Sometimes he lived on the verge of extreme poverty, before at last the place became fashionable and his work became world famous. Leach experimented with Asian glazing and with the earthenware techniques of the English Middle Ages. He combined eastern and western traditions in a new form of ceramic art,

Bernard Leach

which brought whole colonies of potters flocking to Cornwall. When Hamada left St Ives in 1923, Leach's first pupil arrived – Michael Cardew, who was himself soon to become one of the greats, with a pottery of his own in the former Wenford Bridge Pub near Bodmin.

Like Gabo, Leach regarded his works as practical objects that should be perfect in form. Examples can be seen in the fishermen's chapel of St Nicholas: a series of ceramic tiles, his 'Pilgrim Plate', and two flowerpots. In 1940 he published a résumé of all his experiences, *A Potter's Book*, which became a bible for modern potters. His sons David and Michael learned the art in his workshop, and David in turn founded the Lowerdown Pottery in Bovey Tracey, Devon, with his eldest son John in 1956. A member of this ceramic dynasty, and a potter herself, was Leach's wife

Janet, a Texan who had studied in Japan under Hamada. Before Leach died in 1979, she took over the little studio on the edge of St Ives, but she died in 1997 and today only her assistant Trevor Corser is at work there.

Leach and Gabo, Ben Nicholson and Barbara Hepworth: these were the names that gave St Ives a reputation which spread far beyond the confines of the region. They were inclined, however, to keep their distance from the locals. Patrick Heron remembered how he had once suggested going for a beer at the Sloop Inn down by the harbour. 'Oh, no!' cried Nicholson. 'I wouldn't know who I might meet there!' But there was one local man that everyone looked up to, the Hampstead artists and the Downalong fishermen: Alfred Wallis, the great naïve artist of Cornwall.

From his ninth year onwards, Wallis was a sailor, but in 1890 he settled in St Ives as a fisherman, opened a junk shop, became a rag-and-bone man, an ice-cream vendor, and a member of the Salvation Army. When 'Old Iron' was almost 70 his wife died, and he began to paint 'for company', with no training and no personal ambition. In his cottage at 3 Back Road West, Alfred Wallis painted houses, ports, ships, with 'real paint' – as used on ships and houses – and pieces of wood or cardboard or whatever else he could lay his hands on (Frontispiece). His paintings were anti-illusion, in the modern style – memories, imaginary scenes, with very few colours: 'some lively dark browns, shiny blacks, fierce greys, strange whites and a particularly pungent Cornish green.' This was Ben Nicholson's description of Wallis's pictures, which he had happened to see during his first visit to St Ives in August 1928, when he had looked through an open door in Back Road West while returning from Porthmeor Beach. This was one of the revelations of St Ives, and has been quoted ever since as the first miracle at this holy site. Ben Nicholson and his friends, laden with their theories, could only marvel at this simple painter who joined his life so intensely but so naturally to his art, as if the latter were a sailing ship and he the nine-year-old sailor. The fact that London's avant-garde adored and collected his work did not, alas, do Wallis any good. He died in 1942 in the Madron Institution, a poorhouse and lies buried in a graveyard by the sea, next to the new Tate Gallery, where his pictures hang for all to see. His grave was designed by his friend Bernard Leach – painted stone tiles with the Godrevy Lighthouse.

The *Tate* of the West, opened in 1993, is right beside the sea, but for all the beauty of its situation, it is architecturally anonymous. Its modernity is from the 1930's, all cubes and cylinders, squeezed in between houses, beach and hillside. The London architects Eldred Evans and David Shalev designed a rectangular wing with a rotunda open to the sea, resting on pencil-thin supports. This glass rotunda serves simultaneously as entrance hall, sculpture exhibition-hall, and amphitheatre. The view from the roof café windows is splendid, and the slate roof fits in well with the local architecture. The front has a facing of light grey marble splinters on concrete, and as a small gallery in a small town it is unassuming, pleasant, unobjectionable. But at such a showplace one longs for something a bit more daring – the shock of originality that can make even a little building great.

The Tate Gallery on Porthmeor Beach must be the first such building said to have planned a changing room specially for surfers. The idea was that they could leave their boards here and enjoy an artistic break between low and high tide, but in the end the surfers' racks were never made. The first thing that will strike visitors as they go in is a fanfare of colour: pink, red, yellow, turquoise, navy and cobalt blue (inside front cover). Patrick Heron's monumental window (1993) is in the spirit of Matisse and the Hard Edge, with no leading (illustrated on the inncer front cover). The gallery offers a unique opportunity to see the work of the St Ives artists in its place of origin. They were not a school but simply a group of friends, and one cannot even talk of an artists' colony, but just a place where fine art flourished.

Like the Tate Gallery in Liverpool, this one has no collection of its own, but borrows from the vast store at its London headquarters, where there are some 900 works by the artists of St Ives. A regular change of exhibits is the principle here, although account must always be taken of the wear and tear on pictures, particularly through transport. The Tate was not always too quick off the mark to purchase the top quality works of these artists, but all the same there are things that even an expert will enjoy. Apart from the major figures, there are works by their friends and successors, especially the middle generation which came to Cornwall after the Second World War. Theirs is generally abstract art, but it is deeply rooted in the landscape, inspired by the rock formations, the menhirs, and the abandoned mines. The most powerful works stem from the early fifties: paintings by Patrick Heron, Terry Frost, and Peter Lanyon, who met his death in 1964 in a gliding accident. There are fine pictures by Paul Feiler, who was born in Frankfurt, Bryan Wynter and Roger Hilton – both of whom died in 1975, the same year as Barbara Hepworth. One of her assistants was the sculptor Denis Mitchell, who worked in a tin mine near Land's End during the war, and later moved to the Trewarveneth Studios in Newlyn, together with his painter friend John Wells. The St Ives veteran Terry Frost also has a studio overlooking the bay of Newlyn, and he too worked with Barbara Hepworth for a while.

St Ives echoes with many names. It is a hornets' nest of artists, linked by strong threads of love, jealousy, gossip, quite apart – of course – from the painting. In many cases the town has left a greater mark on their lives than on their work. Some came for a short visit and then wanted to stay for ever, while others stayed for ever and longed to get away. The artists who have had most success internationally and who are now at work in Cornwall do not, with good reason, have their studios in St Ives. The Op-Art star Bridget Riley prefers St Merryn, and the abstract artist Alan Davie works in Sancreed. 'All that St Ives School stuff is terribly English,' says Davie. 'I adore the place and the light, but it's not the basic stuff of art.' Christopher Wood, Stanley Spencer, Margaret Mellis, Victor Pasmore all visited and painted in St Ives, however. Besides the major paintings, the Tate Gallery also exhibits lesser known works by famous artists, for instance there was a special Mark Rothko exhibition in 1996. Rothko in St Ives? In 1958 this New York painter visited his friend Peter Lanyon in Cornwall, in his search for a setting that would suit his meditative Abstract Expressionism. What might have happened if he had found his chapel of artistic worship in St Ives instead of Houston?

As you sip your tea up above in the gallery café, it's like sitting on deck with a view of sea and land. And what you are looking at is the same scene that the artists have looked at for generations. They are all part of St Ives now, and part of the power that seeks and creates beauty, and so brings more and more people flocking to this pretty seaside resort. 'The all-too-picturesque has seized hold of this place, too, and seems to have become a copy of bad pictures,' wrote Wolfgang Hildesheimer in 1971 (he had had a studio here for a short time before the war). Certainly there was a danger that St Ives might turn into a third-rate Blackpool, and the Tate Gallery's rescue operation came just in time. The new artistic prestige and the new boom in arty tourism has been hugely profitable for everyone – not least the artists themselves.

Some of them still meet in an old pilchard cellar in Back Street West, at the gallery of the Penwith Society of Arts in Cornwall. Among the founder members of 1949 were Bernard, Ben and Barbara, 'the moderns with their rubbish', as the others used to call them. The 'others' were the orthodox St Ives Society of Artists of 1926, who showed their good works in church – namely, the converted Mariners' Church in Norway Square. The abstract artists have long since turned into traditionalists, but all of them have the same problem of artists everywhere: how to earn a living. A garret in St Ives is no different from a garret anywhere else.

How many artists are there in St Ives? 'Too many,' says one of them. 'A few hundred,' reckons Eric Ward, the harbour master. In Back Road West alone there are 25 studios and five galleries. And that's not counting Ponckle, the cat specialist, and competition from the Far East in the shape of cheap stuff 'made in Taiwan'. Eric Ward himself, when he is not fishing surfers out of the Atlantic in his capacity as helmsman of the St Ives lifeboat, stands at his easel and paints landscapes, portraits, and especially nudes. 'Nude art is difficult to sell to the tourists,' he says, 'but it's very satisfying.'

The man who taught this former fisherman to paint was Roy Ray. Roy is an institution in St Ives, as respected as the harbour master himself. He is the head of the School of Painting, and up in his attic academy in Back Road West he is introducing a dozen amateurs to the art of portraiture. 'It's raining outside,' says a housewife from Australia, on a painting holiday in England. 'Yes,' says Roy, 'and sometimes it rains inside as well.' The rain is as much a part of St Ives as the legendary light. Every Wednesday evening Eric, Ray and their artist friends meet for a session of life drawing at the school, and then afterwards down they go to the 'Sloop Inn' on the quayside. There are plenty of pictures on the walls, and ropes hanging from the ceiling to assist those who are having a rough passage after the seventh pint. The host knows his debt to the reputation of St Ives, and so every Wednesday evening he stands treat with 'a round of pizza for the poor artists'.

One clear spring day, I drove out to *St Just*. The fields were dark green, the fern-covered hills speckled with granite, and the Atlantic an endless blue. There is no more spectacular coastal road in England, and no more isolated studio than that of Karl Weschke on the cliffs of Cape Cornwall. His cottage is the converted pump house of a tin mine. He comes from Thuringia, and is a small, wiry man with a face a bit like Picasso's. He has been living in Cornwall since 1955, 'because it was much cheaper here than in London.' He knew Bernard, Ben and Barbara and all the big names of St Ives, and has become one of them himself – an internationally successful artist, but still an outsider, a German following the traditions of the Expressionists. He is not the only German in St Ives. The most prolific and most amusing German art critic of the postwar era has had a house here for many years. He is Heinz Ohff, former features editor of the Berlin *Tagesspiegel*. As for Weschke's work, some of his strong, dark paintings can be seen in the St Ives Tate Gallery – landscapes with archaic figures, earth-coloured, heavy and elemental, as if, like Edvard Munch, he were listening out for Nature's scream. But his more recent paintings are bright. Could he have been changed by the light of St Ives? 'No,' he says. 'I made a trip to Egypt.'

The Garden of Magic Stones: Barbara Hepworth in St Ives

It was nothing more than a biographical coincidence that brought Barbara Hepworth and Ben Nicholson to Cornwall. This coincidence, however, left an indelible mark on their work and on the myth of St Ives. A friend of theirs in London, the writer Adrian Stokes, had invited them to stay in his house, Little Parc Owles, in Carbis Bay. On 25 August 1939, a week before the outbreak of war, Ben and Barbara and their five-year-old triplets arrived in St Ives. A few months later, they rented a little house called Dunluce, and in 1942 moved into Chy-an-Kerris. 'I had only limited space: a backyard, a room only eight feet high, and endless complaints about my hammering!' Nevertheless, Barbara wrote later, 'at Carbis Bay, during the mid-forties, I did some of my best work.'

This contact with Cornwall's cliffs and bays, Neolithic dolmens and menhirs, and the whole of the ancient, 'pagan' landscape broadened the range of her artistic vocabulary, and for all the abstraction of her work, it always remained bound to organic forms. *Sea form – Porthmeor, Oval form (Penwith landscape) –* many of the titles allude to their counterparts in Nature and to the source of her inspiration. Her sculptures are like washed rocks with holes and hollows, their interiors sometimes painted blue and white, in stone cut from Cornwall. It was during this period that

Barbara
Hepworth in
the garden of
her studio

she began to pierce her sculptures, to incorporate the negative space into her work. It was her most radical phase. The strings in these sculptures were originally Naum Gabo's idea, but they corresponded to the tensions she felt between herself, the sea, wind and hills. Her late figurative works, like *Conversation with Magic Stones* (1973) and the menhir-like *Family of Man* (1970) are related in form to the works of her prehistoric predecessors, but they also have great affinity to those of Brancusi. In Cornwall, Barbara Hepworth found a spiritual and atmospheric parallel to the landscapes of her native Pennines in Yorkshire. Whereas her fellow Yorkshireman and friend Henry Moore generally stuck to the reclining forms of his hills, her own figures were akin to the isolated standing stones of the Cornish countryside.

In 1949 Ben Nicholson left his wife, and nine years later he left St Ives for good. Barbara stayed behind in Trewyn Studio, where she had moved in 1949 with her cats and her sculptures, and there she became ever more famous and ever more lonely. She lived modestly, on steak, salads and cigarettes, until one night in May 1975 her house caught fire and she burned to death.

'Finding Trewyn Studio was a sort of magic,' she wrote. Her house and garden are right in the middle of St Ives, behind high granite walls. In her studio, the tools, chisels, respirator (to keep out the dust), a Wincarnis box, and blocks of stone for the next sculpture all lie ready and waiting (col. pl. 64). The *Barbara Hepworth*

Museum was opened in 1976, and since 1980 has been run by the Tate Gallery in London. It was the then director, Sir Alan Bowness, married to one of Barbara's daughters, who initiated the scheme for a Tate Gallery in St Ives. There are nearly fifty Hepworth sculptures exhibited in the museum, representing all phases of her work, from her very first completely abstract piece *Three Forms* (1934) to *Fallen Images* (1974), which was completed a few months before her death.

The real wonder of Trewyn is the garden (col. pl. 65). It is enclosed in high walls, and the wind rustles through the grass and the bamboo, gulls circle above the trees, and through the branches you can see the church tower. This is every inch an artist's garden, intimate, luxuriant, permeated with her sure instinct for space and light. Between the palms and the camellias and azaleas stand her sculptures, including her most massive piece *Four square (Walk through)* (1966). Her works are to be seen all over St Ives – outside the town hall, in the library, on the Malakoff Platform, in a courtyard between two blocks of flats, Barnaloft and Piazza. In the parish church is a stone relief *Madonna and Child* (1954), in memory of her son Paul, who was killed in an accident. At Longstone Cemetery is a bronze sculpture called *Ascending form (Gloria)*, and here, between Lelant and Carbis Bay, Dame Barbara is buried.

Tintagel: The Ubiquitous Arthur

Cornwall's Atlantic coast stretches for some 85 miles, from Land's End to Morwenstow, on the Devon border. This is the place for hikers and surfers, with quiet bays nestling between tall cliffs. There are two spots in particular that have made a name for themselves among the surfing fraternity. *Perranporth* has three miles of beach, and is England's 'Santa-Monica-next-the-Sea', while *Newquay* has risen from being a little pilchard port to being the surfing capital of the country. Fistral Bay is the setting for international championships, and here the beach boys practise non-stop on their boards. A whole industry has sprung up in Newquay because of this one sport: there are surfboard manufacturers, surfing schools, shops that specialize in surfing equipment and, if you are not already surfeited, there are even surfing magazines. A former European champion lives in Newquay. She is Eden Burberry, who now leads the environmental group Surfers Against Sewage. Pollution of beach and water is a continual problem, not only on this part of the English coast.

Behind the long beach at Perranporth, with its somewhat depressing holiday complex of huts and caravans, there is a tiny chapel which for centuries was covered by the dunes of Penhale Sands. This is St Piran, the earliest known church in south-west England. St Piran, patron saint of the Cornish miners and a follower of the Irish missionary St Patrick, is believed to have built this chapel in the 6th century. It

Trerice

disappeared beneath the sands in the Middle Ages, and was only excavated in 1835. It is a simple, rectangular oratory, but once again it is fast disappearing.

Among the beautiful sights to see are *Trerice*, an Elizabethan estate near Newquay, Padstow Bay where you can enjoy sea bass at Rick Stein's Seafood Restaurant or play golf behind the dunes, and little fishing villages like Port Isaac or Boscastle. Many of the coastal areas, however, have been spoiled by great wedges of bungalows, apartment houses and camping sites. 'A lot of Cornwall has been ruined for ever,' said Lord St Levan. 'In my ten years as President of the Council for the Preservation of Rural England, I was forced to watch Cornwall undergoing more destruction than at any time in her history.'

The roofs of old houses in and outside the West Country are often covered with slate. It came from *Delabole*, which at one time was England's biggest slate quarry, and it used to be shipped out from the port at Boscastle. The best specimens of Delabole slate can be seen in Cornwall's village churchyards – slabs of silvery blue and deep green, the elegantly engraved visiting cards of the dead. Great Britain's first commercial wind farm was opened on the hills of Delabole in 1991. These are the new, steel menhirs of our time, and their rotating arms point towards the ancient myths all around them. For here if anywhere is the centre of King Arthur's country. Historians and archaeologists have never been able to pinpoint the identity of this legendary king, or the location of his castle with the Round Table. Those who have pursued the legend have been so successful in commercialising it that even the last traces of truth have disappeared. What remains is the gift of the poets, who provide the irrefutable 'facts' of fantasy amid the endless topography of a story that could surely only have taken place in Cornwall, the land of myths and magic.

Slaughterbridge. The very name proclaims that this was the spot where Arthur last wielded the magic sword Excalibur in the battle against his nephew Mordred, and indeed there is a memorial stone with a Latin inscription here. Slaughterbridge is only one mile north of Camelford where the A39 roars past, and perhaps the name Camelford is a sign that the court of Camelot was here, though it is said that the court was at Castle-an-Dinas, above St Columb Major, or at Cadbury Castle in Somerset. They seek it here, they seek it there, and they also seek Excalibur. Sir Bedivere threw it – just like a villain disposing of the murder weapon – into Dozmary Pool, where the Lady of the Lake took charge of it. Since then, the wind has never stopped howling around this remote lake on Bodmin Moor. But if it's facts you're after, the fact is that it could be anywhere in Cornwall. If it is in Cornwall at all. If it is in Cornwall at all. Tennyson himself favoured *Loe Pool* near Helston – an astonishing place, a little freshwater lake divided from the sea by a narrow pebble ridge. Here Sir Bedivere carried the dying Arthur in Tennyson's *Morte*, until they reached

> A dark strait of barren land:
> On one side lay the Ocean, and on one
> Lay a great water, and the moon was full.

In Arthur's village of *Tintagel* you will find just about everything except Excalibur itself. The locals have no doubt that this was his place: they profit, therefore he was. Everything is named after him: car parks, ash trays, letter knives, saucers, tea-towels. In the land of Arthur, Arthur is King. The main road is a positive orgy of souvenir shops and holy and unholy grails of all sizes. Real live Knights of King Arthur built King Arthur's Hall in 1933, out of Cornish granite, to house the Round Table. In 'King Arthur's Arms' you can eat genuine Excaliburgers. How did it all come about? Because the chronicler Geoffrey of Monmouth wrote in his *Historia Regum Britanniæ* (1136) that Tintagel Castle was where Arthur lived. And Geoffrey also knew that Arthur died in the year 542. Archaeologists maintain that the ruined castle by the sea dates from the early 13th century. To prove their goodwill, however, they dug up a lot of shards – evidence of Byzantine trade connections – and the remains of an early Celtic monastery. In 1998 they even claimed to have found a piece of slate with Arthur's name, under some pottery that had not been disturbed, even by them, since the 6th century. So is it possible that the British King

Uther Pendragon met Ygrayne, wife of the Duke of Cornwall, here? And that nine months later a Celtic monk, not the magician Merlin, fished little Arthur out of the sea in Merlin's Cave, just as Moses had once been pulled out of the bulrushes? Anything might have happened in Tintagel, for all that remains now is a few ruined walls, and those are the perfect foundations for palaces of poetry. Chrétien de Troyes, Hartmann von Aue, Gottfried von Strassburg, Wolfram von Eschenbach, and in the 15th century Thomas Malory – they all wrote about Arthur without ever having seen Tintagel. And once the imagination had had its fling, there began the age of sight-seeing.

In 1848 Tennyson arrived in Tintagel, and made notes in his diary about the black cliffs, caves, storm and wind, presumably to compare with his imaginings in his epic poem *Idylls of the King,* written some fifteen years earlier. In this particular reincarnation, the legendary King is a true Victorian gentleman, a nostalgic counter to 19th-century industrial development. Tennyson's rival Swinburne was unwilling to lag behind during the Pre-Raphaelite Arthurian boom, and his romance *Tristram of Lyonesse* added to the poetic aura surrounding Tintagel as the court of King Marke, as well as mobilising the Victorian tourists. The whole nation was eager to see where Arthur had been born and where Tristram and Ysolde were buried. As far as the historical King Arthur is concerned, very little is known. He may have been a Celtic knight who defeated the invading Angles and Saxons in the battle of Badon Hill around 516 AD, but was then himself defeated by the invaders. That at least was the tale told in political folklore, which portrayed him as an heroic emblem of British resistance, and as guardian of all courtly virtues. The Tudor King Henry VII's eldest son was given the name of Arthur, and when Henry Purcell's musical score *King Arthur* of 1691 was revived in London in 1995, its contemporary relevance was not lost on the critics. Arthur had united the kingdom, but it was now in danger of being split asunder: 'Our sacred institutions have either collapsed,' wrote *The Observer,* 'or are being voted out of existence by the European parliament.'

'The Once and Future King' is still alive and well in the literature of this century, from T. H. White's Arthurian tetralogy (1958) – the first part of which is the famous *The Sword in the Stone* (1937) – to the best-selling fantasies by Marion Zimmer Bradley and Stephen Lawhead. When he was just a child, John Steinbeck read Malory's *Morte d'Arthur* and called it his 'magic book'. His passion for the English language was aroused by it even more than by Shakespeare, and 'I think my sense of right and wrong, my feeling of *noblesse oblige,* and any thought I may have had against the oppressor and for the oppressed came from this secret book.' During his stay in Somerset (see p. 73) Steinbeck wrote *The Acts of King Arthur and His Noble Knights,* a fragment drawn from his own studies. Jerry Zucker's film *First Knight* (1995) with Sean Connery as Arthur will certainly not be the last on this ever enthralling subject.

Many of Tintagel's old houses were demolished at the turn of the century in order to satisfy requirements for the new age of Arthurian tourism. A crooked little mansion survived, with stone-grey elephant-hide walls struggling to support a slate roof, which itself is bent by the burden of the years and the winds, like an old peasant woman. This is the Old Post Office (14th century), which has been partly refurbished in Victorian style by the National Trust so that it can resume its postal duties. Tintagel in fact becomes more beautiful the further you are away from it. Outside the village, remotely situated on the coast, is the Norman parish church of St Materiana. A walk along the cliffs from here to *Boscastle* is an exhilarating experience. In Boscastle, within shouting distance from the 'Wellington Inn', Napoleon is spurring his white horse Marengo across the sign of the 'Napoleon Inn', disrespectfully known as the 'Nap'. The skeleton of this magnificent Arabian stallion was far too impressive to leave to the French, and so the English kept it to exhibit in London's National Army Museum.

Morwenstow: The Rev. Hawker Has Other Ideas

Morwenstow is as far north as you can go in Cornwall. Between the cliffs is a church without a village, surrounded by a graveyard and three houses. There is a pub with monastic origins and smuggling traditions, a rectory designed by an eccentric priest and poet, and keeping its distance a Tudor mansion – the classic English trinity. You enter Morwenstow's church under the stony gaze of a dragon, a dolphin, a mermaid and a whale. The colonnaded Norman doorway is one of the highlights of St John the Baptist, and the Norman north arcade is the other. Hanging in the spandrels above the massive round pillars, like hunting trophies, are the stone heads of antelopes and hippos. And above the zigzag carvings on the arches there is a whole gallery of monstrous bird and human heads. This was a fitting environment for a man like Robert Stephen Hawker, rector of Morwenstow.

Hawker believed in God, for the most part, but he also believed in the evil eye and in witchcraft, which is scarcely surprising in such a godforsaken place and at

Morwenstow

such a time (1834-75). If strangers ever lost their way and ended up here, they were usually shipwrecked sailors, and they were usually dead. The Reverend Hawker buried them all. For the crew of the *Caledonia*, he stuck the figurehead on the grave. In 1842 he built himself a hut made of driftwood on the cliff, and there he smoked opium pipes and wrote poems and ballads about God and the world, especially his Cornish world. 'Hawker's Hut' is now owned by the National Trust and is open to the public. When the rector visited his flock, he would wear a brimless hat on his head, and fishing boots beneath his cassock, and sometimes he would be accompanied by his pet pig Porky. He decorated the roof of his rectory with chimneys in the shapes of church towers, faithfully modelled on the churches where he had previously served. For over forty years he worked in Morwenstow and far across Cornwall, a poet-priest, individualist and eccentric, and a true Anglican. Shortly before his death, however, Robert Stephen Hawker had second thoughts and converted to Catholicism. If there were an Eccentrics' Corner in Westminster Abbey, the Rector of Morwenstow would surely be given pride of place.

Kings and Queens of England

Anglo-Saxon and Danish Kings

802-839	Egbert
839-855	Ethelwulf
855-860	Ethelbald
860-865	Ethelbert
865-871	Ethelred I
871-899	Alfred the Great
899-924	Edward the Elder
924-939	Athelstan
939-946	Edmund
946-955	Edred
955-959	Edwy
959-975	Edgar
975-978	Edward the Martyr
979-1016	Ethelred II the Unready
1016	Edmund II Ironside
1016-1035	Canute
1035-1040	Harold I
1040-1042	Hardicanute
1042-1066	Edward the Confessor
1066	Harold II

Norman Kings

1066-1087	William I the Conqueror
1087-1100	William II Rufus
1100-1135	Henry I
1135-1154	Stephen

House of Plantagenet

1154-1189	Henry II
1189-1199	Richard I Lionheart
1199-1216	John Lackland
1216-1272	Henry III
1272-1307	Edward I
1307-1327	Edward II
1327-1377	Edward III
1377-1399	Richard II

House of Lancaster

1399-1413	Henry IV
1413-1422	Henry V
1422-1461	Henry VI

House of York

1461-1483	Edward IV
1483	Edward V
1483-1485	Richard III

House of Tudor

1485-1509	Henry VII
1509-1547	Henry VIII
1547-1553	Edward VI
1553-1558	Mary I
1558-1603	Elizabeth I

House of Stuart

1603-1625	James I
1625-1649	Charles I
1649-1653	*Commonwealth*
1653-1658	*Oliver Cromwell, Lord Protector*
1658-1659	*Protectorate*
1660-1685	Charles II
1685-1688	James II
1689-1702	William III and Mary II
1702-1714	Anne

House of Hanover

1714-1727	George I
1727-1760	George II
1760-1820	George III
1820-1830	George IV
1830-1837	William IV

House of Saxe-Coburg-Gotha (Windsor)

1837-1901	Victoria
1901-1910	Edward VII
1910-1936	George V
1936	Edward VIII
1936-1952	George VI
1953-	Elizabeth II

Glossary of Architectural Terms

Apse In Christian architecture, generally the eastern end of the church

Atrium Originally an open, colonnaded inner court in a Roman house; in Christian architecture, a colonnaded court in front of the west door of the church

Bailey Open court of a stone-built castle

Balustrade A series of small, vertical columns used to support a rail on stairs, balconies or roofs

Barrel Vault Roof, consisting of a series of semicircular sections

Basilica Church with three or more aisles, of which the central one is higher than the others and contains windows to let in light. In early Christian architecture this was the favourite form, and set standards for all western church architecture even in its later developments

Boss A stone at the apex of an arch or at the intersection of ribs in a vault. Often ornamental

Bronze Age In Britain, from *c.* 1800 BC to 600 BC

Buttress A pillar built at an angle to the wall to strengthen it and to resist its outward thrust

Capital The very top of a column, pillar or pilaster, with decorative patterns, figures or plants

Cathedral Close From medieval times, the area all round the Cathedral, generally including a wide stretch of lawn, subject to canon law; the lay-out and architecture are typical of English cathedral cities

Chancel Area containing High Altar, reserved for choir and clergy, and some steps higher than the nave. Often separated from the nave by a screen or rails

Chantry or Chantry Chapel A memorial chapel in which, until the time of Edward VI, a mass was said (or sung – chanter) for the soul of the person who endowed it. In cathedrals such chapels are nearly always small, and situated between pillars in the interior, whereas on the Continent they tend to b extensions

Chapter House Separate room in cathedral set aside exclusively for the clergy for business meetings at which a chapter of the Bible would always be read out

Choir Screen A screen with one or more means of access between choir and nave, to separate clergy from laity

Circus Circle of houses with uniform front

Clapper Bridge Bridge made of large slabs of stone, some built up to make piers, supporting longer stones making up the span

Clerestory Upper part of main walls of church, with windows

Cloister Covered walk round inner court of monastery or cathedral (in the latter often an extension)

Clustered pier A pier with several shafts of different diameters reaching up into an arch or the ribs of a vault

Coffered Ceiling Flat or vaulted ceiling, decorated with sunken round or rectangular panels; the decorations are often gilded reliefs or plants

Corbel Block of stone projecting from a wall, supporting another architectural element or decoration on its upper surface

Crescent Ellipse of houses with uniform front

Crossing Intersection of transepts, chancel and nave

Crypt Underground chamber at eastern end of church for relics, tombs of saints and martyrs, and later of priests and sometimes other important people

Decorated Style (c.1300-1400) Typically English form of Gothic (2nd period) with flowing convex, concave lines (ogees) and elaborate ornamentation

Diaper work Surface decoration composed of square or lozenge shapes

Early English Style (c.1190-1300) First period of English Gothic, with severe, narrow forms and emphasis on the vertical (e.g. lancet windows)

Fan Vaulting the ribs radiate out in a fan shape from a central point

Hall Church Church in which all the aisles are of more or less the same height

Helm Spherical, tent or pyramid-shaped roof of a tower

Keep Central tower of a Norman castle with tiny apertures and no visible entrance. Used as a refuge during sieges and also as residence

Iron Age From c. 600 BC to the coming of the Romans

Lady Chapel Since c.1200, often an eastern extension of the Chancel, epitomising the growing veneration of the Virgin in western Christianity

Lantern Circular or polygonal windowed turret crowning roof or dome

Lierne Additional ribs that spring from bosses other than the central one, and link up with another boss

Long Gallery On the top floor of Elizabethan country houses, it runs the full length of the house and was used for games and entertainment in bad weather

Motte Steep mound, central element of eleventh and twelfth-century castles (Motte and Bailey design, with motte set in the bailey and enclosed by a ditch and palisade)

Mullion Vertical posts dividing a window; the individual sections are called 'lights'

Nave The main body of the church between the west entrance and the chancel

Palladian Architecture following the style and principles of the Venetian architect Andrea Palladio (1518-80)

Perpendicular Style (c.1350 – beginning of 16th century) Peak and final period of English Gothic, with filigree vaulting, clear and simple forms and proportions developed from complete mastery and reduction of all preceding forms

Pilaster Vertical rectangular column attached to wall or other area, with base and capital

Piscina Basin for washing the Mass or Communion vessels, with a drain. Usually in or against wall south of the altar

Portico Porch in front of main entrance, borne by columns and usually surmounted by triangular gable

Render Plaster covering of an outer wall

Reredos Structure above and behind the altar

Retable Raised shelf behind altar containing panel or shrine

Retro-choir Section east of choir, often used to contain the shrine of a saint

Rib Member which supports other sections of a vault

Rose Window In Gothic architecture, a round window with tracery radiating from the centre

Sedilia Seats for the priests, usually three, on or in the south wall of the chancel

Solar Upper living room of a medieval house

Stone Age The Old Stone Age (Paleolithic), before *c.* 8000 BC; the Middle Stone Age (Mesolithic), from *c.* 8000 BC to *c.* 3500 BC, overlapping with the New Stone Age (Neolithic), from *c.*3500 BC to *c.* 600 BC

Three-decker pulpit Pulpit with Clerk's Stall below and Reading Desk below Clerk's Stall

Tracery Geometrical Gothic ornamentation, initially only in large windows, but later also on walls, gables etc.

Transept Between nave and chancel, one of the two extensions that form the crossing in a cruciform church

Transom Upper part of main walls of church, with windows

Triforium Passage in church wall above arcades and below clerestory

Tudor Style (*c.*1520-early 17th C.) Mixture of Late Gothic elements with Italian and German Renaissance

Tympanum Arched area above doorway, generally with relief sculpture

Venetian window Three part window, with central section arched and wider than the outer two

Further Reading

Abrams, Lesley and James P. Carley (ed.), *The Archaeology and History of Glastonbury Abbey*, Woodbridge 1991

Arnold, Eve, *Eve Arnold in Britain*, London 1991

Betjeman, Sir John, *Sir John Betjeman's Guide to English Paris Churches*, rev. and updated by Nigel Kerr, London 1993

Bisgrove, Richard, *The Gardens of Gertrude Jekyll*, London 1992

Brown, Jane, *Gardens of a Golden Afternoon: The story of a partnership: Edwin Lutyens and Gertrude Jekyll*, London 1982

Cannadine, David, *The Decline and Fall of the British Aristocracy*, London 1990 (rev. ed. 1992)

Cheatle, J. R. W., *A Guide to the British Landscape*, London 1976

Chippindale, Christopher, *Stonehenge Complete*, London 1983 (rev. ed. 1994)

Clifton-Taylor, Alec, *The Cathedrals of England*, London 1967

Clifton-Taylor, Alec, *The Pattern of English Building*, London 1987

Cobbett, William, *Rural Rudes* (1830), London 1975

Collins, Wilkie, *Rambles Beyond Railways*, London 1851

Compton, Susan (ed.), *British Art in the Twentieth Century: The Modern Movement*, London 1987

Cook, Olive, *The English Country House: An Art and a Way of Life*, London 1974

Defoe, Daniel, *A Tour through England and Wales (1724-26)*, London and New York 1959

Drabble, Margaret and Lewinski, Jorge, *A Writer's Britain*, London 1971

Du Maurier, Daphne, *Vanishing Cornwall*, Harmondsworth 1972

Eagle, Dorothy and Carnell, Hilary, *The Oxford Literary Guide to the British Isles*, Oxford, 1977

Fisher, Adrian and Georg Gerster, *The Art of the Maze*, London 1990

Fleming, Laurence and Alan Gore, *The English Garden*, London 1979

Fowles, John and Barry Brukoff, *The Enigma of Stonehenge*, London 1980

Girouard, Mark, *Life in the English Country House: a social and architectural history*, Harmondsworth 1980

Girouard, Mark, *The English Town*, New Haven and London 1990

Godwin, Fay, *Our Forbidden Land*, London 1990

Grigson, Geoffrey, *The Faber Book of Poems and Places*, London 1980

Hadfield, John (ed.), *The Shell Book of English Villages*, London 1985

Hewison, Robert, *The Heritage Industry*, London 1987

Hildesheimer, Wolfgang, *Zeiten in Cornwall*, Frankfurt 1971

Hunt, John Dixon and Peter Willis, *The Genius of the Place: The English Landscape Garden 1620-1820*, London 1975

Hutton, Graham and Edwin Smith, *English Parish Churches*, London 1976

Hyams, Edward Solomon, *The Changing Face of England*, Harmondsworth 1974

Jackson-Stops, Gervase and James Pipkin, *The English Country House: A grand tour*, London 1984

Jackson-Stops, Gervase and James Pipkin, *The Country House Garden: A grand tour*, London 1987

Jacobs, Michael and Malcolm Warner, *The Phaidon Companion to Art and Artists in the British Isles*, Oxford 1980

James, Henry, *English Hours (1905)*, London 1960

Jekyll, Gertrude, *Classic English Gardens*, New York and London 1995

Jenner, Michael, *A Traveller's Companion to the West Country*, London 1990

Krier, Leon, *Architecture and Urban Design 1967-1992*, London 1993

Lees-Milne, James, *William Beckford*, London 1976

Lutyens, Mary, *Edwin Lutyens*, London 1980 (rev. ed. 1991)

Marsh, Kate (ed.), *Writers and their Houses*, London 1993

McCullin, Don, *Open Skies*, London 1989

McCullin, Don, *Unreasonable Behaviour: an autobiography*, London 1990

Myerson, Jeremy, *Makepeace: A Spirit of Adventure in Craft and Design*, London 1995

Naipaul, V. S., *The Enigma of Arrival*, London 1987

Newby, Howard, *Country Life: A Social History of Rural England*, London 1987

Nicolson, Nigel, *Great Houses of Britain*, London 1973

Palmer, Alan and Veronica, *Royal England*, London 1983

Pevsner, Nikolaus, *The Englishness of English Art*, London 1955

Pevsner, Nikolaus, *The Buildings of England*, Harmondsworth 1951

Priestley, J. B., *The English*, Harmondsworth 1975

Rackham, Oliver, *The History of the Countryside*, London 1986

Rackham, Oliver, *Illustrated History of the Countryside*, London 1994

Randall, Gerald, Church Furnishings and Decoration in England and Wales, London, 1980

Richmond, I. A., *Roman Britain*, Harmondsworth 1963

Schinkel, Karl Friedrich, *English Journey*, (ed. David Bindman and Gottfried Riemann), Yale 1993

Sitwell, Edith, *Bath*, London 1932

Soper, Tony and Le Messurier, Brian, *A Natural History Guide to the Coast*, London 1993

Spens, Michael, *The Complete Landscape Designs and Gardens of Geoffrey Jellicoe*,

London 1994

Taylor, Christopher, *Dorset*, London 1970

Taylor, John, *A Dream of England: Landscape, Photography and the Tourist's Imagination*, Manchester 1994

Theroux, Paul, *The Kingdom by the Sea: A Journey Around the Coast of Great Britain*, London 1983

Thomas, Nicholas, *A Guide to Prehistoric England*, London 1976

Tooby, Michael, *Tate Gallery St Ives: An Illustrated Companion*, London 1993

Trevelyan, George Macaulay, *English Social History*, Harmondsworth 1984

Trueman, A. E., (rev. J. B. Whittow and J. R. Hardy) *Geology and Scenery in England and Wales*, London, 1971

Whybrow, Marion, *St Ives 1883-1993: Portrait of an Art Colony*, Woodbridge 1994

Wilson, Simon, *Holbein to Hockney: A History of British Art*, London 1979

Picture Credits

24, 44, 46, 50 and 51 by David Lyons; colour plates 7, 8, 11, 26, 28, 30, 31, 33, 34, 35, 36, 45, 48, 49 and 62 by Peter Sager; colour plates 12, 14 and 37 by courtesy of the Tate Gallery, London; colour plates 20, 58, 59, 60 and 67 by courtesy of Peter Sager/DuMont Buchverlag; colour plate 27 by courtesy of the Roman Bath Museum, Bath; colour plate 39 by courtesy of the National Portrait Gallery, London; colour plate 40 by courtesy of the British Museum, London; colour plates 61, 63, 65 and 66 by courtesy of the Tate Gallery, St Ives; colour plate 68 by courtesy of the University of Liverpool Art Gallery and Collections; colour plates 13, 15, 52, 53, 54, 55 & 64 courtesy of Pallas Athene.

Maps and plans by Berndtson & Berndtson, Fürstenfeldbruck.

Some Practical Hints A-Z

Accommodation There is something for all tastes and budgets, from camping sites to manor houses. The cosiest, and particularly practical and economic for the go-as-you-please tourist, is Bed and Breakfast (B & B), which may also offer a unique insight into other people's private lives. See the annually updated *Good Bed and Breakfast Guide* (Penguin) and *The Great British Bed & Breakfast* (KGP Publishing).

Hotels are relatively expensive, in some cases unashamedly so bearing in mind their quality. Ask to see the room, and don't necessarily take the first one offered (it's often second best). See *The Good Hotel Guide* (Vermilion) and *The Which? Hotel Guide* (Which? Ltd). For luxury hotels at luxury prices, contact the Pride of Britain Group, PO Box 1353, Andover, Hampshire, tel. 01264 736604.

Unusual accommodation in restored historic houses, e.g. Luttrell's Tower, James Wyatt's 18th-C. folly near Southampton, can be rented from the Landmark Trust, Shottesbrooke, Maidenhead, Berkshire, tel. 01628 825925.

More than 225 beautifully situated holiday homes, from farmhouses to castles and water towers, are available from the National Trust (Holiday Cottages, PO Box 536, Melksham, Wiltshire SN12 8SX). If you want real peace and quiet, e.g. in monasteries, hermitages, meditation centres, you'll find a selection in George Target's original guidebook *Out of this World* (Bishopsgate Press Ltd). See also *The Good Holiday Cottage Guide 1999* (Swallow Press) and *Special Places to Stay in Britain* (Alastair Sawday Publishing).

For groups and conferences, good deals are offered at university halls of residence during the Easter and summer vacations. Information from: British Universities Accommodation Consortium, PO Box 581, University Park, Nottingham NG7 2RG, tel. 01602 504571.

For farm holidays, contact Cornish Farm Holidays, tel. 01726 861200, web-site, www.cornish-farms.co.uk; or Dorset Farm and Country Holidays, tel. 01935 872550; or Let Devon Farms Accommodate You, tel. 01404 871342. Self-catering farm holidays in Devon can be arranged through Helpful Holidays, tel. 01647 433593, or in Dorset through Heart of Dorset, tel. 01305 848252. Exmoor holiday specialists are Exmoor Holidays, tel. 01598 710702. Camping barns on Exmoor, Dartmoor and the Tarka Trail can be organized by North Devon Holiday Homes, tel. 01271 376322.

For more information, contact the West Country Tourist Board, tel. 01392 425426, web-site www.wctb.co.uk; or the Devon Tourist Information Service, tel. 01392 437581.

See also Youth Hostels

Angling There are many facilities on coasts and rivers. See the annual handbook *Where to Fish* (Harmsworth Publishing). Licences may be obtained from local tourist offices.

Cycling More and more cycle tracks are being created in England. For information, contact Cyclists Touring Club (CTC), Cotterell House, 69 Meadrow, Godalming, Surrey GU7 3HS, tel. 01483 417217.

See also Sustrans

Drink For a long time it used to be said that the English didn't drink when they were thirsty, but they were thirsty when it was time to drink. To some extent this still applies in the country, where pubs often keep to the traditional 3-6 p.m. break regardless of the 1988 licensing laws revolution. Egon Ronay's *Best Pubs in Great Britain*, updated every year, lists over 1,000 pubs, including some from Tudor and stagecoach times. It's always worth asking for local beers, like Wadworth's 6X, known as Waddies, in Wiltshire.

A refreshing alternative is cider. The best comes from Somerset and Devon 'from the wood'. Farmhouse cider and a museum are to be found at Sheppy's, a family firm founded in the 19th century: Three Bridges, Bradford-on-Tone (3 miles SW of Taunton) Mon-Sat 8.30-18, Sun 12-14. Tel. 01823 461233

Julian Temperley sells Somerset Royal cider brandy at Passvale Farm, Burrow Hill, Kingsbury Episcopi, Martock, Mon-Sat 9-17.30. Tel. 01460 240782

The Romans tried, and so of course did the Normans: wine-making in England can be regarded either as a sport or as an eccentricity. Nevertheless, it is on the increase. For information, contact The English Vineyards Association, 38 West Park, London SE9 4RH. But don't drink and drive.

Eating Out Somerset Maugham thought that anyone who wanted to eat well in England would have to eat three breakfasts a day. With the regrettable advance of the so-called Continental Breakfast, that is no longer true, but complaints about English food (and weather) are equally anachronistic. 'The miracle of English cuisine: flavoursome, juicy and sensuous' (*Die Zeit*) can be enjoyed even in the villages and small towns of the West Country. Fresh ingredients from the garden or the market, and international sophistication make these gourmet restaurants well worth a detour. See the annually updated *Good Food Guide* (Consumers Association), which has become a gourmets' bible since its first publication in 1951. The same association publishes a *Vegetarian Good Food Guide*.

Tea rooms can be a great source of pleasure, and cream teas are a speciality – particularly in Devon and Cornwall. Make sure the scones are homemade, and tuck into lashings of strawberry jam and clotted cream.

The West Country is a great region for cheese. Vying with the best that Europe can produce are Cornish Yarg, Devon Oke, Somerset Brie, Brendon Blue (made from goat's milk), Beenleigh Blue (from sheep's milk), Dorset Blue Vinney, and of course the world-famous Cheddar. Two useful addresses for cheese-lovers: Chewton Cheese Dairy, Chewton Mendip (NE of Wells), and Ticklemore Cheese, 1 Ticklemore St, Totnes, Devon.

In the churchyard at St Buryan's in Cornwall, I found the following epitaph for William Simpson Paris (1867):

Our life is but a winter's day,
Some only breakfast and away,
Others to dinner stay and are full fed,
The oldest only sups and goes to bed,
Large is his debt who lingers out the day,
Who goes the soonest has the least to pay.

Eclipse On Wednesday 11 August 1999, Cornwall experienced a total eclipse of the sun lasting 2 minutes and 6 seconds. Despite predictions of widespread chaos, mass starvation and unprecedented prosperity for the Cornish tourist trade, the eclipse was in organizational terms the biggest non-event in Cornwall's history. For those who ignored the doomsayers and who managed to avoid the line of total cloud cover, it was a magical and never-to-be-repeated experience, with the diamond ring effect, Bailey's beads and other staples of pre-eclipse conversation in full view. Others had to be content with the knowledge that the event is in fact due to be repeated on an almost annual basis in parts of the world where there are cloud-free skies.

English Heritage (EH) Independent, but partly funded by the government as the successor organization to the Ministry of Works, it owns and administers over 400 historic sites and buildings, including Stonehenge. It protects and maintains houses and gardens, prehistoric monuments, as well as castles, ruined abbeys, industrial and municipal sites. It also gives grants to the National Trust, historic churches, and important private estates. London headquarters: Fortress House, 23 Savile Row, London W1X 2HE tel. 020 7973 3396.

In recent years the concept of English Heritage has become an important issue. The increasingly popular, practical but not always unproblematic relationship between conservation and tourism is analysed by Robert Hewison in *The Heritage Industry* (London 1987), in which he argues against the complete commercialization of the past: heritage seen as the enemy of history.

Folly Fellowship This is a charity dedicated to the preservation of follies 'of varying quality and peculiarity'. It enjoys, records, photographs, gossips and researches follies. Contact the Membership Secretary, 41 Bincore Road, Enfield, Middlesex EN2 7RD; web-site www.heritage.co.uk/ heritage/follies.

Gardens The West Country is particularly rich in glorious gardens. As well as gardens attached to NT or other country houses, many private gardens are open for a few days a year. Consult the annually updated *Gardens of England and Wales* (universally referred to as the 'Yellow Book'), published by the National Gardens Scheme.

Short descriptions of over 900 British gardens, with addresses and best visiting times, are published in the *Good Gardens Guide* (Vermilion), also updated yearly.

A history of both traditional and unusual English gardens is Penelope Hobhouse's *The Private Gardens of England* (London 1986).

Worth visiting is the only Museum of Garden History (St Mary-at-Lambeth, Lambeth Palace Rd, London SE1 7LB, tel. 020 7261 1891, open Mon-Fri 10.30-16, Sun 10.30-17).

Information Local Tourist Information Centres are always helpful. The West Country Tourist Board, 60 St Davids Hill, Exeter EX4 4SY, publishes useful brochures and maps; tel. 01392 425426, e-mail, post@wctb.co.uk, website, www.wctb.co.uk.

National Trust (NT) Three English philanthropists – a social reformer, a clergyman, and a lawyer – founded the 'National Trust for Places of Historic Interest or Natural Beauty' in 1895. This highly influential private institution is financed by members' subscriptions, donations, entrance money, foundations, and a whole chain of flourishing souvenir shops and tea rooms. Next to the Crown and the State, the NT is the third biggest land-owner in Britain. It owns, administers, and restores castles, country houses, estates, farmhouses, gardens, forests, battlefields, bird sanctuaries, pubs, dovecotes, industrial monuments, barns, mills, cider presses, and whole villages and islands. It has over 2.6 million members, some 11.7 million paying visitors a year, and an annual turnover of around £170 million, making it the most powerful conservation body in England.

Its acquisitions have a not inconsiderable influence on the tastes and values of the nation. This most admirable and most enviable institution does, however, have its critics. They dub it the National Dust, and accuse it of one-sidedly preserving the traditions of the aristocracy and the pastoral past – a 'fossilisation of taste' (*Observer*). Until the 1970's, the Trust appeared to be mainly focused on saving historic houses that were under threat, but since the mid 1980's it has concentrated more on protecting Nature and the countryside. This 'green policy' has rescued some of the most beautiful British landscapes, which include about a sixth of the English coast – over 550 miles – thanks to Enterprise Neptune, a campaign begun in 1964. See the informative and richly illustrated history by Merlin Waterson: *The National Trust, The First Hundred Years* (1995).

Members pay an annual subscription, for which they can visit all the houses, gardens and other properties free of charge. Headquarters of the NT are at 42-44 Queen Anne's Gate, London SW1, tel. 020 7222 9251.

Railways The Paignton and Dartmouth Steam Railway passes through stunning countryside, while the Bristol to Weymouth line offers a gentle cross-country journey, with special ticket offers. Paignton-Dartmouth enquiries tel. 01345 125625. Bristol-Weymouth enquiries tel. 0870 900 0766

Riding Exmoor and Dartmoor are the best areas for holidays on horseback, with riding lessons and pony trekking on offer at farms and accredited riding schools. For further information, contact: The British Horse Society, National Equestrian Centre, Stoneleigh, Kenilworth, Warwickshire, tel. 01203 696969

Walking 'Why walk? To clear the mind, thoughts drifting effortless to the surface like tea leaves,' says walk artist Hamish Fulton.

The West Country is great walking country, especially on the Quantock and Mendip Hills in Somerset and the moors of Devon and Cornwall: Exmoor, Dartmoor and Bodmin Moor. For long-distance enthusiasts, there is the Hardy Way (211 miles, following the tracks of Dorset's famous author), the South-West Coast Path (600 miles from Studland/Dorset to Minehead/ Somerset) and the Tarka Trail (181 miles across Exmoor). For further information contact The Ramblers' Association (the umbrella organisation for about 400 local groups and 800 affiliated groups) at 1-5 Wandsworth Rd, London SW8 2XX, open Mon-Fri 9.30-17.30. Tel. 020 7339 8500; website, www.ramblers.org.uk

Youth Hostels For addresses and information, contact: Youth Hostels Association (YHA), 8 St Stephens Hill, St Albans, Herts AL1 2DY, tel. 01727 855215

Places to See, with Opening Times

NT = National Trust, EH = English Heritage, P = Private, TIC = Tourist Information Centre
Ring ahead to check opening times on Bank Holidays and over Christmas. Groups should book.

Bristol

at-Bristol, Deanery Road, Harbourside: unique learning and leisure destination including Explore-at-Bristol, a hands-on science centre, and Wildscreen-at-Bristol, where visitors can experience the natural world. Opens Spring 2000. Tel. 0117 914 9452

Architecture Centre, Narrow Quay: exhibitions about the built environment in a redundant sail maker's workshop. Tue-Fri 11-17, Sat-Sun 12-17. Tel. 0117 922 1540

Arnolfini, 16 Narrow Quay: major contemporary art gallery, founded 1961. Exhibitions, films, performances. Mon-Sat 10-19, Sun 12-18. Tel. 0117 929 9191

Bristol Blue Glass, Great Western Dock: glass blowing. Daily 9-17. Tel. 0117 929 8900

Blaise Castle House Museum, Henbury Rd, Henbury: 18th C. collection. Park. Mon-Wed & Sat-Sun 10-16.45. Tel. 0117 950 6789

Bristol Cathedral, College Green: (Anglican) Evensong Mon-Fri 17.15, Sat & Sun 15.30. Tel. 0117 926 4879

Bristol Industrial Museum, Prince's Wharf: Apr-Oct, Sat-Wed 10-17; Nov-Mar, Sat & Sun only. Tel. 0117 925 1470

Bristol Old Vic, King St: Theatre Royal, opened 1766, Britain's oldest working theatre. Tel. 0117 987 7877

City Museum & Art Gallery, Queen's Rd: archaeology, natural and industrial history of the region; old and modern art (Bristol School). Daily 10-17. Tel. 0117 922 3571

The Exploratory, Bristol Old Station, Temple Meads: highly interactive museum of science and technology. Daily 10-17. Tel. 0117 907 5000

The Georgian House, 7 Great George St: Home of sugar merchant and friend of Wordsworth, John Pretor Pinney, 1791. Vivid presentation of life in Georgian townhouse. Apr-Oct, Sat-Wed 10-17. Tel. 0117 921 1362

Harveys Wine Museum, 12 Denmark St; firm founded 1796. Mon-Sat 10-17. Tel. 0117 927 5036

The Red Lodge, Park Row: Elizabethan merchant's house (c.1590), with reconstructed 17th-C. town garden. Sat-Wed 10-17. Tel. 0117 921 1360

Royal West of England Academy, Queen's Rd, Clifton, Mon-Sat 10-17.30, Sun 14-17. Tel. 0117 973 5129

SS Great Britain, including the **Maritime Heritage Centre**, Great Western Dock, Gas Ferry Road. Open daily except 24-25 Dec. Apr-Oct 10-17, Nov-Mar 10-16. Tel. 0117 929 1843

St George's, Brandon Hill: recording studio. Occasional concerts in Georgian church. Programme & tickets, tel. 0117 923 0359

Tourist Information Centre, St Nicholas Church, St Nicholas Street. Mon-Sat 9.30-17.30, Sun 11-16. Tel. 0117 926 0767; bristol@ tourism.bristol.gov.uk. Further information at www.cityguide.co.uk

Watershed Media Centre, 1 Canon's Rd: contemporary photography, film, media events, 8.30-20.30. Cafe 10.30-23.00, Sun 11-19. Tel. 0117 927 6444

Cornwall

Antony (Torpoint, 5 miles W of Plymouth) 18th-C. country house of Carew family with a wealth of paintings, tapestries, embroideries and a collection of furniture from the 19th C. Apr-Oct, Tue-Thur; June-Aug, also Sun 13.30-17.30. NT. Tel. 01752 812191
    Adjacent 100 acre Woodland Garden, owned by family trust, has many native and exotic trees and shrubs, over 300 kinds of camellia, 18th-C. dovecote, and bathhouse 1789. Apr-Oct, daily, 13.30-17.30. NT. Tel. 01752 812191

Camborne (SW of Truro, A3047 at Pool). Camborne School of Mines: exhibition of geology & mineralogy, open all year Mon-Fri 9-17. Tel. 01209 714866

Cotehele (nr Calstock, 14 miles NW of Plymouth) Tudor country house on west bank of Tamar, terraced gardens, chapel. Apr-Oct, 11-17 (exc. Fri). NT. Tel. 0157 351346

Chysauster Ancient Village (NE of Penzance, 3 miles NW of Gulval) Remains of prehistoric village, Apr-Sept 10-18; Oct 10-17. EH. Tel. 0117 975 0716

Falmouth Arts Gallery, Municipal Buildings, The Moor. Permanent collection and changing exhibitions of Cornish art. Mon-Fri 10-17, Sat 10-13, closed Bank Holidays. Tel. 01326 313863

Fowey Daphne du Maurier Literary Centre, South Street. Exhibition, video, talks & walks concerning du Maurier & other literary figures of the area. May-Sept 10-17. Tel 01726 833619

Geevor Tin Mining Museum (Pendeen, nr St Just, NW of Penzance) Guided tours above and underground, exciting and claustrophobic. Mar-Oct, Sun-Fri & Bank Holiday Sat only 10-17; July-Aug, daily 10-17; Nov-Feb, tel. to check. Tel. 01736 788662

Glendurgan Garden (4 miles SW of Falmouth) Subtropical garden with maze, Mar-Oct, Tue-Sat 10.30-17.30. NT. Tel. 01326 250906

Godolphin (5 miles NW of Helston) 15th-C. country house, with Elizabethan and Carolean additions and colonnaded façade (c.1635), birthplace of Cavalier poet, Sidney Godolphin, Queen Anne's High Treasurer and owner of the famous Godolphin Arabian, ancestor of all thoroughbreds today. The early gardens are being restored. May-June, Thur 14-17; July & Sep, Tue & Thur 14-17; Aug, Tue 14-17, Thur 10-13, 14-17. Tel. 01736 762409

Heligan Gardens (S of St Austell, B3273, between Pentewan & St Ewe) Laid out in 18/19 C., restored 1994-98: 'The Lost Gardens of Heligan', magical mixture of gardens, forest and wilderness. 10-18. Tel. 01726 845100

Isles of Scilly The wild paradise in the Gulf Stream is an archipelago of more than 100 islands off the SW coast of Cornwall, three hours boat ride from Penzance (or 20 minutes flying time from heliport). The 2,000 Scillonians live on five inhabited islands of St Mary's, Tresco, St Martin's, St Agnes, and Bryher. The capital, the village of Hugh Town (population 1500), is on St Mary's, the biggest island. Harold Wilson, famous for taking his holidays on the Scillies, is now buried there. Many megalithic tombs, spectacular rocks and sandy beaches, seabirds and subtropical climate. Bananas and lemons, Indian fan ferns and Burmese honeysuckle grow in abundance in terraced gardens of former Benedictine abbey on Tresco. 10-16. Tel. 01720 424105

Additional attraction in garden: 'Valhalla', a collection of figureheads from shipwrecks. The islanders used to live off such wrecks, as well as flowers and fishing. Principal industry now tourism. Almost the whole archipelago is protected, and belongs to the Duke of Cornwall, Prince Charles. Information, St Mary's, Porthcressa Bank. Tel. 01720 422536

Lands End (9 miles W of Penzance) Highly commercialized, but visitors' centre exhibition good of its kind. The Lizard is a more evocative bit of country and further south.

Lanhydrock (3 miles S of Bodmin, B3268) Jacobean & Victorian country house with gardens, park and Pre-Raphaelite paintings (inc. Spencer Stanhope), Apr-Oct, Tue-Sun 11-17.30. NT. Tel. 01208 73320

Megalithic sites There are many megalithic sites in Cornwall, much visited by tourists and New Age pagans alike. For the most mysterious, try the holy well at Sancreed, or the fogou at Trelissick, or the cromlech and pierced stone at Lanyon Quoit and Men an Tol (NW of Madron and Penzance). Ancient stones walks, leaflets, maps and beautiful prints at the Men an Tol Studio, Bosullow. Tel. 01736 68282.

Minack Theatre (Porthcurno, 3 miles SE of Land's End) Open air theatre on the cliffs. Tel. 01736 810181

Mount Edgcumbe House (Rame Peninsula, S of Plymouth, A38-A374-A3247, or Plymouth-Cremyll ferry for foot passengers only): Tudor house of Edgcumbe family, 1547-54, burned down in Second World War, rebuilt 1958-64; 18th-C. west wing regarded by David Garrick as 'the haunt of the Muses, the Mount of Parnassus', now popular with sightseers: formal gardens and landscaped park with collection of camellias and spectacular coastal path from Plymouth Sound to Whitsand Bay. House: 1

Apr-1 Oct, Wed-Sun 11-16.30. Park: all year. Tel. 01752 822236

Newlyn (S of Penzance): Newlyn Art Gallery, New Rd: local, national & international contemporary art. Mon-Sat 10-17. Tel. 01736 331578

Pilchard Works. 'How the Cornish Pilchard has shaped the social, industrial and artistic life of Cornwall'. Working Museum Award Winner. Mar-Oct, Mon-Fri 10-18, Sat 10-14; group bookings all year round. Tel. 01736 332112

Newquay: Dairy Land Farm World (4 miles SE of Newquay) Apr-Oct and Dec, daily 7.30-17, school holidays 10-17. Tel. 01872 510349

Pencarrow House (nr Washaway, 4 miles NW of Bodmin, A389/B3266) Georgian country house of Molesworth-St Aubyns family, 1765-75. 18th-C. paintings, furniture and porcelain, rock and woodland gardens, over 600 varieties of rhododendron, collection of conifers, especially an avenue of araucaria. Araucaria's English name is said to have originated in Pencarrow in 1834, when a house guest touched the prickly leaves and exclaimed: 'It would puzzle a monkey!' Easter-1 June, 13.30-17, 1 June-10 Sept, 11-17, 11 Sept-15 Oct 13.30-17, & Bank Holiday Mon 11-17. Tel. 01208 841369

Pendennis Castle (SE of Falmouth) Coastal fort of Henry VIII on mouth of Fal, 1546. Apr-Sept 9.30-18, Oct-Mar 9.30-16. EH. Tel. 01326 316594. St Mawes castle on the opposite side has the same opening times

Penzance: Penlee House Gallery & Museum, Morrab Rd: specializes in artists of Newlyn school from 1880's to 1920's. Open all year, Mon-Sat 10.30-16.30; July-Aug, also Sun 12-16.30. Tel. 01736 363625

The Rooster and the Rat (originally The Wolf at the Door), Bread St: Gallery of contemporary art, especially regional. Mon-Sat

10-17.30. Tel. 01736 360573

Trengwainton Garden (nr Penzance): tropical, exotic plants. Mar-Oct, Wed-Sat 10.30-17.30 (Mar, Oct 10.30-17). Tel. 01736 363021/368410

Poldark Mine (Wendron nr Helston, 6 miles S of Redruth, B3297) Tin mine museum, including underground tours. Apr-Oct 10-17.30. Tel. 01326 563166

Pool Cornish Engines (nr Redruth, A3047) Two restored 19th-C. engine houses. Apr-Oct 11-17. NT. Tel. 01209 216657

Porthcurno (3 miles SE of Land's End, B3315): Porthcurno Tunnels, telegraph station of 1870, since 1994 museum of vintage wireless & telegraph communications. Apr-Oct, Fri 11-15; July-Sept, Wed 11-15. Tel. 01209 612142

Prideaux Place (Padstow, 13 miles NE of Newquay, B3276) 16th-C. home of Prideaux-Brune family, rebuilt in Neo-Gothic style c.1810, 16th C. panelling, long gallery: garden and deer park overlooking Camel estuary. Easter Sun-7 Oct, Sun-Thur 13.30-17; Bank Holiday Mon 11-17. Tel. 01841 532411/2

Restormel Castle (between Bodmin and Lostwithiel) Ruined castle on hill overlooking River Fowey, 12/13th-C., which Pevsner regards as Cornwall's most perfect example of military architecture. Apr-Oct 10-18. Tel. 01208 872687

Sennen Cove (2 miles NE of Land's End, A30) Fishing village with broad bay for bathing. 19th-C. Round House now gallery for arts and crafts. Cover's Gallery, Mar-Nov, Mon-Sat 10-17. Tel. 01736 871546

St Germans (W of Plymouth, between A38 & A374) Beautifully situated village on mouth of River Tiddy.

St Germanus: Augustinian Priory Church, 12/13th-C. One of the most magnificent churches in the West. With two west towers (one square, one octagonal), grandiose Norman colonnaded porch, east window by Burne-Jones & Morris (1902), Monument to Edward Eliot by Rysbrack (1722), his first major commission after coming to England in 1720.

Port Eliot: Georgian manor house near church, former priory, mainly by Sir John Soane, 1802-06, park by Humphry Repton, 1792-93. P.

Almshouses: picturesque terrace of six, with loggia and balcony, 17th-C.

St Ives: Barbara Hepworth Museum and Sculpture Garden, Barnoon Hill: Tue-Sun 10.30-17; July-Aug also open Mon. Garden may close earlier in winter. Tel. 01736 796226

The Leach Pottery, The Stennack, Mon-Fri, 10-17, also Sat in summer. Tel. 01736 796398

The New Craftsman, 24 Fore Street, Mon-Sat 10-17, July-Aug 10-17.30, Sat 10-17, Sun 11-17. Tel. 01736 795652

The Penwith Galleries, Back Rd West, Tue-Sat 10-13, 14.30-17. Tel. 01736 795579

Salthouse Gallery, Norway Square: Exhibitions of contemporary art, Mon-Sat 10.30-17.30. Tel. 01736 795003

St Ives School of Painting, Back Rd West: est. 1939, holiday and evening courses. Tel. 01736 797174 & 797180

Tate Gallery St Ives, Porthmeor Beach. Tue-Sun 10.30-17; July-Aug also open Mon. Tel. 01736 796226

Wills Lane Gallery, Wills Lane: works by St Ives artists, Mon-Sat 10.30-16.30. Tel. 01736 795723

St Michael's Mount (nr Marazion, 3 miles E of Penzance, A394) Rocky island with medieval castle, Apr-Oct, Mon-Fri 10.30-17.30. Tel. 01736 710265

Tintagel (N of Wadebridge, W of A39) The Old Post Office: Tiny 14th-C. manor house, 19th-C. Post Office, Apr-Oct 11-17.30. NT. Tel. 01840 770024

Tintagel Castle (NW of village): 12/13th-C.

ruin with Arthurian atmosphere. Apr- Oct 10-18; Nov-Mar 10-16. EH. Tel. 01840 770328

Trebah (SW of Mawnan-Smith, 4 miles SW of Falmouth) Mid 19th-C. garden in broad bay on River Helford, subtropical plants and rainforest vegetation. Open every day of the year 10.30-17. Tel. 01326 250448

Tregrehan (2 miles E of St Austell, A390, opposite Britannia Inn) Early 19th-C. garden, collection of camellias, Victorian hothouses. Mid Mar-mid June daily (exc. Easter Sun), 10.30-17. Tel. 01726 814389

Trelissick (4 miles S of Truro, B3289) Late Georgian country estate of 1825. Extensive gardens and woodland paths above mouth of River Fal: ferns, figs, hydrangeas, camellias etc. Garden, parkland, woodland and riverside walks, pottery and gallery open to public. Apr-Sep, Mon-Sat 10.30-17.30, Sun 12.30-17.30; Oct-Mar, Mon-Sat 10.30-17, Sun 12.30-17. NT. Tel. 01872 862090

Trelowarren (3 miles SE of Helston) Manor house, pottery, crafts gallery, restaurant, woodland walks, camping site. Christian fellowship squatting in Elizabethan house (restored) Gothick chapel. Tue-Sun 11-17. Tel. 01326 221224

Trerice (3 miles SE of Newquay, A392/A3058) Elizabethan country estate, 1571, garden, small lawnmower museum, Apr-Sept 11-17.30 (exc. Tue & Sat); daily in Aug; Oct 11-17. NT. Tel. 01637 875404

Trewithen (A390 between Truro & St Austell) Early Georgian manor, 1715-40, by Sir Robert Taylor, completed 1764. Landscaped garden with outstanding collection of magnolias, azaleas & rhododendrons. Garden: Mar-Sept. Mon-Sat 10-16.30; Apr-May daily. House: Apr-July, Mon & Tues 14-16. Tel. 01726 882763/4

Truro: Royal Cornwall Museum, River St: large mineral collection, industrial archaeology, prehistory, Cookworthy chinaware, paintings and drawings (Hogarth et al.), Mon-Sat 10-17. Tel. 01872 272205; e-mail, courtney.rcmric @btinternet.com

Truro Cathedral. Sung evensong weekdays 17.30, Sun 18. Tel. 01872 276782

Wheal Martyn China Clay Heritage Centre, Carthew (on B3274 N of St Austell). Story of china clay. Historic trail, nature trail, panoramic views over current workings. Apr-Oct 10-18. Tel. 01726 850362

Devon

A la Ronde (2 miles N of Exmouth, A376) 16-cornered cottage orné of 1796, with eccentric interiors: walls lined with shells, feather frieze and what not. Folly built by two spinsters, Jane and Mary Parminter. Apr-Oct, Sun-Thurs 11-17.30. NT. Tel. 01395 265514

Arlington Court (7 miles NE of Barnstaple, A39) Regency country house, 1820-23, with collection of model ships, pewter, coaches etc. Park with Jacob's sheep. Apr-Oct 11-17.30 (exc. Sat). Park: all year. NT. Tel. 01271 850296

Barnstaple Ancient town, oldest borough in England, granted charter 930 AD. Saxon street outline still visible. Norman castle mound. Cattle market every Friday. Has won 'Britain in Bloom' and European 'Entente Florale' competition winner more often than any other town in Britain. Centre of laver collecting: 'Forget Viagra, local laver now in!'

Museum of North Devon, The Square. Art, pottery, military and maritime history of the area plus *Tarka the Otter*. Tue-Sat 10-16.30. Tel. 01271 346747

Queen Anne's Walk, 1609 merchants' exchange remodelled as arcade 1708, much carved, with statue of Queen Anne and wall panels depicting the Armada. Barnstaple

Heritage Centre specialising in maritime history now open. Tel. TIC 01271 375000

St Anne's Chancel: John Gay's school, with his carved desk

Guildhall, Butchers Row, 17th-C. oak panelling, 16th- & 17th-C. silver and gold. (Barnstaple has thriving goldsmith industry and is particularly famous for its spoons.) Free tours by appointment. Tel. TIC 01271 375000

Berry Pomeroy Castle (2.5 miles E of Totnes) Picturesque ruin (14th-16th C.). The first owner was Sir Edward Seymour, brother of Jane Seymour, and after her death in childbirth he became Protector of her son Edward VI. Monument to the Seymours (1613) and outstanding choir screen in St Mary's. EH. Apr-Nov 10-18. Tel. 01803 866618

Bickleigh Castle (4 miles S of Tiverton, A 396) Castle and estate dating back 900 years. Tudor interiors, Norman chapel, 18th-C. wrought iron gate. Park with Gingko Biloba, Judas and tulip trees etc. Easter, then May-Sept 14-17 (exc. Sat). Tel. 01884 855363

Bicton Bicton Park Gardens (nr East Budleigh, 8 miles SE of Exeter, A376) Extensive early 18th & 19th-C. garden, with collection of agricultural implements. All year, 10-18; winter 10-16. Tel. 01395 568465

Nearby: Bicton College of Agriculture, with arboretum. All year every day 10.30-17. Tel. 01395 568353

Bicton Mausoleum: chapel by A. W. N. Pugin, one of his last major commissions (1850). He designed the Minton tiles, stained glass windows, painted ceiling and the monument to John, Lord Rolle, owner of Bicton.

Bideford The Big Sheep, sheep racing. Mar-Oct, daily at 3.20 p.m. Tel. 01237 472366

Bovey Tracey (13.5 miles SW of Exeter, A38/A382) Riverside Mill, arts and crafts centre of Devon Guild of Craftsmen. Daily 10-17.30. Tel. 01626 832223

Bovey Tracey Tourist Information Centre, Station Rd: claims to have the sixth most visited website in Britain! www.dartmoor.co.uk. Tel. 01626 832047

Bradley Manor (SW of Newton Abbot, 7 miles NW of Torquay, A381) Small 15th-C. country house surrounded by woodland and riverside meadows. Apr-Sept, Wed 14-17; also first two Thurs in Apr & last two Thurs. in Sept. NT. Tel. 01626 354513

Buckfast Abbey (half mile S of Ashburton, A38) 1137-1539 Cistercian abbey, taken over in 1882 by French Benedictines. Monastery church rebuilt 1907-38 in Norman and Early Gothic style (with copies of altar and font from German cathedrals). Famous for its commercially produced drink, Buckfast Wine, which has been blamed for juvenile delinquency in Glasgow (where it is known as Electric Soup). Home until his death of Brother Adam, world renowned apiarist. Open every day. Opposite Shell Museum with Victorian arts and crafts. Tel. 01364 642519

Buckland Abbey (10 miles N of Plymouth, A386) 13th-C. Cistercian abbey, Drake's house with maritime museum, silver and china crafts studio. Apr-Oct 10.30-17.30 (exc. Thur); Nov-Mar, Sat & Sun 14-17. NT. Tel. 01822 853607

Cadhay Manor (nr Ottery St Mary, E of Exeter A30/B3176) Tudor country house with park. July-Aug, Tue-Thur 14-18; groups by appointment. Tel. 01404 812432

Castle Drogo (Drewsteignton, S of A30 between Exeter & Okehampton) Lutyens castle (1910-30) in picturesque spot above River Teign: terraced garden, croquet lawn (where public can play), woodland walks across northeast edge of Dartmoor. Apr-Oct 11-17.30 (exc. Fri). NT. Tel. 01647 433306

Chagford (E. Dartmoor, A382/B3206) Former tin-mining town. St Michael with Renaissance monument (1575) and processional cross made out of aluminium from first Zeppelin to be shot down over England in 1916

Cockington (between Torquay and Paignton) Picturesque village with Perpendicular church, 16/17th-C. manor house, old smithy, thatched Drum Inn (by Lutyens, 1934)

Coleton Fishacre Garden (E of Dartmouth, 3 miles S of Kingswear) Subtropical garden, laid out 1925-48; collection of rare exotic trees and shrubs in spectacular coastal setting. Garden: Mar, Sun 14-17; Apr-Oct, Wed-Sun 10.30-17.30/dusk. House: May-Oct, Wed-Sun & Bank Holiday Mon 11-16. NT. Tel. 01803 752466

Compton Castle (1 mile N of Marldon, W of Torquay, A381) Fortified manor house (14th-16th C.). Home of Sir Walter Raleigh's half brother Humphrey Gilbert, who in 1583 founded the first English colony, Newfoundland. Apr-Oct, Mon, Wed & Thur 10-12.15, 14-17. NT. Tel. 01803 872112

Dartington Hall (2 miles NW of Totnes) Elizabethan manor house, centre of agriculture, arts and crafts, international summer courses, gardens and park. Tel. 01803 866051
High Cross House: Easter-Oct, Tue-Fri 10.30-16.30, Sat & Sun 14-17. Tel. 01803 864114
Cider Press Centre: Mon-Sat, 9.30-17.30; Easter-Christmas 10.30-17.30. Tel. 01803 864171

Dartmouth Castle Situated at mouth of River Dart, begun 1481. Military history with spectacular view. Apr-Oct 10-18; Nov-Mar, Wed-Sun 10-16. EH. Tel. 01803 833588

Endsleigh House (Milton Abbot, 4 miles NW of Tavistock, B3362) Designed by Jeffrey Wyatville, 1810, in cottage orné style for 6th Duke of Bedford, with magnificent landscaped garden by Humphry Repton, shell house,

arboretum. Now a country house hotel (see p. 000). Apr-Sept, Sat & Sun 12-16, Tue & Fri by appointment. Tel. 01822 870248

Exeter Royal Albert Memorial Museum, Queen St: English oils and watercolours, costumes, porcelain. Mon-Sat 10-17. Tel. 01392 265858
Cathedral: Evensong Mon-Fri 17.30, Sat 15, Sun 15. Tel. 01392 255573
Exeter Phoenix, Bradninch Place, Gandy St: theatre, films, exhibitions, café. Mon-Thur 10-20; Fri-Sun 11-20.30. Tel. 01392 667055
Maritime Museum, The Haven: 150 sailing and steamships from all over the world. Open for occasional summer exhibitions only. Tel. 01392 251139
University of Exeter, Streatham Campus, full university status since 1955: arts and sciences, education, Celtic culture (Institute of Cornish Studies). Tel. 01392 263263

Exmouth (S of Exeter, A376) The Barn, Foxhole Hill: art nouveau house, 1897, by E. S. Prior, a pupil of Norman Shaw. P.

Flete (Ermington, 10 miles E of Plymouth, A379/B3121) Victorian house, 1878, built in Neo-Elizabethan style around a small Elizabethan house. Outstanding example of picturesque country house architecture by Norman Shaw, who created the first garden suburb (Bedford Park in London, 1880). May-Sept, Wed & Thur 14-17. Garden: every weekend, 14-17. Tel. 01752 830308

Fursdon (Cadbury, 6 miles S of Tiverton, A3072) Late Georgian country house with older origins, 700-year family history, garden. Easter-Sept, Thur & Bank Holiday Mon 14-17. Tours at 14.30 & 15.30. Tel. 01392 860860

Hartland Abbey (nr Stoke, 14 miles W of Bideford, A39/B3248) Former 12th-C. Augustinian monastery, Tudor country house with 18th- & 19th-C. alterations and extensions. Spectacular coast. Open Easter Sun & Mon;

May-Sept, Wed, Thur & Sun 14-17.30; July-Aug, also Tue. Tel. 01237 441264

Honiton (A30/A35) Famous for lace since arrival of Flemish weavers in Middle Ages. Allhallows Museum, High St: lace collection. Apr-Oct 10-17 (exc. Sun). Tel. 01404 44966

Killerton (6 miles NE of Exeter, B3181) Late Georgian country house, 1778. Costume collection, Neo-Norman chapel by Cockerell, 1841, hill garden with rare trees. House: Mid Mar-Oct 11-17.30 (exc. Tue). Park: all year, 10.30 till dusk. NT. Tel. 01392 881345

Kingsbridge (SE of Plymouth, A379/A381) William Cookworthy Museum, 108 Fore St: Life & work of first English porcelain manufacturer. Easter-Sept, Mon-Sat 10-17; Oct, Mon-Fri 10.30-16. Tel. 01548 853235

Knightshayes Court (2 miles N of Tiverton, A396) Country house of Victorian lace manufacturer, designed 1869-74 by William Burges. Victorian interiors by John Diblee Crace, 1874ff., paintings (including Constable and Rembrandt), garden with topiary. Apr-Oct: park 11-17.30; house: (exc. Fri) 11-17.30. NT. Tel. 01884 254665

Limebridge Docton Mill, 13th C. mill, with gardens. Mar-Oct, daily 10-17. Tel. 01237 441369

Lundy Island Granite island, famous for birdlife. At entrance to Bristol Channel. 17 inhabitants. NT, administered by Landmark Trust, which rents out holiday homes. Ferries from Bideford and Ilfracombe. Groups only by appointment. Tel. 01237 470422

Marwood Hill (4 miles N of Barnstaple, A361) Garden with camellias, magnolias, willows, wisteria etc. All year 11-17. Tel. 01271 342528

Morwellham Quay (S of Tavistock, A390) In 19th C. England's biggest copper port, restored in Tamar Valley as industrial monument. Open all year, summer 10-17.30; winter 10-16.30. Tel. 01822 832766

Okehampton (W of Exeter, A30) Museum of Dartmoor Life, West St; also National Park Visitors' Centre. Easter-Oct, Mon-Sat 10-17; June-Sept, also Sun 10-17; Nov-Mar, weekdays only 10-16. Tel. 01837 52295

Overbecks Museum and Garden (Sharpitor, 1 mile S of Salcombe) Terraced garden with agave, myrtle, camphor trees and other exotic plants; spectacular situation on Salcombe Bay. Small museum of regional and natural history. Garden: all year 10-20. Museum: Apr-Oct 11-17.30 (exc. Sat). NT. Tel. 01548 842893 & 843238

Plymouth Arts Centre, 38 Looe St: exhibitions, concerts, films, workshops, vegetarian restaurant. Mon-Sat 10-20, Sun 17-19.30. Tel. 01752 660060

City Museum & Art Gallery, Drake Circus: paintings by Reynolds, Angelica Kauffmann etc., drawings by Rubens, Constable, Rembrandt, Titian etc. Porcelain and model ships. Important silver (including the Eddystone Salt). Lively temporary exhibition programme. Tue-Fri 10-17.30, Sat 10-17. Tel. 01752 304774

Elizabethan House, 32 New St: 16th-C. town house with contemporary interior. Apr-Oct, Wed-Sun 10-17. Tel. 01752 264878

Merchant's House, 32 St Andrew's: Jacobean home of the Mayor. Easter-Sept, Tue-Fri 10-13, 14-7.30, Sat 10-13, 14-17.

The National Marine Aquarium: thousands of marine creatures. Open daily 10-18. Tel. 01752 220084

Plymouth Dome, The Hoe: information centre on history of city, open all year 9-17.30. Tel. 01752 603300

Robert Lenkiewicz Studio, Barbican: open odd hours! Tel. 01752 263208

The Royal Citadel, Plymouth Hoe: England's largest 17th-C. fortress in continuous military use since King Charles II built it. Guided tours only May-Sept, daily, 14 & 15.30. Tel. 01752 775841/266496

Powderham Castle (7.5 miles S of Exeter, A379) 14-19th-C., designed by Wyatt. Easter-Oct 10-17.30 (exc. Sat). Tel. 01626 890243

Princetown (Dartmoor, B3212/B3357) Moorland Visitors' Centre, Duchy Hotel. First class exhibition area & books, maps, advice. Open summer 10-17; Nov-Apr 10-16. Tel. 01822 890414

Rosemoor Garden (nr Great Torrington, SE of Bideford, A386/B3220) Garden & arboretum in wooded valley of River Torridge. Branch of Royal Horticultural Society, with variety and quality one would expect. Special collections of ilex and cornus. Apr-Sept 10-18, Oct-Mar 10-17. Tel. 01805 624067

Saltram House (3 miles E of Plymouth, A38) Early Georgian country house, interior by Robert Adam, collections of furniture, porcelain and paintings. Apr-Oct. House: Sun- Thur 12.30-17.30. Park, kitchen & art gallery: 10.30-17.30. NT. Tel. 01752 336546

Shute Barton (2.5 miles SW of Axminster) Medieval manor house, begun in 1380, with later alterations and extensions. Tudor gatehouse. Apr-Oct, Wed & Sat 14-17.30. NT. Tel. 01297 34692

Tapeley Park (2 miles N of Bideford, A39) Country house overlooking mouths of Taw and Torridge, rebuilt 1901 in Edwardian Neo-Georgian style, with older nucleus (18th-C. plaster ceilings). William Morris furniture and opera costumes (house previously owned by the Christie family of Glyndebourne). Terraced garden & park with shell house etc. Easter-Oct 10-17. Tel. 01271 860528

Tavistock Centre of tin and copper mining till well into 19th C. On western edge of Dartmoor. Ruined Benedictine abbey (founded 974).

St Eustachius, 15th-C. church, east window of north aisle by Morris & Co, Drake statue by Edgar Boehm (1883).

Pannier Market: established 1105, every Fri, cheese & antiques

Teignmouth Seaside town famous for its winkles until they were rustled by Portuguese and Welsh winklepickers

Tiverton John Greenway, rich cloth merchant, donated Perpendicular south porch (1517) of St Peter.

Birthplace of miniaturist painter Richard Cosway (1740).

Blundell's School, Station Rd: founded by textile manufacturer Peter Blundell in 1604.

Tiverton Castle: built by Henry I, collection of arms. Easter-Sept, Sun-Thurs 14.30- 17.30. Tel. 01884 253200

Tiverton Museum, St Andrew St: lace, clocks, dolls, smithy, steam locomotive, etc. Open Feb-Christmas, Mon-Sat 10.30-16.30. Tel. 01884 256295

Torquay Torre Abbey, The King's Drive: former Premonstratensian abbey (1196), now museum with Agatha Christie's study and Remington typewiter etc. Easter-Oct, 9.30-18. Tel. 01803 293593

Kents Cavern Showcaves, Ilsham Rd, Wellswood: stalactite cave, one of England's earliest prehistoric cave dwellings. Open all year. Tel. 01803 294059

Totnes Charming one-street town up a hill.

South Devon Railway – steam train trips to Staverton and Buckfastleigh along the river Dart. Tel. 01364 642338

Ugbrooke House (Chudleigh, A380, between Exeter & Torquay) Robert Adam's first house in 'castle' style, 1764-68, Four wings with corner turrets and inner court. Original building, home of Clifford family; park by Capability

Brown. Mid July-early Sept, Tue-Thur & Sun. Park: 13-17.30. House (guided tours) 14 & 15.45. Tel. 01626 852179

Yelverton Garden House, interesting walled garden. Mar-Oct, daily 10.30-17. Tel. 01822 854769

Dorset

Abbotsbury (9 miles NW of Weymouth, B3157) Swannery of Benedictine abbey, known to have existed since 1393. Luxuriant garden. Mid Mar-Oct daily 10-17. Tel. 01305 871684

Athelhampton (5 miles NE of Dorchester, A35) Charming 15/16th-C. country house with gardens and Victorian topiary. Garden of the Year 1997. Mar-Oct daily (exc. Sat) 10.30-17; Nov-Feb Sun only 10.30-17. Tel. 01305 848363

Blandford Forum (15.5 miles NE of Dorchester, A354) Market town on Stour, Georgian rebuilding after 1731. St Peter & St Paul (1739), Town Hall, Market Place. Birthplace of Victorian sculptor, painter & designer Alfred Gilbert (Eros, Piccadilly Circus)

Bournemouth Russell-Cotes Art Gallery & Museum, East Cliff: paintings, sculptures, ceramics, furniture, contemporary art and items from East Asia. Closed for refurbishment until spring 2000. Tel. 01202 451800

Casa Magna, The Shelley Rooms, Beechwood Avenue, Boscombe: Shelley memorabilia. Tue-Sun 14-17 all year. Tel. 01202 303571

Bovington National Tank Museum. Battle Day, last Sunday in July. Daily 10-17. Tel. 01929 405096

Brownsea Island In Poole Harbour, Henry VIII castle, views and bathing. Apr-Sept 10-18. NT

Canford Manor (in Canford Magna, 2 miles NW of Bournemouth) Typical Victorian country house, reconstructed by Charles Barry, who designed Houses of Parliament. Now an independent school.

Cattistock (NW of Dorchester, A356) St Peter and St Paul, 'the masterpiece among Dorset churches' (Pevsner), designed by Sir Gilbert Scott (1857) and his son George Gilbert Scott (1874): south aisle with stained glass windows by Morris (1882); font with Late Victorian foliage decoration by Burlison & Grylls

Chettle House (6 miles NE of Blandford, A354) Queen Anne house by Thomas Archer, c.1710-15, with garden. Easter-Sept, 11-17 (exc. Tue & Sat). Tel. 01258 830209

Chilcombe House (5 miles E of Bridport, A35) Garden of painter John Hubbard and his wife Caryl, begun 1965, with exquisite variety of plants and colours. June, Wed 14-18. Tel. 01308 482234

Clouds Hill (10 miles E of Dorchester) Country cottage of T. E. Lawrence. Apr-Oct, Wed-Fri & Sun 12-17. NT. Tel. 01929 405616

Compton Acres Gardens (Poole, Canford Cliffs) Garden with many sculptures. Mar-Oct 10-18 (last admission 17.15). Tel. 01202 700778

Corfe Castle (SE of Wareham, A351) Ruins of royal castle in National Trust village. Mar-Oct 10-17.30. NT Tel. 01929 481294

Cranborne Manor (17 miles N of Bournemouth, B3078) Hunting lodge of James I, 1608-11, on edge of Cranborne Chase, ancient hunting grounds. Country home of Viscount Cranborne. Only gardens open to public (designed by John Tradescant in early 17th C.). Mar-Sept, Wed 9-17. Tel. 01725 517248

Dean's Court (2 miles N of Wimborne Minster, B3073) Early Georgian country house,

1725. Only park and garden (herb garden, 200+ species) open to public occasional days, Apr-Sept. For appointments tel. TIC 01202 886116

Dorchester Market Day: Wednesday

Dorset County Museum, High West St: local museum with prehistoric and Roman finds, memorabilia of Thomas Hardy and the great dialect poet William Barnes. July-Aug, daily 10-17; rest of year Mon-Sat 10-17. Tel. 01305 262735

Old Crown Court: displays about Tolpuddle Martyrs, six farm labourerers who were transported to Australia in 1834 for swearing an oath of loyalty to the union. Pardoned in 1836, they became heroes to the labour movement and symbols of the freedom of association.

Max Gate, Alington Avenue: Hardy designed this house, where he lived from 1885 till his death in 1928. Apr-Sept, Mon, Wed & Sun 14-17. NT. Tel. 01305 262538

Tutankhamun Exhibition: replica of tomb. Mon-Fri 9.30-17, Sat 10-17, Sun 10-16.30. Tel. 01305 269571

Edmondsham House (Cranborne, N of Wimborne, B3081) 16th-C. country house with mid 18th-C. wings. Victorian kitchen garden with organic vegetables. Easter, Apr & Oct, Wed 14-17. Tel. 01725 517207

Forde Abbey (4 miles SE of Chard, A30/B3162) 12th-15th C. Cistercian abbey with park & gardens. House (fine tapestries): Apr-Oct, Sun & Wed 13-16.30. Gardens: daily 10-16.30. Tel. 01460 221290

Hardy's Cottage (Higher Bockhampton, 3 miles NE of Dorchester) Thomas Hardy's birthplace. Apr-Oct daily (exc. Fri & Sat) 11-17. NT. Tel. 01305 262366

Kingston Lacy (2 miles NW of Wimborne Minster, B3082) 17th-C. country house with important art collection. Apr-Oct. House: Sat-Wed 12-17.30. Park: daily 11-18. NT. Tel. 01202 883402

Lulworth (1 mile E of Lulworth Cove) 17th-C. castle, open daily, 10-18 summer, 10-16 winter. Tel. 01929 400510

Lulworth Cove is a textbook example of the geology of coastal scenery, showing the effect of the sea on the different rocks – Portland stone, Purbeck marble and chalk.

Mapperton (5 miles NE of Bridport, A3066) Tudor manor house, extended in 1660's, beautiful estate together with church and stables in remote valley. 17th-20th C. terraced and hill gardens. Mar-Oct 14-18. House by appointment. Tel. 01308 863348

Milton Abbas (7 miles SW of Blandford Forum, A354) Neo-Gothic manor house by William Chambers and James Wyatt, now a school. Open to public only in holidays, 10-18.30. Tel. 01258 880489

Parnham Parnham House (nr Beaminster, 4.5 miles N of Bridport, A3066) Elizabethan country house, school and workshops of furniture designer John Makepeace. Apr-Oct, Sun & Tue-Thur 10-17. Tel. 01308 862204

Poole Scaplen's Court, High St: 15th-C. merchant's house. Here and in Waterfront Museum (Poole Quay) history of everyday life. Museum open all year, Mon-Sat 10-15, Sun 12-15; Apr-end summer, Mon-Sat 10-17, Sun 12-17. Tel. 01202 683138

Portland Castle (S of Weymouth) One of the best preserved of Henry VIII's coastal fortresses, *c*.1540. Apr-Oct 10-18. EH. Tel. 01305 820539

Purse Caundle Manor (4 miles E of Sherborne, A30) 15th/16th-C. country house. May-Sept, Thur & Sun 14-17. Tel. 01963 250400

Sandford Orcas (2 miles N of Sherborne) Mid 16th-C. manor house with garden. May-Sept, Sun 14-18, Mon 10-18. Tel. 01963 220206

Sherborne Market Days: Tue & Sat

Sherborne Castle: built by Sir Walter Raleigh, with landscape park by Capability Brown. Castle: Apr-Oct, Tues, Thur, Sat-Sun 12.30-17. Grounds: daily (exc. Wed) 12.30-17. EH. Tel. 01935 813182

Waterston Manor (Lower Waterston, 1 mile NW of Puddletown, A35/B3142) 17th-C., splendid Elizabethan gable, 1586. P

Weymouth One of the first seaside resorts, patronised by George III.

Sea Life Park, Lodmoor Country Park: large collection of marine life. Daily 10-17. Tel. 01305 761070

Wimborne Minster Market Day: Fri; flea market: Sat & Sun

Priest's Museum and Garden, 23 High St: townhouse with Victorian shop, kitchen & garden. Apr-Oct, Mon-Sat 10.30-17; June-Sept, also Sun 14-17. Tel. 01202 882533

Wolfeton House (1 mile N of Dorchester, A37) Early 16th-C. manor house, beautiful stone, woodwork and plaster. May-Sept, Sun, Tue & Thur 14-18.

Riding House c.1610: oldest surviving riding school in England. Can be seen by appointment. Tel. 01305 263500

Somerset

Barrington Court (5 miles NE of Ilminster, A303) Tudor country house, c.1515, heavily remodelled, with small garden by Gertrude Jekyll. First estate acquired by NT, in 1907. Garden only, Apr-Sept 11-17.30 (exc. Fri), closed 1999. Restaurant. NT. Tel. 01460 241938

Bath Bath Abbey: Heritage vaults, multimedia history of church and city ('Hear the voices of fashionable visitors to Bath'), Mon-Sat 10-16. Tel. 01225 422462

Beckford's Tower, Lansdown Rd: built 1827

by William Beckford; small exhibition, fine view, Victorian cemetery. Currently closed for renovation and unlikely to reopen before 2000. Tel. 01225 460705

The Book Museum, Manvers St: includes special exhibition 'Bath in Literature'. Mon-Fri 9-13, 14-17.30; Sat 9.30-13. Tel. 01225 466000

Building of Bath Museum, The Paragon: outstanding museum; do not miss. Architectural history of Georgian city, with special library of Georgian architecture. Mid Feb-Nov, Tue-Sun 10.30-17. Tel. 01225 333895

Georgian Garden, Gravel Walk (between Royal Crescent and Queen Square): at rear of Circus, laid out in 1760's, reconstructed 1985. May-Oct, Mon-Fri 9-16.30. Tel. TIC 01225 477101

Guildhall Banqueting Room, High St: 1775-79, with interiors in Adam style, and portraits of dignitaries. Tel. 01225 477724

Herschel House Museum, 19 New King St: home of the astronomer, with small town garden. Mar-Oct 14-17; Nov-Feb, Sat & Sun 14-17. Tel. 01225 311342

Holburne Museum and Craft Study Centre, Great Pulteney St: founded 1884 in former Sydney Hotel (1796), famous silver collection, porcelain, glass, miniatures, paintings (including portraits by Gainsborough, Romney and Raeburn). Tue-Sat 11-17 (Mon-Sat after Easter), Sun 14.30-17.30. Tel. 01225 466669

Museum of Costume, Assembly Rooms (by Wood the Younger, 1769-71): large collection from 17th C. till today, including exhibition of wedding dresses & 'patriotic underwear' from First World War. Open all year daily 10-17. Tel. 01225 477789

Museum of East Asian Art, 12 Bennett St: from 7000 BC till 18th C. Most important collection of Chinese jade in Europe. Established 1993 by Brian McElney, a British lawyer from Hong Kong. Oct-Mar, Mon-Sat 10-17, Sun 12-17; Apr-Sep, Mon-Sat 10-18, Sun 10-17. Tel. 01225 464640

National Centre of Photography, Milson St: Headquarters of Royal Photographic Society, the oldest such society in the world. Museum with changing exhibitions. Open daily 9.30-17.30. Tel. 01225 462841

Prior Park (2 miles SE, A36): Palladian country house by Wood the Elder (1734), now a school. Landscape garden open to public daily (exc. Tue) 12-17.30. NT. Tel. 01225 833422

Roman Baths Museum and Pump Room, Abbey Churchyard: views of hot spring and items excavated inc. bronze head of Minerva. In 18th C. Pump Room coffee, lunch, tea to accompaniment of Pump Room Trio. Hot spa water can be sampled: chalybeate and horrid. Apr-July & Sept 9-18; Aug 9-18 & 20-22; Oct-Mar 10.30-17

No 1 Royal Crescent: restored Georgian residence (1767). Mid Feb-Oct, Tue-Sun 10.30-17; Nov 10.30-16. Tel. 01225 428126

Theatre Royal, Sawclose: first royal theatre outside London, opened 1805, rebuilt after fire of 1862, restored 1982 following original Georgian interior design by George Dance. Tel. 01225 448844

Victoria Art Gallery, Bridge St: paintings, watercolours, crafts, English and Bohemian glass, clock collection. Tue-Fri 10-17.30, Sat 10-17, Sun 14-17. Tel. 01225 477233

Beckington (S of Bath, A36) Topiary in front garden on main street: privet hedge in shape of a Dreadnought Battleship, created by sheepshearer Charlie Thorne in late 1940's, as reminder of 'HMS Queen Elizabeth', on which he served during both world wars. P.

Brympton d'Evercy (W of Yeovil) Beautiful country house with Tudor west front and 17th-C. south front. Family home, sold in 1992, and now private house. P.

Carhampton (A39 nr Dunster) St John the Baptist, outstanding choir screen, with 15th/16th-C. original paintwork (restored)

Cheddar Gorge Spectacular gorge partly owned by NT. Protected habitat of Cheddar Pink ancestors of local pinks. Grazed by Soay sheep to restore balance of local habitat.

Cheddar Showcaves (Cheddar Gorge) Highly commercialised stalactite caves; Cheddar and other cheeses. Open all year daily, summer 10-17; winter 10.30-16.30. Tel. 01934 742343

Chewton Mendip Rolling countryside of Mendip hills.
Chewton Cheese Dairy. Daily (exc. Thurs & Sun) 7.30-15. Tel. 01761 241666

Claverton Manor (2 miles SE of Bath, A36) The American Museum, est. 1961. Country house (1820, by Sir Jeffrey Wyatville) where Sir Winston Churchill made his first political speech; the documents of colonisation of America: Indian culture, furniture, crockery, tools and utensils of Shakers, Quakers & Pennsylvania Dutch, large collection of quilts, gallery of naïve art, arboretum consisting solely of American trees and shrubs. Apr-Oct, Tue-Sun 14-17. Tel. 01225 460503

Cleeve Abbey (Washford, A39 SE of Cistercian monastery, founded 1198, unusually well preserved: 16th-C. refectory, 13th-C. gatehouse. Apr-Sep, daily 10-18; Oct-Mar 10-16. EH. Tel. 01984 640377

Clevedon Court (nr Clevedon, W of Bristol, B3130) 14th-C. country house with Thackeray room, collection of Nailsea glass and Eltonware ceramics; terraced garden. Apr-Oct, Wed, Thur & Sun, 14-17. NT. Tel. 01275 872257

Coleridge Cottage (Nether Stowey, 7.5 miles W of Bridgwater, A39) Samuel Taylor Coleridge's attractive home, 1797-1800. Here, in the pretty rolling countryside of the Quantocks, Coleridge wrote *Frost at Midnight* and started work on his contribution to the *Lyrical Ballads*. Apr-Sept, Tue-Thur & Sun 14-17. NT. Tel. 01278 732662

Combe Sydenham Country Park (Monksilver, SE of Minehead, B3188) Elizabethan manor (1580); parterres with old roses, herb garden, deer park. Apr-Sept, daily

8.30-17. House only by appointment (guided tours). Tel. 01984 656284

Croscombe (A371, E of Wells) St Mary, 15th/16th C., almost entirely Jacobean church fittings (pulpit, benches, choir screen)

Dunster Castle (3 miles SE of Minehead, A39) 13th-C. and earlier castle, converted to manor house in 17th C., and extended by Anthony Salvin c.1870. Artistic highlights from late Stuart period: plaster ceiling in Dining Room (1681), leaf and flower carvings on staircase (c.1680). Terraced garden, park. Home of Luttrell family from 1376 till 1976. Castle: Sat-Wed, Mar-Sept, 11-17; Oct 11-16. Gardens and park: daily, Apr-Sept 10-17; Jan-Mar & Oct-Dec 11-16. NT. Tel. 01643 821314

Folly Tower, Conygar Hill: round tower, c.1760-70

Farleigh Hungerford (SE of Bath, A36/A366) 14th-C. ruined castle, chapel (medieval window sections, arms collection). Apr-Oct 10-18; Nov-Mar, Wed-Sun 10-16. EH. Tel. 01225 754026

Forde Abbey (nr Chard) Cistercian abbey: magnificent house with tapestries, and rich gardens. Daily 10-16.30. Tel. 01460 220231

Frome: 18th-C. wool-trade town. Holy Trinity Church, Trinity St: Burne-Jones windows (1880*ff*). Usually open daily 9.30-12. Tel. 01373 453425

Gaulden Manor (nr Tolland. 8.5 miles NW of Taunton, A358/B3224) Small medieval country estate. Rich stucco decorations in hall, mid 17th-C. Series of small gardens with great charm. Easter, May-beginning Sept, Thur & Sun 14-17. Tel. 01984 667213

Glastonbury The Tribunal, High St: Lake Village Museum: prehistoric and Iron Age finds from pile-dwellings; complete Iron Age dug-out boat. Apr-Sept, Sun-Thurs 10-17, Fri-Sat 10-17.30; Oct-Mar, Sun-Thurs 10-16, Fri-Sat 10-16.30. Tel. 01458 832954

Glastonbury Abbey: extensive ruins from 1184. Holy Thorn tree grown from the Crown of Thorns; resting place of the Holy Grail brought by Joseph of Arimathea. Reputed grave of Arthur and Guinevere. Medieval abbot's kitchen. Modern visitor centre display. June-Aug 9-16; Sept-May 9.30-dusk. Tel. 01458 832267

Town full of New Age shops

Hadspen Garden (2 miles SE of Castle Cary, A371) Classic Victorian country-house garden, restored by Penelope Hobhouse. Mar-Sept, Thur-Sun 10-17. Tel. 01749 813707

Hatch Court (Hatch Beauchamp, 6 miles SE of Taunton, A358) Mansion in Palladian style, 1755. Bath stone with Georgian elegance. House & garden: May-Sept daily 10-17.30. Tel. 01823 480120

Hestercombe Gardens (Cheddon Fitzpaine, 4 miles N of Taunton, A361) Edwardian garden, 1904-06, a highlight of the Lutyens- Jekyll partnership. Orangery, pergola, ponds, steps etc. all perfect examples of Lutyens' garden architecture. Restored in accordance with Jekyll's plant designs. Open daily 10-17. Tel. 01823 413923

Ilminster Dillington House: residential courses from drawing to history. Tel. 01460 55866

Lullington (A36/A361, nr Frome) Norman village church with richly decorated font and north porch

Lytes Cary Manor (E of Taunton, A303/A372) Medieval estate, chapel c.1350, Hall c.1420, Great Chamber 16th-C., garden. Apr-Oct, Mon, Wed & Sat 14-18. NT. Tel. 01985 843600

Mells (2.5 miles W of Frome) Village church of St Andrew, 15th-C., with monument by Mullins for Edward Horner, 1920-22. Splendid Burne-Jones 'peacock' memorial inside. The poet Siegfried Sassoon (1886-1967) is buried in the churchyard. Lutyens designed the village war memorial.

Milton Lodge Gardens (1/2 mile N of Wells, A39/Old Bristol Rd) Hill garden with panoramic view of Wells Cathedral and the Vale of Avalon; arboretum. Easter-Oct 14-18 (exc. Sat). Tel. 01749 672168

Montacute House (4 miles W of Yeovil, A3088) Elizabethan mansion with formal garden, landscaped garden and portraits from the National Portrait Gallery. House: Apr-Oct, 12-17.30 (exc. Tue). Park: 11-17.30. NT. Tel. 01935 823289

Muchelney Muchelney Abbey (2 miles S of Langport) Remains of Benedictine Abbey, founded 939, and Priest's House (14th/15th C.), only by appointment. Apr-Oct , daily 10-18, EH. Tel. 01458 250664
Church with topless angels.
Muchelney Pottery: studio pottery and practical objects by John Leach, grandson of Bernard. Mon-Fri 9-13, 14-17, Sat 9-13. Tel.

Perry's Cider Mills (Dowlish Wake, 2 miles SE of Ilminster) Museum and sales, Mon-Fri 9-17.30, Sat 9-16.30, Sun 10-13. Tel. 01460 52681

Shepton Mallet (A37/A361) Sts Peter and Paul: Perpendicular barrel vault with 350 coffers and over 300 bosses – one of the finest wooden roofs in Somerset

Sherborne Garden (Pear Tree House, Litton, 6 miles N of Wells, A39/B3114) Garden & mini-arboretum, specialising in hollies. In Hollywood-on-Avon, there are over 150 types of ilex. June-Oct, Sun & Mon 11-18.30. Tel. 01761 241220

Stanton Drew (A37 nr Bath) Three Bronze Age stone circles, most important prehistoric monument in Somerset

Stoke St Gregory (7 miles E of Taunton) Willows and Wetlands Visitor Centre. Daily 9-17. Tel. 01823 490249

Stoke sub Hambdon (5 miles W of Yeovil, between A3088 and A303) Village at foot of Hamdon Hill, where biscuit-coloured Ham Hill stone was cut.
Priory, North St: 14th/15th-C. complex of buildings for priests of St Nicholas chapel (now destroyed). NT. Apr-Oct daily 10-18. Tel. 01985 843600

Street (A39, 2 miles S of Glastonbury) Largest British shoe factory and huge factory outlet shopping village, C & J Clark. Show Museum, High St. Mon-Fri 10-16.45, Sat 10-17, Sun 11-17. Tel. 01458 840064

Tintinhull House Garden (5 miles NW of Yeovil, S of A303) Small, diverse 20th-C. garden, looked after for some time by gardening expert and authoress Penelope Hobhouse. Apr-Sept, Wed-Sun 14-18. NT. Tel. 01935 822545

Wells Beautiful cathedral town.
Market days: Wed & Sat
The Bishop's Palace, Market Place (next to Cathedral): Apr-Oct, Tue-Fri 10.30-18; Aug daily 10.30-18, Sun 14-18. Tel. 01749 678691
Cathedral: Evensong with Cathedral choir daily 17.15, Sun 15. Cathedral concerts, including Wells Bach Choir & Orchestra. Tel. 01749 674483
Wells Museum, 8 Cathedral Green: 18th-C. house, finds from Mendip caves etc. Apr-Oct, daily 10-17.30 (Jul-Aug 10-20); Nov-Mar, Wed-Sun 11-16. Tel. 01749 673477

Weston-super-Mare: Victorian seaside resort with somewhat bleak charm. Accused in 1998 of colouring its seas blue on the town brochure: people 'do swim at Weston', explained the council.
Birthplace of John Cleese; reputed hometown of best-selling author Jeffrey Archer (Baron Archer of Weston-super-Mare)

Wookey Hole showcaves: Open daily summer 10-17; winter 10.30-16.30. Tel. 01749 672243

Wiltshire

Avebury (6 miles W of Marlborough, B4003/A4361) Avebury Manor: early 16th C. and later, with monastic origins. Garden with topiary. Apr-Oct 11-17.30 (exc. Mon & Thur). NT. Tel. 01672 539250

Aexander Keiller Museum: important prehistoric finds. Apr-Oct 10-18; Nov-Mar, Wed-Sun 10-16. Tel. 01672 539250

Bowood House (between Calne & Chippenham, A4/A432) 18th-C. family home of Earl of Shelburne. South front and Library by Robert Adam, 1770. Exhibition in Adam's Orangery and former stables: 19th-C. watercolours and drawings (Lear, Richard Bonington), Lord Byron's Albanian costume etc. Landscaped park by Capability Brown, 1763-66, with waterfall, grotto and temple. Lansdowne family mausoleum by Robert Adam, 1761. Arboretum with over 200 varieties of tree and shrub. Laboratory where Joseph Priestley discovered oxygen. Easter-Oct, daily 11-18. Tel. 01249 812102

Bradford-on-Avon Charming small town with Saxon church and tithe barn.

Charlton Park House (1 mile NE of Malmesbury, A429) Jacobean home of Earls of Suffolk, 1607, remodelled in Georgian style c.1770. May-Oct, Mon & Thur 14-18.

Corsham Court (4 miles W of Chippenham, A4) Elizabethan-Georgian country home of 6th Lord Methuen. Furniture by Adam, Chippendale et al. Important art collection (Fra Filippo Lippi, Sofonisba Anguisciola, Elsheimer, Tintoretto, Veronese, Rubens, van Dyck etc.) & Michelangelo sculpture. Landscaped park by Capability Brown &

Humphry Repton. Arboretum with some 340 varieties of tree. Mid Mar-Sept 11-17 (exc. Mon); Oct-mid Mar (closed December) weekends only, 14-16. Tel. 01249 701610

The Courts (nr Holt, 2.5 miles E of Bradford-on-Avon, B3107) 18th-C. house (not open to public) with Edwardian garden, 1900-11, topiary, aquatic plants and wild flowers. Apr-Oct 13.30-17.30 (exc. Sat). NT. Tel. 01225 782340

Devizes (9 miles SE of Chippenham, A360/A361) Small town with three medieval churches. In his father's inn on the Market Place, now the Bear Hotel, Sir Thomas Lawrence painted his first portraits (of the guests). West of town, at Caen Hill, 29 locks of Kennet and Avon Canal, designed 1810 by John Rennie (87 miles Bristol-Reading), restored in 1990 as leisure facility

Museum, 164 Long St: probably the finest prehistoric collection in Europe. Mon-Sat 10-17. Tel. 01380 727369

Great Chalfield Manor (2.5 miles NE of Bradford-on-Avon) Late medieval house (1480) in romantic setting. Apr-Oct, Tue-Thur 12.15-16.30. NT. Tel. 01225 782239

Heale Gardens (Middle Woodford, 4 miles N of Salisbury, between A360 & A345) Carolean house and gardens in Avon Valley. Japanese bridge and teahouse, 1910, lily ponds by Harold Ainsworth Peto, unwalled kitchen garden. Open all year, daily 10-17. Tel. 01722 782504

Iford Manor (6 miles SE of Bath, A36) Home of Edwardian garden architect Harold Ainsworth Peto, who lived here from 1899 until his death in 1933. Italian terraced garden in characteristic style, with (over-)abundance of antique-style urns, columns, statues, cloister etc. Romantic setting in Frome Valley. HHA Garden of the Year 1998. May-Sept, Tue-Thur, Sat & Sun 14-17; Apr & Oct, Sun 14-17. Tel. 01225 422328

Lacock (A350, 3 miles S of Chippenham) 13th-C. Augustinian monastery, manor house since 1540, home of W. H. Fox Talbot. Apr-Oct 13-17.30 (exc. Tue). Tel. 01249 730227

Fox Talbot Museum of Photography: Mar-Oct 11-17.30. Phone for information about winter weekends. NT. Tel. 01249 730459

Longford Castle (3 miles S of Salisbury, A338) Elizabethan castle with triangular ground plan, designed by John Thorpe, 1578-91. Family home of Earls of Radnor. Important art collection. Visits only by appointment: The Estate Office, Salisbury, Wilts SP5 4ED. Tel. 01722 411616

Longleat House (4 miles SW of Warminster) Classic Early English Renaissance 'prodigy'-house; landscaped garden by Capability Brown. Mazes and safari park. House: Easter-Oct 10-18, winter 10-16. Park: mid Mar-Oct 11-17. Tel. 01985 844400

Lydiard Park (Lydiard Tregove, 4.5 miles W of Swindon, M4 exit 16) House, 1743. Furniture, family portraits. 15th-C. church in park, with outstanding frescoes, wrought iron and Renaissance monuments (The Golden Cavalier). Mar-Oct, Mon-Sat 10-17, Sun 14-17; Nov-Feb, Mon-Fri 10-13, 14-16, Sat 10-16, Sun 14-16. Tel. 01793 770401

Marlborough (12.5 miles S of Swindon, A345/A4) Small town with renowned public school, founded 1843. Famous pupils include William Morris, William Golding, Sir John Betjeman, Anthony Blunt. The school chapel contains Pre-Raphaelite wall pictures by Spencer Stanhope (1872-79) and a Morris window. A Gainsborough portrait was recently, and shamefully, sold.

High St: Georgian colonnades, and weekly market Wed & Fri.

Old Wardour Castle (NE of Shaftesbury, north A30) 14th-C. ruin in 18th-C. landscaped park. Apr-Sept, daily 10-18; Oct, daily 10-17;

Nov-Mar, Wed-Sun 10-16. EH. Tel. 01722 336855

Philipps House (Dinton, 8 miles W of Salisbury, B3089) Neoclassical house by Jeffrey Wyatville, 1816. Apr-Oct, Mon 13-17, Sat 10-13. Park open daily all year. NT. Tel. 01985 843600

Salisbury Cathedral: evensong sung Mon-Sat 17.30, Sun 15. Tel. 01722 555120

Mompesson House, The Close: Queen Anne town house with Georgian decorations and garden. Apr-Oct 12-17.30 (exc. Thur & Fri). NT. Tel. 01722 335659

Salisbury & South Wiltshire Museum, The Close: city history, Stonehenge finds, pictures by Turner. Mon-Sat 10-17, July- Aug, Sun 14-17. Tel. 01722 332151

Market Days: Tue & Sat

Stonehenge (N of Salisbury) The site can be hired privately most days in the early morning before the public are admitted to allow small groups to walk among the stones. At public times the stones are roped off and one may approach to only about five yards from them. June-Aug, daily 9-19; Sept-mid Oct 9.30-18; mid Oct-mid Mar 9.30-16. EH. Tel. 01980 624715

Stourhead (Stourton, between Shaftesbury & Frome, B3092/north A303) Surely the greatest 18th-C. landscaped park. House partly by Colen Campbell; furniture, paintings. Park: all year 9-dusk. House: Apr-Oct, Sat-Wed 12-17.30. NT. Tel. 01747 841152

King Alfred's Tower (3 miles from house): nearly 50 yards high, built in brick by Flitcroft, 1772, park folly with view. Apr-Oct 14-17.30 (exc. Mon & Fri). NT

Swindon (M4, exit 15) Great Western Railway Museum, Faringdon Rd, with Isambard Kingdom Brunel archives. Mon-Sat 10-17, Sun 14-17. Tel. 01793 493189

Museum & Art Gallery, Bath Rd: a strong

collection of 20th-C. British art. Mon-Sat 10-17.30, Sun 14-17.30. Tel. 01793 493188

National Monuments Record Centre. Tel. 01793 414600

Railway Village Museum, 34 Faringdon Rd: turn of century railway worker's home in Brunel's purpose-built village. Mon-Sat 10-17, Sun 14-17. Tel. 01793 466555

Westwood Manor (1 mile SW of Bradford-on-Avon) 15th-C. with 16th-C. extensions. Topiary garden. Apr-Sept, Tue, Wed & Sun 14-17. NT. Tel. 01225 863374

Wilton House (2.5 miles W of Salisbury, A30) Rooms by Inigo Jones (*c.*1650). Claims to be first stately home to be opened to public (by Earl of Pembroke, 1776); rich art (Rembrandt) and furniture (William Kent) collections, *c.* 7000 tin soldiers, park, rose garden and Japanese water garden. Apr-Oct 10.30-17.30. Tel. 01722 746720

Hotels and Restaurants

H = Hotel, B & B = Bed and Breakfast, R = Restaurant, GF = Good Food

> *'There is nothing which has yet*
> *been contrived by man by which*
> *so much happiness is produced as by*
> *a good tavern or inn'*
> *(Dr Samuel Johnson, 1776)*

Bristol

Avon Gorge Hotel, Sion Hill: overlooking gorge in Clifton, Bristol's noblest district. H + R. Tel. 0117 973 8955

Berkeley Square Hotel, 15 Berkeley Square: central H + R. Tel. 0117 925 4000

Harveys, 12 Denmark St: cellar restaurant nr Harveys Wine Museum, with superb wine list. GF. Tel. 0117 927 5034

Howards, 1a & 2a Avon Crescent, Hotwells: bistro. GF. Tel. 0117 926 2921

Hunt's, 26 Broad St. GF. Tel. 0117 926 5580

Markwicks, 43 Corn St: Georgian cellar restaurant. GF. Tel. 0117 926 2658

Melbourne's, 74 Park St: good value GF. Tel. 0117 922 6996

The Old Duke, 45 King St: pub with live jazz (Mon, Tues, Wed, Fri, Sun lunchtime & Sun evening). Tel. 0117 927 7137

Rocinante's, 85 Whiteladies Rd: organic food. GF. Tel. 0117 973 4482

Swallow Royal Hotel, College Green: Victorian luxury H + R. (1863) near Cathedral, with swimming pool & fitness centre. Tel. 0117 925 5100

Watershed Cafe & Bar, 1 Canons Rd: cafe & restaurant on quayside, with jazz (Thur evening). Tel. 0117 927 6444

Thornbury (N of Bristol, A38/B4061) Thornbury Castle, Castle St: Tudor H + GF, with vineyard. ('Henry VIII slept here.') Tel. 01454 281182

Cornwall

Bolventor (A30, between Launceston & Bodmin) Jamaica Inn, made famous by Daphne du Maurier's novel (1936): inn on Bodmin Moor, with Museum of Curiosity, high point of Victorian taxidermy, containing Walter Porter's life's work (Feb-Dec, 10.30 till dusk). Snacks. Tel. 01566 86838

Blackwater (NE of Redruth, A30) Pennypots, GF. Tel. 01209 820347

Bodinnick (E of Fowey) Old Ferry Inn, 16th-C., on mouth of Fowey. H + R. Tel. 01726 870237

Botallack (nr St Just, N of Land's End, B3306) Count House Restaurant. Tel. 01736 788588

Calstock (between Plymouth & Tavistock, off A390) Danescombe Valley Hotel, small, remote H + GF in Tamar valley. Tel. 01822 832414

Clowance House (nr Praze-on-Beeble, 12.5 miles NE of Penzance, B3280), 18th/19th-C. country estate with holiday village. Tel. 01209 831111

Falmouth Penmere Manor, Mongleath Rd: Georgian family H + R set in five acres of sub-tropical gardens and woodland. Tel. 01326 211411

Fowey (S of Bodmin) Food for Thought, Town Quay: fish specialities. GF. Tel. 01726 832221

Golant (4 miles N of Fowey) Cormorant, hotel on River Fowey with good fish. Tel. 01726 833426

Helford (The Lizard, E of Helston) The Shipwrights Arms: pub-restaurant beautifully situated overlooking bay. Tel. 01326 231235

Lamorna Cove (S of Penzance, B3315) Lamorna Cove Hotel, small H + R overlooking bay. Tel. 01736 731411

Mawgan (3 miles SE of Helston, A3083/B3293) Yard Bistro, former coach house of Trelowarren Manor. GF. Tel. 01326 22595

Mawgan Porth (between Newquay & Padstow, B3276) Tredragon Hotel, small H + R on Atlantic. Tel. 01637 860213

Mawnan-Smith (SW of Falmouth) Meudon Hotel: small, coastal H + R with garden & private beach. Tel. 01326 250541
Nansidwell Country House Hotel, Arts and Crafts H + R with excellent organic food. Tel. 01326 250340

Mousehole (S of Penzance, B3315) Lobster Pot, South Cliff. H + R: seafood specialities. Tel. 01736 731251

Mullion (The Lizard, S of Helston, A3083/B3296) Polurrian Hotel, Polurrian Cove: clifftop family H + R. Tel. 01326 240421

Padstow (NW of Bodmin, A389) The Seafood Restaurant, Riverside: 'the best seafood restaurant in the UK' (*The Times*). GF. Tel. 01841 532485
Nearby hotel & bistro, St Petroc's House, 4 New St. Tel. 01841 532700. Both owned by Rick Stein, author of *English Seafood Cookery*.
Fish and chips in the town square some of the best in England

Penzance The Abbey, Abbey St: comfortable H + R overlooking harbour, run by ex-model Jean Shrimpton. Tel. 01736 366906

Polperro (SW of Liskeard, A387) The Kitchen, The Coombes. GF. Tel. 01503 272780

Port Isaac (9 miles SW of Tintagel) Old School Hotel, Victorian quayside H + R. Tel. 01208 880721
Port Gaverne Hotel: H + R. GF, with fish specialities. Tel. 01208 880244
Slipway, harbour front: 16th-C., fish specialities. B & B, H + GF. Tel. 01208 880264

Rame (SW of Plymouth) Polhawn Fort Hotel: restored coastal fort of 1862. Self-catering. Tel. 01752 822864

St Agnes (between St Ives & Newquay) Railway Inn: 17th-C. inn with strange collection of shoes etc.

St Ives Boskerris Hotel, Boskerris Rd: family H + R on quiet Carbis Bay. Tel. 01736 795295
Garrack Hotel, Burthallen Lane: small H + R overlooking Porthmeor Beach. Tel. 01736 796199
Pedn-Olwa,The Warren, Porthminster Beach: H + R with view of sea & harbour. Tel. 01736 796222
Pig'n'Fish, Norway Lane: fish specialities Tue-Sat, dinner only. GF. Tel. 01736 794204
Talland House, Talland Rd: Virginia Woolf's childhood holiday home 1882-95. Holiday flats. Tel. 01736 796368

St Keyne (2.5 miles S of Liskeard, B3254) Well House: Edwardian country house H + GF. Tel. 01579 342001

St Mawes (opposite Falmouth) Rising Sun: Quayside H + R. Tel. 01326 270233

Trenale (1/2 mile N of Tintagel, off Boscastle Rd) Trebrea Lodge: small country house H + R. Tel. 01840 770410

Veryan (NE of Falmouth, A3078) Nare Hotel, Carne Beach: remote beach H + R. Tel. 01872 501279

Widegates (5 miles S of Liskeard, B3253) Coombe Farm: B & B + R. Tel. 01503 240223

Zennor (W of St Ives, B3306) Boswednack Manor: family B & B (n/s, vegetarian) on coast, remote, simple. Tel. 01736 794183

Isles of Scilly

St Martin's St Martin's Hotel, Lowertown: seashore H + R. Tel. 01720 422092

St Mary's Atlantic Hotel: H + R. Tel. 01720 422417

Tresco Island Hotel: H + GF (no cars on island). Tel. 01720 422883

Devon

Barnstaple Lynwood House, Bishops Tawton Rd (A377): Victorian house on southern outskirts. B & B + GF. Tel. 01271 43695

Broadhembury (NW of Honiton, A373) Drewe Arms: picturesque village pub. GF (fish specialities). Tel. 01404 841267

Burgh Island (Bigbury-on-Sea, SE of Plymouth, B3392) Island Hotel, 1929 (see p. 000). H + R. Tel. 01548 810514

Chagford (W of Exeter, A382/B3206) Gidleigh Park: country home of Edwardian shipping magnate on eastern edge of Dartmoor, luxurious hospitality. H + GF. Tel. 01647 432367

Clovelly Red Lion Hotel, The Quay: 17th C., good fish. H + R. Tel. 01237 431237

Cockington (nr Torquay) The Drum Inn, designed by Edwin Lutyens, 1934

Croyde (nr Braunton, NW of Barnstaple, A361/B3231) The Whiteleaf: small B & B by the sea, with charm and haute cuisine. GF. Tel. 01271 890266

Dartmouth (S of Torquay) The Carved Angel, South Embankment: famous gourmet R, with tableware by potter Colin Kellam. GF. Tel. 01803 832465
Royal Castle, 11 The Quay: popular H + R with list of famous guests. Tel. 01803 833033

Dittisham (5 miles N of Dartmouth) Fingals, Old Coombe Manor Farm: 17th-C. H + R. Tel. 01803 722398

Doddiscombsleigh (6 miles SW of Exeter, B3193) Nobody Inn, on eastern edge of Dartmoor. B & B + R. Tel. 01647 52394

Drewstaignton (W of Exeter, between A30 & A382) Hunts Tor House: small B & B + GF on edge of Dartmoor. Tel. 01647 21228

East Buckland (SE of Barnstaple, between A361 & A399) Lower Pitt: traditional longhouse on edge of Exmoor. B & B + GF. Tel. 01598 760243

Endsleigh House (Milton Abbot, 4 miles NW of Tavistock, B3362) Exclusive fishing H + GF on River Tamar. Tel. 01822 87248

Exeter St Olaves Court Hotel, Mary Arches St: Georgian merchant's house. H + GF. Tel. 01392 217736
Lamb's, 15 Lower North St. GF. Tel. 01392 254269
Royal Clarence, Cathedral Yard. H + R. Tel. 01392 258464

Exmouth Barnaby's Restaurant, 9 Tower St: former coffin-maker's. GF. Tel. 01395 269459

Hartland Hartland Quay: clifftop H + R in northwest corner of Devon, with open-air swimming pool & beach. Tel. 01237 4218

Haytor (2.5 miles W of Bovey Tracey, B3387) The Bel Alp House; Edwardian country house H + R on Dartmoor. Tel. 01364 661292

Holbeton (between Plymouth & Kingsbridge, south of A379) Al ston Hall Country House Hotel: small Edwardian H + R, with fitness facilities. Tel. 01752 830555

Huntsham (5 miles NE of Tiverton, between A361 & A3227) Huntsham Court: Victorian country house H + R, eccentric, musical ambiance. Tel. 01398 6365 & 366

Lewdown (between Launceston & Okehampton, S A30) Lewtrenchard Manor: home of Victorian clergyman, novelist and hymn-writer Sabine Baring-Gould ('Onward Christian Soldiers'; 'Curious Myths of the Middle Ages'). H + GF. Tel. 01566 783256

Lifton (3 miles E of Launceston, A30) Arundell Arms: anglers' H + R. Tel. 01566 784244

Lydford (7.5 miles SW of Okehampton, A386) Castle Inn, on western edge of Dartmoor. B & B + R. Tel. 01822 82242

Lympstone (N of Exmouth, A376) River House, The Strand: R with rooms, on shores of River Exe, overlooking Powderham Castle. GF. Tel. 01395 265147

Lynmouth (W of Minehead, A39) Rising Sun Hotel: harbourside cottage accommodation, 'Shelley was here'. H + R. Tel. 01598 753223

Mary Tavy (4 miles NE of Tavistock, A386) The Stannary: 16th/19th-C. B & B + GF on western edge of Dartmoor, with vegetarian cuisine. Tel. 01822 810897

Plymouth Chez Nous, 13 Frankfort Gate. GF. Tel. 01752 266793

Salcombe (SW of Torquay, A381) Soar Mill Cove Hotel. H + R. Tel. 01548 561566

Marine Hotel, Cliff Rd: small H + R beside sea. Tel. 01548 842251

Saunton (NE of Barnstaple. B3231) Saunton Sands Hotel: 1930's H + R, with beach, surfing and golf. Tel. 01271 890212

South Molton (NW of Tiverton, A361) Whitechapel Manor: 16th-C. manor house on edge of Dartmoor. H + GF. Tel. 01769 573377

Tavistock Neil's, 27 King St. GF. Tel. 01822 615550

Torquay Capers, 7 Lisburne Square. GF. Tel. 01803 291177

The Imperial Hotel, Park Hill Rd: luxury H + R above Torbay. Tel. 01803 24301

Mulberry House, 1 Scarborough Rd: Victorian guest house. B & B + GF. Tel. 01803 213639

Osborne Hotel, Hesketh Crescent, Meadfoot: Regency H + GF, with fitness facilities. Tel. 01803 213311

Regina: harbourside H + R (as 'Bath House', home of Elizabeth Barrett Browning, 1838-41) Tel. 01803 292904

Table, 135 Babbacombe Rd, Babbacombe. GF. Tel. 01803 324292

Woolacombe (NW of Barnstaple, A361/B3343) Woolacombe Bay Hotel, South St: beach H + R with fitness facilities. Tel. 01271 870388

Dorset

Beaminster (N of Bridport, A3066) Bridge House Hotel, Prout Bridge: 15th-C. H + GF. Tel. 01308 862200

Dorchester Casterbridge Hotel, 49 High East St: Georgian B & B. Tel. 01305 264043

Evershot (between Dorchester & Yeovil, W of A37) Summer Lodge: 18th/19th-C. country house H + GF. Tel. 01935 83424

Farnham (8 miles NE of Blandford Forum, A354) The Museum Hotel: formerly museum of Victorian country estate, now pub B & B with character. Tel. 01725 516261

Gillingham (5 miles NW of Shaftesbury, B3081) Stock Hill House: Victorian country house with spectacular garden. H + GF: classic Austrian + international. Tel. 01747 823626

Loders (NE of Bridport, between A35 & A3066) Loders Arms: village pub with GF. Tel. 01308 22431

Lower Bockhampton (nr Dorchester) Yalbury Cottage: small country H + R. Tel. 01305 262382

Lyme Regis Alexandra Hotel, Pound St: centrally situated H + R, 1735. Tel. 01297 442010

Maiden Newton (7 miles NW of Dorchester, A356) Le Petit Canard, Dorchester Rd. GF. Tel. 01300 20536
　　Maiden Newton House: small manor house H + R. Tel. 01300 20336

Shaftesbury La Fleur de Lys, 25 Salisbury St. GF. Tel. 01747 53717

Shave Cross (NW of Lyme Regis, Marshwood Vale) Shave Cross Inn: 14th-C. with garden & draught beer. R.

Shipton Gorge (2 miles E of Bridport, S of A35) Innsacre: former farmhouse. B & B. GF. Tel. 01308 56137

Studland (3 miles N of Swanage, Isle of Purbeck) The Manor House, Beach Rd: small country house H + R above Studland Bay. Tel. 01929 450288

Sturminster Newton (between Sherborne & Blandford, A357) Plumber Manor, Hazelbury Bryan Rd: Jacobean H + R. Tel. 01258 72507

Swanage (Isle of Purbeck, A351) Gallery, 9 High St. GF. Tel. 01929 427299

Wareham Priory Hotel, Church Green: former monastery on River Frome. H + GF. Tel. 01929 551666

West Bay (1/2 mile S of Bridport, E of Lyme Regis, A35) Riverside: fish restaurant by sea, unpretentious presentation, ambitious cuisine. GF. Tel. 01308 22011

West Bexington (5 miles SE of Bridport, B3157) Manor Hotel, Beach Rd: H + GF near Chesil Beach. Tel. 01308 897616

Weymouth Perry's, 4 Trinity Rd: harbourside restaurant. GF. Tel. 01305 785799

Somerset

Barwick (2 miles S of Yeovil, off A37) Little Barwick House: R with rooms. GF. Tel. 01935 423902

Bath Clos du Roy, 1 Seven Dials: first-class, gourmet food. Tel. 01225 444450
　　The Hole in the Wall, 16 George St: legendary gourmet restaurant. GF. Tel. 01225 425242
　　The Pump Room, Stall St: Georgian treatment room. Coffee, lunch, tea with chamber music, daily 10-17.30
　　The Queensberry Hotel, Russell St: small, central Georgian H + R. GF. The Olive Tree (Queensberry restaurant). H + GF. Tel. 01225 447928
　　The Royal Crescent Hotel, 16 Royal Crescent: small, luxury H + GF in Georgian crescent. Tel. 01225 739955
　　Sally Lunn's, 4 North Parade Passage: 17th-C. bakery with excavated cellars and kitchens from Roman times. Home to the Sally Lunn bun, larger cousin of the famous Bath Bun, which caused Jane Austen a bit of trouble in 1801 ('...disordering my stomach with Bath

bunns...'). R. Tel. 01225 461634

Somerset House, 35 Bathwick Hill: Regency B & B in southeast of city. Tel. 01225 466451

Woods, 9-12 Alfred St: small R opposite Assembly Rooms. GF. Tel. 01225 314812 & 422493

Bishop's Lydeard (NW of Taunton, A358) Cedar Falls Health Farm: 18th-C. country house H + R with fitness centre & golf course. Tel. 01823 433233

Bruton (between Frome & Yeovil, A359) Clair de Lune, 2-4 High St: B & B (1 room) + GF. Tel. 01749 813395

Truffles, 95 High St. GF. Tel. 01749 812255

Combe Hay (S of Bath, between A367 & B3110) Wheatsheaf: pub with garden, game & fish dishes. R. Tel. 01225 833504

Dunster Luttrell Arms, 36 High St: 15-C. residence of Abbots of Cleeve, has been an inn since 1651. H + R. Tel. 01643 821555

Exford (Exmoor, B3224) Crown Hotel: 17th-C. inn with riding. H + R. Tel. 01643 83554

Glastonbury Number 3, 3 Magdalene St: small Georgian B & B + GF. Tel. 01458 832129

Hinton Charterhouse (6 miles SE of Bath, A36/B3110) Homewood Park: Georgian country house H + GF. Tel. 01225 723731

Holford (Quantock Hills, A39) Alfoxton Park: Wordsworth and his sister Dorothy lived here. H. Tel. 01278 74211

Hunstrete (W of Bath, A39/A368) Hunstrete House: country house H + GF. Tel. 01761 490490

Langley Marsh (N of Wiveliscombe, W of Taunton, B3227) Langley House Hotel: Georgian family H + GF. Tel. 01984 623318

Montacute (4 miles W of Yeovil, A3088) Milk House, The Borough: organic food. B & B + GF. Tel. 01935 823823

Porlock (W of Minehead, A39) Anchor Hotel and Ship Inn, Porlock Weir: Victorian harbourside H + R. Tel. 01643 862753

Shepton Mallet (E of Wells, A371) Bowlish House, Wells Rd: Georgian R with rooms, on outskirts of town. GF. Tel. 01749 342022

Simonsbath (Exmoor, B3223/B3358) Simonsbath House: country house H + R. Tel. 01643 831259

Ston Easton (between Bath and Wells, A39/A37) Ston Easton Park: Georgian country house with Repton park, luxury H + GF. Tel. 01761 241631

Taunton The Castle, Castle Green: town centre H + GF (exquisite cuisine). Tel. 01823 272671

Wells Ritcher's, 5 Sadler St. GF. Tel. 01749 679085

Swan Hotel, 11 Sadler St: 15th-C. H + R opposite Cathedral. Tel. 01749 678877

West Bagborough (NW of Taunton, A358) Higher House: family B & B, nr Quantock Hills. Tel. 01823 432996

Williton (E of Minehead, A39) White House Hotel, H + GF. Tel. 01984 632306 & 632777

Winsford (10 miles SW of Minehead, A396) Royal Oak: village H + R on Exmoor. Tel. 01643 85455

Wiltshire

Bradford-on-Avon (SE of Bath) Woolley Grange, Woolley Green (B3105, NE of Bradford): country house H + GF with garden, swimming pool & tennis. Tel. 01225 864705

Bradford Old Windmill, 4 Masons Lane. B & B. Tel. 01225 866842

Castle Combe (nr Chippenham) Manor House Hotel: H + R. Tel. 01249 782206

Chiseldon (4 miles SE of Swindon, A346/B4005) Chiseldon House Hotel, New Rd: Regency H + GF. Tel. 01793 741010

Colerne (6 miles NE of Bath, between A4 & A20) Lucknam Park: Georgian country house H + GF with leisure & beauty spa. Tel. 01225 742777

Crudwell (between Malmesbury & Cirencester, A429) Crudwell Court: 17th-C. rectory. Family H + GF. Tel. 01666 577194

Easton Grey (W of Malmesbury, B4040) Whatley Manor: luxury country house H + R on Avon. Tel. 01666 822888

Horningsham (SW of Warminster) The Bath Arms: H + R on Longleat estate. Tel. 01985 844308

Lacock (3 miles S of Chippenham, A30) At the Sign of the Angel, 6 Church St: 15th/16th-C. village H + R. Tel. 01249 730230

Redlynch (6 miles SE of Salisbury, A338/B3080) Langley Wood: small R with rooms on edge of New Forest. GF. Tel. 01794 390348

Salisbury Harper's, 6-7 Ox Row, The Market Square. GF. Tel. 01722 333118

Crustaceans, 2-4 Ivy St: fish restaurant. Tel. 01722 333948

Teffont Evias (W of Salisbury, B3089) Howard's House Hotel: Elizabethan coutry-house H + GF. Tel. 01722 716392 & 716821

Warminster Bishopstrow House: Georgian luxury H + GF. Tel. 01985 212312

Events and Local Customs

January

'Wassailing the Apple Trees' in Carhampton (Somerset), to rid them of evil spirits: January 1

February

Hurling the Silver Ball in St Ives (Cornwall)

April

Hobby Horse in Minehead (Somerset): procession with grotesque horse: April 30

May

Royal Bath and West (Agricultural) Show, Shepton Mallet (Somerset)

Hobby Horse procession in Padstow (Cornwall): May 1

Furry Dance through streets of Helston (Cornwall): May 8

Chippenham International Folk Music Festival (Wiltshire)

Blessing of the Water in Christchurch (Dorset): May 8

Bath International Festival: music, dance, theatre: mid May to beginning of June

Devon County Show, Exeter: third week

June

Three Spires Festival of the Arts, Truro (Cornwall): concerts in Cathedral, theatre, exhibitions etc: end June/beginning July

Summer season at Minack Theatre, Porthcurno (Cornwall): till September

Royal Cornwall Show, Wadebridge (Cornwall)

Glastonbury Abbey Pilgrimage (Somerset): last Saturday in June

Summer Solstice Druid ceremonies at Stonehenge and Avebury (Wiltshire), and on Glastonbury Tor (Somerset): June 21

July

Tolpuddle Trade Union Festival: Procession in memory of Tolpuddle Martyrs, third Sunday

John Knill Ceremony: eccentric festival started by a bachelor in 18th C. Ten 10-year-old girls in white dance to a fiddle round the Knill Monument, a pyramid in Steeple Rd, St Ives (Cornwall): every 5th year on July 25 (next ceremony due 2001)

Exeter Festival, Devon

Dartington International Summer School (Devon) music lessons and seminars: till end August

Summer Festival of Music and Drama, St Endellion (Cornwall): till August

August

Start of hunting season with Devon and Somerset Staghounds: first week

Bristol International Hot Air Balloon Fiesta: second week

Church Music Festival, choral and organ concerts, alternating yearly between cathedrals of Chichester, Salisbury (Wiltshire), and Winchester

Bude Jazz Festival (Cornwall): end August

Fowey Royal Regatta (Cornwall): mid August

International Festival of Folk Arts, Sidmouth (Devon): beginning August

Bristol Flower Show, Durdham Downs: last week

September

Great Steam Dorset Steam Fair, South Down, Tarrant Hinton (near Blandford Forum, Dorset): early September

Widecombe Fair (Devon): traditional cattle fair on Dartmoor (second Tuesday)

Salisbury Festival (Wiltshire): music, theatre, exhibitions, children's events etc: two weeks, beginning and mid September

Frome Cheese Show (Somerset)

October

Wessex Carnivals (at night). Hundreds of mobile floats, millions of lightbulbs – Bridgwater, Taunton, Weston-super-Mare, Shepton Mallet, Wells and Glastonbury: check TICs for dates

Shark and Deep-Sea Fishing Festival in Looe (Cornwall)

Cider Barrel Rolling Race in Taunton (Somerset) during Carnival

November

Guy Fawkes' Day: major event, especially in Bridgwater (Somerset) & Ottery St Mary (Devon)

PALLAS GUIDES

OTHER BOOKS IN THIS SERIES

EAST ANGLIA
Peter Sager is an unsung genius
Val Hennessy, Daily Mail

WALES
Peter Sager has opened my eyes to my own country
Mavis Nicholson, South Wales Echo

ANDALUCIA
Michael Jacobs is an engaging, wonderfully informative and
ever-surprising companion
Jan Morris

CZECH AND SLOVAK REPUBLICS
Highly informative and quite admirable
The Art Newspaper

POLAND
No one interested in Polish culture, landscape, people and life in Poland
should be without this book
Polamerica

FORTHCOMING

SOUTH-EAST ENGLAND
TIBET LAOS   ROMANIA YEMEN
DORDOGNE   PROVENCE
ISRAEL AND THE HOLY LAND

PALLAS GUIDES

VENICE FOR PLEASURE

J. G. LINKS

This magic book: not only the best guidebook to that city ever written,
but the best guidebook to *any* city ever written
Bernard Levin, The Times

One of the most delightful and original guides ever
Jan Morris

The world's best guidebook
William Boyd, The Spectator

One of those miraculous books that gets passed by hand,
pressed urgently on friends
Sean French, New Statesman

AMSTERDAM EXPLORED

DEREK BLYTH

Ideally you would take Derek Blyth with you to Amsterdam, but
Amsterdam Explored is almost as good
The Times

FLEMISH CITIES EXPLORED

DEREK BLYTH

No one should travel to Bruges without a copy
Val Hennessy, Daily Mail

MADRID OBSERVED

MICHAEL JACOBS

He is the ideal companion we all dream of but rarely find
Irish Independent

Index

Doddiscombsleigh 237
dolmens *see* prehistoric sites
Donhead St Mary 32
Donne, John (*c.*1572-1631) 24
Doone Valley 76
Dorchester **57f**, 60, 63, 227, 228, 238
Dorchester, Caroline, Countess of 51
Dorchester, Joseph Damer, 1st Earl of 51
Dorset **45ff**, 238
Dowlish Wake 231
Doyle, Sir Arthur Conan (1859-1930) 160
Dozmary Pool 197
Drake, Sir Francis (*c.*1543-96) 137, 141, 152, *153*, 154, *156*, 222, 225
Drew, Julius 160
Drewsteignton 159, 222, 237
Drogo 160 *and see* Castle Drogo
drugs 90
Druids 14, 215
Dunkery Beacon 73, **75**
Dunster **78**, 240
  Dunster Castle 230, *col. pl. 25*
Durdham Downs 215
Durham Cathedral 52
Durlston Head **53**
Durrington 11
Dyck, Sir Anthony van (1599-1641) 24, 49, 155, 232, *col. pl. 3*

E

Eagle's Nest **182**
East Avon, River 46
East Buckland 237
East Budleigh **140**, 222
East Dart, River 159
East Knoyle **29**
East Lulworth 53
Easton **120**
Easton Grey 241
Eavis, Michael 90
Eddystone 154
Edgar, King (944-75) 89
Edgcumbe family 170, 219
Edgcumbe, Richard (d. 1489) 170
Edgeworth, Maria (1767-1849) 126

Edmondsham House 227
Edmund I, King (?922-46) 89
Edmund, King (Ironside) (?981-1016) 54, 89
Edward I, King (1239-1307) 159
Edward III, King (1312-77) 114, 168
Edward IV, King (1442-83) 174
Edward VI, King (1537-53) 169, 222
Edward VIII, King (1894-1972) 151
Edward, the Black Prince (1330-76) 153, 168
Edward the Confessor, St and King (*c.*1002-66) 54
Edward, the Martyr (?963-78) 54, 69
Egdon Heath 56
Egypt 49, 179, 193
Eisenberg, Baron d' 24
Eisenhower, General Dwight D. (1890-1969) 188
Elfrida 54
Elizabeth I, Queen (1533-1603) 25, 121, 137, 139, 140, 153, 154
Elizabeth II, Queen (b. 1926) 62, 65, 88, 137, 153
Elizabeth of York, Queen (1465-1503) 57
Elmer 40
Elmhirst, Leonard 149
Elsheimer, Adam (1578-1610) 232
Ely Cathedral 52
Emett, Ronald 65
Endsleigh House 237
English Heritage 16, 212
Enzenberger, Hans Magnus 129
Epstein, Sir Jacob (1880-1959) 149
Equator, the 176
Erasmus, Desiderius (1466-1536) 89
Ermington 223
Ethelred, King (d. 871) 48
Ethelred the Unraed, King (968-1016) 54
Evans, Eldred 190
Everard, Edward 124
Evershot 238
Exe, River 75, 144, 238
Exeter, 138, **140**, *141*, 215, 223, 237
  Exeter Cathedral, 52, 142, *142*, *143*, 223, *col. pls. 46 & 47*

Exeter Phoenix 223
  Maritime Museum 223
  University of Exeter 223
Exford 240
Exmoor 73, 75f, 132, 137, 164
  Exmoor National Park 75
  Exmoor ponies *see* ponies
Exmouth 221, 223, 237

F

Faisal, Emir, King of Iraq 55
Fal, River 175, 219, 221
Falklands, the 155
Falmouth 175, **176**, 181, 218, 219, 235
Farleigh Hungerford 230
farm holidays 211
Farnham 239
Feiler, Paul (b. 1918) 191
Fenton, Roger (1819-69) 91
Fielding, Henry (1707-54) 90
Filton 119
Fisher, Adrian 50
Fisher, John (1748-1825), Bishop of Salisbury 18
Fisher, John, Archdeacon of Salisbury 18
fishing 179
Fistral Bay 195
Flaxman, John (1755-1826) 143
Fleming, Thomas *166*
Flemish 78
Flitcroft, Henry (1697-1769) 30, 233
Folly Fellowship 213
Fonthill Abbey 25-29, *26*, **26**, 126
Fonthill Gifford **26**
fonts 54, 163, *163*, *172*, 173
Forbes, Stanhope (1857-1947) 180
Forde Abbey **66**, 227, 230
Foreman, Michael 188
Fossil Forest **53**
fossils 64
Foster, Sir Norman (b. 1935) 43, *col. pl. 11*
Foulston, John 179
Fowey 174f, 215, 218, 236
Fowey, River 173, 174, 220, 235
Fowles, John (b. 1926) 64
Fox, George (1624-91) 172

M

N

Maps

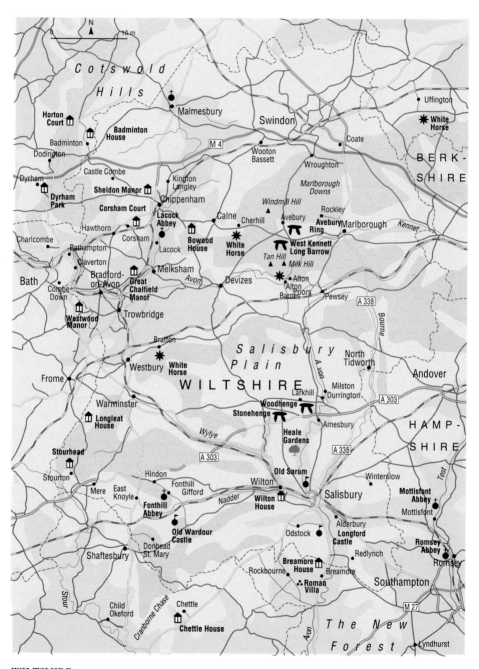

N
0 _____ 10 m

Cotswold Hills

Horton Court
Badminton House
Badminton
Dodington
Castle Combe
Dyrham
Dyrham Park
Charlcombe
Bathampton
Claverton
Bath
Combe Down
Westwood Manor
Bradford-on-Avon
Great Chalfield Manor
Trowbridge
Hawthorn
Sheldon Manor
Kington Langley
Chippenham
Corsham Court
Lacock Abbey
Corsham
Lacock
Bowood House
Melksham
White Horse
Avon
Devizes
Calne
Cherhill
Malmesbury

Swindon
Wooton Bassett
Wroughton
Marlborough Downs
Windmill Hill
Rockley
Avebury
Avebury Ring
West Kennett Long Barrow
Tan Hill
Milk Hill
Alton
Alton Priors
Barnes
Pewsey
Marlborough
Kennet
A 338
Bourne

M 4

Coate
Uffington
White Horse

BERK-SHIRE

Frome
Warminster
Longleat House
Stourhead
Stourton
Mere
East Knoyle
Hindon
Fonthill Gifford
Fonthill Abbey
Donhead St. Mary
Shaftesbury

Bratton
Westbury
White Horse

Salisbury Plain

WILTSHIRE

Woodhenge
Stonehenge

Larkhill
Milston
Durrington
Amesbury

North Tidworth
Andover

HAMP-SHIRE

A 303

Heale Gardens

A 303
Nadder
Wilton
Wilton House
Old Sarum
Salisbury
Winterslow
Mottisfont Abbey
Mottisfont

Test

Wylye

Odstock
Alderbury
Longford Castle
Redlynch
Romsey Abbey
Romsey

Old Wardour Castle

Child Okeford

Cranborne Chase
Chettle
Chettle House

Rockbourne
Breamore House
Breamore
Roman Villa

Southampton

M 27

Stour

Avon

The New Forest
Lyndhurst

WILTSHIRE

265

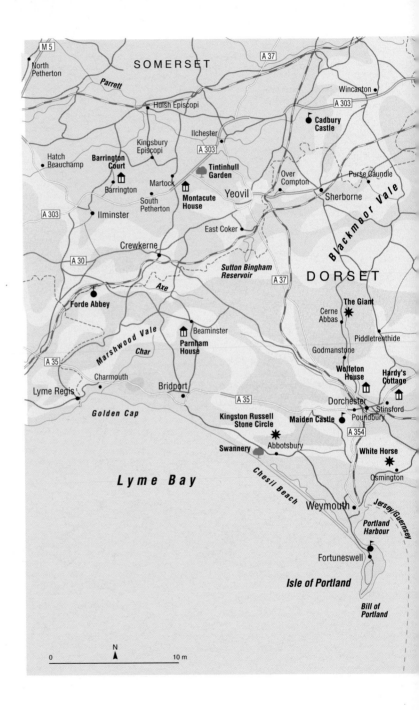

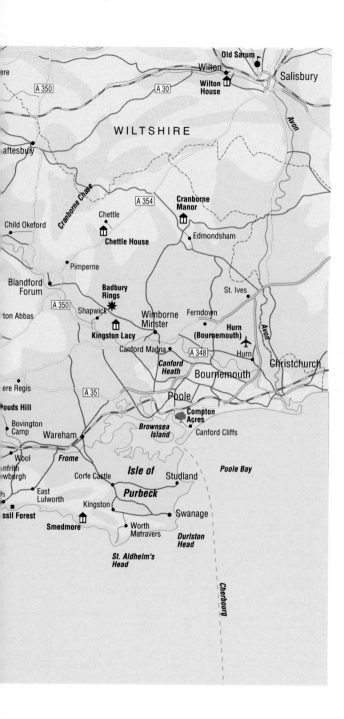

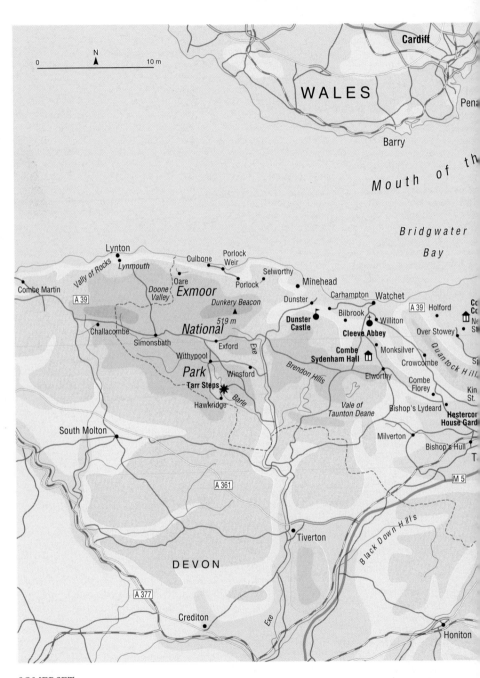

SOMERSET

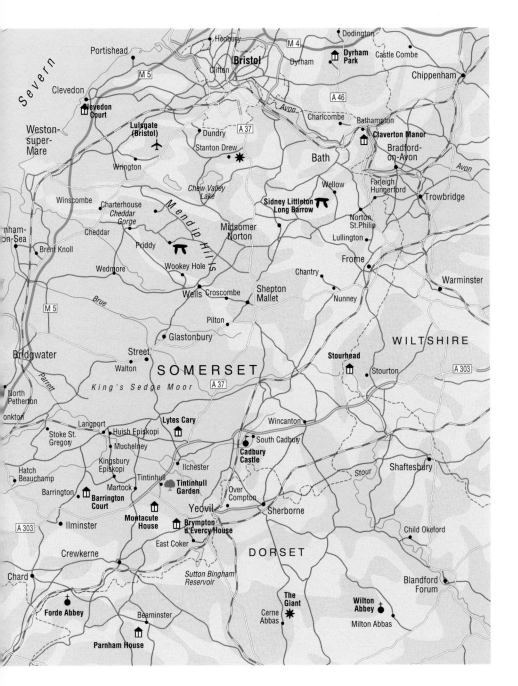

Severn

Portishead

Clevedon

Weston-super-Mare

M 5

Clevedon Court

Lulsgate (Bristol)

Henbury

Bristol

M 4

Clifton

Dyrham

Dyrham Park

Castle Combe

Chippenham

A 46

Avon

Charlcombe

Bathampton

Claverton Manor

Bradford-on-Avon

Avon

Dundry

A 37

Stanton Drew

Bath

Chew Valley Lake

Wellow

Farleigh Hungerford

Trowbridge

Winscombe

Charterhouse

Cheddar Gorge

Mendip Hills

Sidney Littleton Long Barrow

Norton St.Philip

Warminster

Cheddar

Priddy

Midsomer Norton

Lullington

Frome

nham-on-Sea

Brent Knoll

Wedmore

Wookey Hole

Chantry

Wells

Croscombe

Shepton Mallet

Nunney

M 5

Brue

Pilton

Glastonbury

WILTSHIRE

Bridgwater

Street

Walton

SOMERSET

King's Sedge Moor

A 37

Stourhead

Stourton

A 303

North Petherton

onkton

Langport

Huish Episkopi

Lytes Cary

Wincanton

Stoke St. Gregory

Muchelney

South Cadbury

Cadbury Castle

Shaftesbury

Hatch Beauchamp

Kingsbury Episkopi

Ilchester

Stour

Barrington

Tintinhull

Tintinhull Garden

Over Compton

Barrington Court

Martock

Montacute House

Yeovil

Ilminster

Brympton d'Evercy House

Sherborne

Child Okeford

A 303

Crewkerne

East Coker

DORSET

Chard

Sutton Bingham Reservoir

Blandford Forum

Forde Abbey

Beaminster

The Giant

Cerne Abbas

Wilton Abbey

Milton Abbas

Parnham House

Parrett

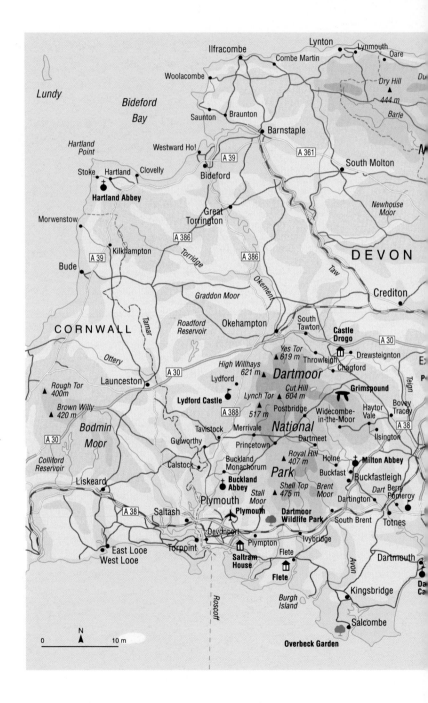

Lundy

Bideford Bay

Ilfracombe
Lynton
Lynmouth
Oare
Combe Martin
Dry Hill
▲
444 m
Du
Barle

Woolacombe

Hartland Point
Saunton
Braunton
Westward Ho!
Barnstaple
A 39
A 361
Stoke Hartland Clovelly
Bideford
South Molton
Hartland Abbey
Great Torrington
DEVON
Morwenstow
A 386
Newhouse Moor
Kilkhampton
Torridge
A 386
Taw
Bude
A 39
Crediton
Graddon Moor
Okement
CORNWALL
Roadford Reservoir
Okehampton
South Tawton
Castle Drogo
A 30
Tamar
Ottery
Yes Tor
▲ 619 m
Throwleigh
Drewsteignton
Teign
Rough Tor
▲ 400m
Launceston
A 30
High Willhays
621 m ▲
Lydford
Dartmoor
Chagford
E
Brown Willy
▲ 420 m
Lydford Castle
Cut Hill
▲ 604 m
Lynch Tor ▲
Grimspound
Bovey Tracey
A 388
517 m
Postbridge
Widecombe-in-the-Moor
Haytor Vale
Bodmin Moor
A 30
Tavistock
Merrivale
National
Dartmeet
Ilsington
A 38
Colliford Reservoir
Gulworthy
Princetown
Royal Hill
▲ 407 m
Holne
Milton Abbey
Liskeard
Calstock
Buckland Monachorum
Park
Buckfast
Buckfastleigh
Berry Pomeroy
Buckland Abbey
Shell Top
▲ 475 m
Brent Moor
Dart
Saltash
A 38
Plymouth
Stall Moor
Dartington
South Brent
Totnes
Plymouth
Dartmoor Wildlife Park
Devonport
Plympton
Ivybridge
Dartmouth
Torpoint
Flete
East Looe
West Looe
Saltram House
Flete
Da
Ca
Avon
Kingsbridge
Burgh Island

Roscoff

N
▲
0   10 m

Salcombe
Overbeck Garden

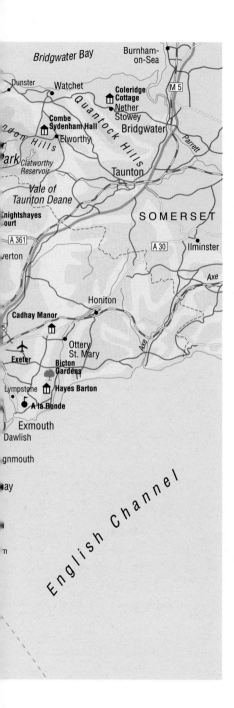

Bridgwater Bay

Burnham-on-Sea

Dunster

Watchet

Coleridge Cottage

Nether Stowey

Combe Sydenham Hall

Bridgwater

Elworthy

Clatworthy Reservoir

Taunton

Vale of Taunton Deane

SOMERSET

Knightshayes Court

A 361

A 30

Ilminster

verton

Axe

Honiton

Cadhay Manor

Ottery St. Mary

Axe

Exeter

Bicton Gardens

Lympstone

Hayes Barton

A la Ronde

Exmouth

Dawlish

gnmouth

ay

m

English Channel

CORNWALL

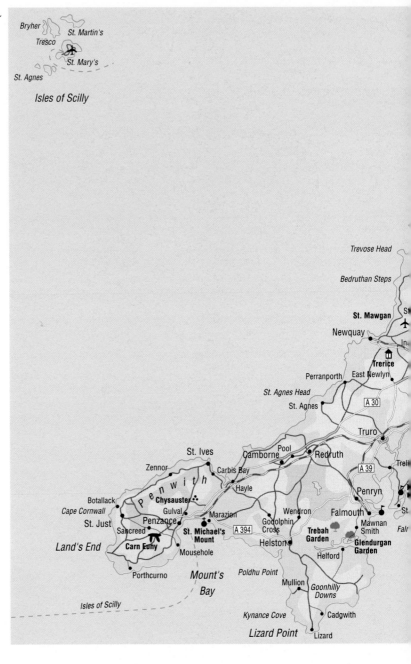

Bryher

Tresco

St. Martin's

St. Mary's

St. Agnes

Isles of Scilly

Trevose Head

Bedruthan Steps

St. Mawgan

Newquay

Trerice

Perranporth   East Newlyn

St. Agnes Head

St. Agnes

A 30

Truro

St. Ives

Pool

Camborne   Redruth

Zennor

A 39

Carbis Bay

Penryn

Hayle

Botallack

Chysauster

Falmouth

Cape Cornwall

Gulval

Wendron

Mawnan
Smith

St. Just

Penzance

Marazion

Godolphin
Cross

**Trebah
Garden**

Sancreed

**St. Michael's
Mount**

A 394

**Glendurgan
Garden**

Land's End

Carn Euny

Helston

Mousehole

Helford

Porthcurno

Mount's

Poldhu Point

Bay

Mullion

Goonhilly
Downs

Isles of Scilly

Kynance Cove

Cadgwith

Lizard Point

Lizard

272

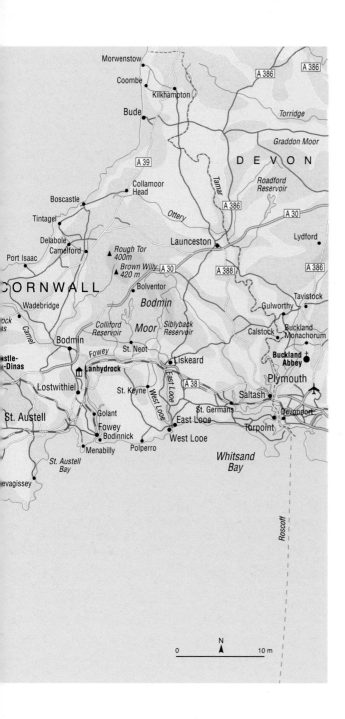

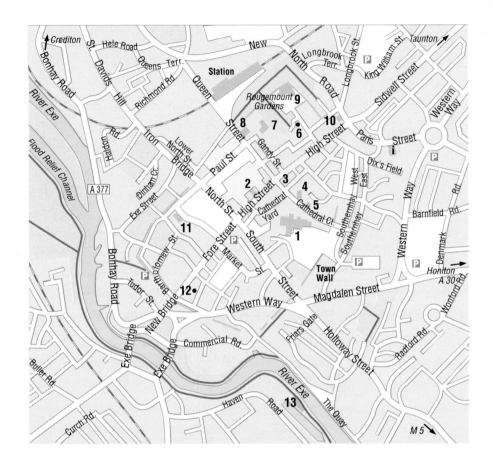

Exeter
1. Cathedral   2. Guildhall   3. Ship Inn   4. St Martin   5. Mol's Coffee House   6. Rougemont
Gardens   7. Exeter and Devon Arts Centre   8. Royal Albert Memorial Museum   9. Rougemont
Castle   10. Underground Passages   11. St Nicolas Priory   12. Stepcote Hill   13. Maritime Museum